THE PENGUIN FREUD LIBRARY

General Editor:
Angela Richards (1973–82)
Albert Dickson (1982–   )

VOLUME 5

THE PSYCHOPATHOLOGY OF EVERYDAY LIFE

Sigmund Freud

Sigmund Freud was born in 1856 in Moravia; between the ages of four and eighty-two his home was in Vienna: in 1938 Hitler's invasion of Austria forced him to seek asylum in London, where he died in the following year. His career began with several years of brilliant work on the anatomy and physiology of the nervous system. He was almost thirty when, after a period of study under Charcot in Paris, his interests first turned to psychology, and another ten years of clinical work in Vienna (at first in collaboration with Breuer, an older colleague) saw the birth of his creation, psychoanalysis. This began simply as a method of treating neurotic patients by investigating their minds, but it quickly grew into an accumulation of knowledge about the workings of the mind in general, whether sick or healthy. Freud was thus able to demonstrate the normal development of the sexual instinct in childhood and, largely on the basis of an examination of dreams, arrived at his fundamental discovery of the unconscious forces that influence our everyday thoughts and actions. Freud's life was uneventful, but his ideas have shaped not only many specialist disciplines, but the whole intellectual climate of the last half-century.

D1347790

THE PENGUIN FREUD LIBRARY
VOLUME 5

•

THE PSYCHOPATHOLOGY OF EVERYDAY LIFE

Sigmund Freud

•

Translated from the German by Alan Tyson

Edited by James Strachey
assisted by Angela Richards and Alan Tyson

The present volume
edited by Angela Richards

PENGUIN BOOKS

PENGUIN BOOKS

Published by the Penguin Group
Penguin Books Ltd, 27 Wrights Lane, London W8 5TZ, England
Penguin Putnam Inc., 375 Hudson Street, New York, New York 10014, USA
Penguin Books Australia Ltd, Ringwood, Victoria, Australia
Penguin Books Canada Ltd, 10 Alcorn Avenue, Toronto, Ontario, Canada M4V 3B2
Penguin Books (NZ) Ltd, Private Bag 102902, NSMC, Auckland, New Zealand

Penguin Books Ltd, Registered Offices: Harmondsworth, Middlesex, England

Zur Psychopathologie des Alltagslebens first published 1901
First English translation by A. A. Brill published 1914
Published in Pelican Books 1938

Present English translation (by Alan Tyson) first published in
The Standard Edition of the Complete Psychological Works of Sigmund Freud,
Volume VI, by the Hogarth Press and the Institute of Psycho-Analysis,
by arrangement with Ernest Benn 1966
Published by Ernest Benn 1966

'Sigmund Freud: A Sketch of his Life and Ideas'
first published in *Two Short Accounts of Psycho-Analysis* in Pelican Books 1962

The Psychopathology of Everyday Life
Published in Pelican Books 1975
Reprinted in Penguin Books 1991
5 7 9 10 8 6

Translation copyright © Alan Tyson, 1960
Editorial matter copyright © Angela Richards and the
Institute of Psycho-Analysis, 1960, 1962
Additional editorial matter copyright © Angela Richards, 1973, 1976
All rights reserved

Printed in England by Clays Ltd, St Ives plc
Set in Monotype Bembo

CONTENTS

VOLUME 5

THE PSYCHOPATHOLOGY OF
EVERYDAY LIFE
(1901)

INTRODUCTION TO THE
PENGUIN FREUD LIBRARY

The Penguin Freud Library (formerly *The Pelican Freud Library*) is intended to meet the needs of the general reader by providing all Freud's major writings in translation together with an appropriate linking commentary. It is the first time that such an edition has been produced in paperback in the English language. It does not supplant *The Standard Edition of the Complete Psychological Works of Sigmund Freud*, translated from the German under the general editorship of James Strachey in collaboration with Anna Freud, assisted by Alix Strachey and Alan Tyson, editorial assistant Angela Richards (Hogarth Press, 24 volumes, 1953–74). The *Standard Edition* remains the fullest and most authoritative collection published in any language. The present edition does, however, provide a large enough selection to meet the requirements of all but the most specialist reader – in particular it aims to cater for students of sociology, anthropology, criminology, medicine, aesthetics and education, all of them fields in which Freud's ideas have established their relevance.

The texts are reprinted unabridged, with corrections, from the *Standard Edition*. The editorial commentary – introductions, footnotes, internal cross-references, bibliographies and indexes – is also based upon the *Standard Edition*, but it has been abridged and where necessary adapted to suit the less specialized scope and purposes of the *Penguin Freud Library*. Some corrections have been made and some new material added.

Selection of Material

This is not a complete edition of Freud's psychological works – still less of his works as a whole, which included important contributions to neurology and neuropathology dating from the early part of his professional life. Of the psychological writings, virtually all the major works have been included. The arrangement is by subject-matter, so that the main contributions to any particular theme will be found in one volume. Within each volume the works are, for the main part, in chronological sequence. The aim has been to cover the whole field of Freud's observations and his theory of Psychoanalysis: that is to say, in the first place, the structure and dynamics of human mental activity; secondly, psychopathology and the mechanism of mental disorder; and thirdly, the application of psychoanalytic theory to wider spheres than the disorders of individuals which Freud originally, and indeed for the greater part of his life, investigated – to the psychology of groups, to social institutions and to religion, art and literature.

In his 'Sigmund Freud: A Sketch of his Life and Ideas' (p. 11 ff. below), James Strachey includes an account of Freud's discoveries as well as defining his principal theories and tracing their development.

Writings excluded from the Edition

The works that have been excluded are, (1) The neurological writings and most of those very early works from the period before the idea of psychoanalysis had taken form. (2) Writings on the actual technique of treatment. These were written specifically for practitioners of psychoanalysis and for analysts in training and their interest is correspondingly specialized. Freud never in fact produced a complete text on psychoanalytic treatment and the papers on technique only deal with selected points of difficulty or theoretical interest. (3) Writings which cover the same ground as other major works which have been included; for example, since the *Library* includes the *Introductory Lectures on Psychoanalysis* and the *New Lectures*, it was decided to leave out several of the shorter expository works in which Freud surveys the whole subject. Similarly, because the *Interpretation of Dreams* is included, the shorter writings on this topic have been omitted. (4) Freud's private correspondence, much of which has now been published in translation[1]. This is not to imply that such letters are without interest or importance though they have not yet received full critical treatment. (5) The numerous short writings such as reviews of books, prefaces to other authors' works, obituary notices and little *pièces d'occasion* – all of which lose interest to a large extent when separated from the books or occasions to which they refer and which would often demand long editorial explanations to make them comprehensible.

All of these excluded writings (with the exception of the works on neurology and the private letters) can be found in the *Standard Edition*.

Editorial Commentary

The bibliographical information, included at the beginning of the Editor's Note or Introduction to each work, gives the title of the German (or other) original, the date and place of its first publication and the position, where applicable, of the work in Freud's *Gesammelte Werke*, the most complete edition at present available of the works in German (published by S. Fischer Verlag, Frankfurt am Main). Details of the first translation of each work into English are also included, together with the *Standard Edition* reference. Other editions are listed only if they contain significant changes. (Full details of all German editions published in Freud's lifetime and of all English editions prior to the *Standard Edition* are included in the *Standard Edition*.)

The date of original publication of each work has been added to the half-title page, with the date of composition included in square brackets wherever it is different from the former date.

Further background information is given in introductory notes and footnotes to the text. Apart from dealing with the

1. [See the list, p. 24 *n.* below, and the details in the Bibliography, p. 345 ff.]

time and circumstances of composition, these notes aim to make it possible to follow the inception and development of important psychoanalytic concepts by means of systematic cross-references. Most of these references are to other works included in the *Penguin Freud Library*. A secondary purpose is to date additions and alterations made by Freud in successive revisions of the text and in certain cases to provide the earlier versions. No attempt has been made to do this as comprehensively as in the *Standard Edition*, but variants are given whenever they indicate a definite change of view. Square brackets are used throughout to distinguish editorial additions from Freud's text and his own footnotes.

It will be clear from this account that I owe an overwhelming debt to the late James Strachey, the general editor and chief translator of the *Standard Edition*. He indeed was mainly responsible for the idea of a *Penguin Freud Library*, and for the original plan of contents. Miss Anna Freud and Mrs Alix Strachey, both now deceased, gave advice of the greatest value. I am grateful to the late Mr Ernst Freud for his support and to the Publications Committee of the Institute of Psycho-Analysis for help in furthering preparations for this edition.

ANGELA RICHARDS

SIGMUND FREUD

A SKETCH OF HIS LIFE AND IDEAS

SIGMUND FREUD was born on 6 May 1856 in Freiberg, a small town in Moravia, which was at that time a part of Austria-Hungary. In an external sense the eighty-three years of his life were on the whole uneventful and call for no lengthy history.

He came of a middle-class Jewish family and was the eldest child of his father's second wife. His position in the family was a little unusual, for there were already two grown-up sons by his father's first wife. These were more than twenty years older than he was and one of them was already married, with a little boy; so that Freud was in fact born an uncle. This nephew played at least as important a part in his very earliest years as his own younger brothers and sisters, of whom seven were born after him.

His father was a wool-merchant and soon after Freud's birth found himself in increasing commercial difficulties. He therefore decided, when Freud was just three years old, to leave Freiberg, and a year later the whole family settled in Vienna, with the exception of the two elder half-brothers and their children, who established themselves instead in Manchester. At more than one stage in his life Freud played with the idea of joining them in England, but nothing was to come of this for nearly eighty years.

In Vienna during the whole of Freud's childhood the family lived in the most straitened conditions; but it is much to his father's credit that he gave invariable priority to the charge of Freud's education, for the boy was obviously intelligent and was a hard worker as well. The result was that he won a place in the 'Gymnasium' at the early age of nine, and for the last six of the eight years he spent at the school he was regularly

top of his class. When at the age of seventeen he passed out of
school his career was still undecided; his education so far had
been of the most general kind, and, though he seemed in any
case destined for the University, several faculties lay open to
him.

Freud insisted more than once that at no time in his life did
he feel 'any particular predilection for the career of a doctor.
I was moved, rather', he says, 'by a sort of curiosity, which
was, however, directed more towards human concerns than
towards natural objects.'[1] Elsewhere he writes: 'I have no
knowledge of having had any craving in my early childhood
to help suffering humanity ... In my youth I felt an over-
powering need to understand something of the riddles of the
world in which we live and perhaps even to contribute
something to their solution.'[2] And in yet another passage in
which he was discussing the sociological studies of his last
years: 'My interest, after making a lifelong *détour* through the
natural sciences, medicine, and psychotherapy, returned to the
cultural problems which had fascinated me long before, when
I was a youth scarcely old enough for thinking.'[3]

What immediately determined Freud's choice of a scientific
career was, so he tells us, being present just when he was
leaving school at a public reading of an extremely flowery
essay on 'Nature', attributed (wrongly, it seems) to Goethe.
But if it was to be science, practical considerations narrowed
the choice to medicine. And it was as a medical student that
Freud enrolled himself at the University in the autumn of
1873 at the age of seventeen. Even so, however, he was in no
hurry to obtain a medical degree. For his first year or two he
attended lectures on a variety of subjects, but gradually concentrated first on biology and then on physiology. His very
first piece of research was in his third year at the University,
when he was deputed by the Professor of Comparative

1. [*An Autobiographical Study* (1925*d*), near the opening of the work.]
2. ['Postscript to *The Question of Lay Analysis*' (1927*a*).]
3. ['Postscript (1935) to *An Autobiographical Study*' (1935*a*).]

Anatomy to investigate a detail in the anatomy of the eel, which involved the dissection of some four hundred specimens. Soon afterwards he entered the Physiological Laboratory under Brücke, and worked there happily for six years. It was no doubt from him that he acquired the main outlines of his attitude to physical science in general. During these years Freud worked chiefly on the anatomy of the central nervous system and was already beginning to produce publications. But it was becoming obvious that no livelihood which would be sufficient to meet the needs of the large family at home was to be picked up from these laboratory studies. So at last, in 1881, he decided to take his medical degree, and a year later, most unwillingly, gave up his position under Brücke and began work in the Vienna General Hospital.

What finally determined this change in his life was something more urgent than family considerations: in June 1882 he became engaged to be married, and thenceforward all his efforts were directed towards making marriage possible. His fiancée, Martha Bernays, came of a well-known Jewish family in Hamburg, and though for the moment she was living in Vienna she was very soon obliged to return to her remote North-German home. During the four years that followed, it was only for brief visits that he could have glimpses of her, and the two lovers had to content themselves with an almost daily interchange of letters. Freud now set himself to establishing a position and a reputation in the medical world. He worked in various departments of the hospital, but soon came to concentrate on neuroanatomy and neuropathology. During this period, too, he published the first inquiry into the possible medical uses of cocaine; and it was this that suggested to Koller the drug's employment as a local anaesthetic. He soon formed two immediate plans: one of these was to obtain an appointment as *Privatdozent*, a post not unlike that of a university lecturer in England, the other was to gain a travelling bursary which would enable him to spend some time in Paris, where the reigning figure was the great Charcot. Both of these aims, if they were realized, would, he felt, bring him real advantages, and in 1885, after a hard struggle, he achieved them both.

The months which Freud spent under Charcot at the Salpêtrière (the famous Paris hospital for nervous diseases) brought another change in the course of his life and this time a revolutionary one. So far his work had been concerned entirely with physical science and he was still carrying out histological studies on the brain while he was in Paris. Charcot's interests were at that period concentrated mainly on hysteria and hypnotism. In the world from which Freud came these subjects were regarded as barely respectable, but he became absorbed in them, and, though Charcot himself looked at them purely as branches of neuropathology, for Freud they meant the first beginnings of the investigation of the mind.

On his return to Vienna in the spring of 1886 Freud set up in private practice as a consultant in nervous diseases, and his long-delayed marriage followed soon afterwards. He did not, however, at once abandon all his neuropathological work: for several more years he studied in particular the cerebral palsies of children, on which he became a leading authority. At this period, too, he produced an important monograph on aphasia. But he was becoming more and more engaged in the treatment of the neuroses. After experimenting in vain with electro-therapy, he turned to hypnotic suggestion, and in 1888 visited Nancy to learn the technique used with such apparent success there by Liébeault and Bernheim. This still proved unsatisfactory and he was driven to yet another line of approach. He knew that a friend of his, Dr Josef Breuer, a Vienna consultant considerably his senior, had some ten years earlier cured a girl suffering from hysteria by a quite new procedure. He now persuaded Breuer to take up the method once more, and he himself applied it to several fresh cases with promising results. The method was based on the assumption that hysteria was the product of a psychical trauma which had been forgotten by the patient; and the treatment consisted in inducing her in a hypnotic state to recall the forgotten trauma to the accompaniment of appropriate emotions. Before very long Freud began to make changes both in the procedure and in the underlying theory; this led eventually to a breach with Breuer, and to the ultimate development by Freud of the whole system of ideas to which he soon gave the name of psychoanalysis.

From this moment onwards – from 1895, perhaps – to the very end of his life, the whole of Freud's intellectual existence revolved around this development, its far-reaching implications, and its theoretical and practical repercussions. It would, of course, be impossible to give in a few sentences any consecutive account of Freud's discoveries and ideas, but an attempt will be made presently to indicate in a disconnected fashion some of the main changes he has brought about in our habits of thought. Meanwhile we may continue to follow the course of his external life.

His domestic existence in Vienna was essentially devoid of episode: his home and his consulting rooms were in the same house from 1891 till his departure for London forty-seven years later. His happy marriage and his growing family – three sons and three daughters – provided a solid counterweight to the difficulties which, to begin with at least, surrounded his professional career. It was not only the nature of his discoveries that created prejudice against him in medical circles; just as great, perhaps, was the effect of the intense anti-semitic feeling which dominated the official world of Vienna: his appointment to a university professorship was constantly held back by political influence.

One particular feature of these early years calls for mention on account of its consequences. This was Freud's friendship with Wilhelm Fliess, a brilliant but unbalanced Berlin physician, who specialized in the ear and throat, but whose wider interests extended over human biology and the effects of periodic phenomena in vital processes. For fifteen years, from 1887 to 1902, Freud corresponded with him regularly,

reported the development of his ideas, forwarded him long
drafts outlining his future writings, and, most important of all,
sent him an essay of some forty thousand words which has
been given the name of a 'Project for a Scientific Psychology'.
This essay was composed in 1895, at what might be described
as the water-shed of Freud's career, when he was reluctantly
moving from physiology to psychology; it is an attempt to
state the facts of psychology in purely neurological terms.
This paper and all the rest of Freud's communications to Fliess
have, by a lucky chance, survived: they throw a fascinating
light on the development of Freud's ideas and show how much
of the later findings of psychoanalysis were already present in
his mind at this early stage.

Apart from his relations with Fliess, Freud had little outside
support to begin with. He gradually gathered a few pupils
round him in Vienna, but it was only after some ten years, in
about 1906, that a change was inaugurated by the adhesion of
a number of Swiss psychiatrists to his views. Chief among
these were Bleuler, the head of the Zurich mental hospital, and
his assistant Jung. This proved to be the beginning of the first
spread of psychoanalysis. An international meeting of psychoanalysts gathered at Salzburg in 1908, and in 1909 Freud and
Jung were invited to give a number of lectures in the United
States. Freud's writings began to be translated into many
languages, and groups of practising analysts sprang up all over
the world. But the progress of psychoanalysis was not without
its set-backs: the currents which its subject-matter stirred up
in the mind ran too deep for its easy acceptance. In 1911 one
of Freud's prominent Viennese supporters, Alfred Adler,
broke away from him, and two or three years later Jung's
differences from Freud led to their separation. Almost
immediately after this came the First World War and an
interruption of the international spread of psychoanalysis.
Soon afterwards, too, came the gravest personal tragedies –
the death of a daughter and of a favourite grandchild, and the
onset of the malignant illness which was to pursue him

relentlessly for the last sixteen years of his life. None of these troubles, however, brought any interruption to the development of Freud's observations and inferences. The structure of his ideas continued to expand and to find ever wider applications – particularly in the sociological field. By now he had become generally recognized as a figure of world celebrity, and no honour pleased him more than his election in 1936, the year of his eightieth birthday, as a Corresponding Member of the Royal Society. It was no doubt this fame, supported by the efforts of influential admirers, including, it is said, President Roosevelt, that protected him from the worst excesses of the National Socialists when Hitler invaded Austria in 1938, though they seized and destroyed his publications. Freud's departure from Vienna was nevertheless essential, and in June of that year, accompanied by some of his family, he made the journey to London, and it was there, a year later, on 23 September 1939, that he died.

It has become a journalistic cliché to speak of Freud as one of the revolutionary founders of modern thought and to couple his name with that of Einstein. Most people would however find it almost as hard to summarize the changes introduced by the one as by the other.

Freud's discoveries may be grouped under three headings – an instrument of research, the findings produced by the instrument, and the theoretical hypotheses inferred from the findings – though the three goups were of course mutually interrelated. Behind all of Freud's work, however, we should posit his belief in the universal validity of the law of determinism. As regards physical phenomena this belief was perhaps derived from his experience in Brücke's laboratory and so, ultimately, from the school of Helmholtz; but Freud extended the belief uncompromisingly to the field of mental phenomena, and here he may have been influenced by his teacher, the psychiatrist Meynert, and indirectly by the philosophy of Herbart.

First and foremost, Freud was the discoverer of the first instrument for the scientific examination of the human mind. Creative writers of genius had had fragmentary insight into mental processes, but no systematic method of investigation existed before Freud. It was only gradually that he perfected the instrument, since it was only gradually that the difficulties in the way of such an investigation became apparent. The forgotten trauma in Breuer's explanation of hysteria provided the earliest problem and perhaps the most fundamental of all, for it showed conclusively that there were active parts of the mind not immediately open to inspection either by an on-looker or by the subject himself. These parts of the mind were described by Freud, without regard for metaphysical or terminological disputes, as the unconscious. Their existence was equally demonstrated by the fact of post-hypnotic suggestion, where a person in a fully waking state performs an action which had been suggested to him some time earlier, though he had totally forgotten the suggestion itself. No examination of the mind could thus be considered complete unless it included this unconscious part of it in its scope. How was this to be accomplished? The obvious answer seemed to be: by means of hypnotic suggestion; and this was the instrument used by Breuer and, to begin with, by Freud. But it soon turned out to be an imperfect one, acting irregularly and uncertainly and sometimes not at all. Little by little, accordingly, Freud abandoned the use of suggestion and replaced it by an entirely fresh instrument, which was later known as 'free association'. He adopted the unheard-of plan of simply asking the person whose mind he was investigating to say whatever came into his head. This crucial decision led at once to the most startling results; even in this primitive form Freud's instrument produced fresh insight. For, though things went along swimmingly for a while, sooner or later the flow of associations dried up: the subject would not or could not think of anything more to say. There thus came to light the fact of 'resistance', of a force, separate from the subject's conscious will, which was refusing to collaborate with the investigation. Here was one basis for a very fundamental piece of theory, for a hypothesis of the mind as something dynamic, as consisting in a number of mental forces, some conscious and some unconscious, operating now in harmony now in opposition with one another.

Though these phenomena eventually turned out to be of universal occurrence, they were first observed and studied in neurotic patients, and the earlier years of Freud's work were largely concerned with discovering means by which the 'resistance' of these patients could be overcome and what lay behind it could be brought to light. The solution was only made possible by an extraordinary piece of self-observation on Freud's part – what we should now describe as his self-analysis. We are fortunate in having a contemporary first-hand description of this event in his letters to Fliess which have already been mentioned. This analysis enabled him to discover the nature of the unconscious processes at work in the mind and to understand why there is such a strong resistance to their becoming conscious; it enabled him to devise techniques for overcoming or evading the resistance in his patients; and, most important of all, it enabled him to realize the very great difference between the mode of functioning of these unconscious processes and that of our familiar conscious ones. A word may be said on each of these three points, for in fact they constitute the core of Freud's contributions to our knowledge of the mind.

The unconscious contents of the mind were found to consist wholly in the activity of conative trends – desires or wishes – which derive their energy directly from the primary physical instincts. They function quite regardless of any consideration other than that of obtaining immediate satisfaction, and are thus liable to be out of step with those more conscious elements in the mind which are concerned with adaptation to reality and the avoidance of external dangers. Since, moreover, these primitive trends are to a great extent of a sexual or of a destructive nature, they are bound to come in conflict with the more social and civilized mental forces. Investigations along this path were what led Freud to his discoveries of the long-disguised secrets of the sexual life of children and of the Oedipus complex.

In the second place, his self-analysis led him to an inquiry into the nature of dreams. These turned out to be, like neurotic symptoms, the product of a conflict and a compromise between the primary unconscious impulses and the secondary conscious ones. By analysing them into their elements it was therefore possible to infer their hidden unconscious contents; and, since dreams are common phenomena of almost universal occurrence, their interpretation turned out to be one of the most useful technical contrivances for penetrating the resistances of neurotic patients.

Finally, the painstaking examination of dreams enabled Freud to classify the remarkable differences between what he termed the primary and secondary processes of thought, between events in the unconscious and conscious regions of the mind. In the unconscious, it was found, there is no sort of organization or coordination: each separate impulse seeks satisfaction independently of all the rest; they proceed uninfluenced by one another; contradictions are completely inoperative, and the most opposite impulses flourish side by side. So, too, in the unconscious, associations of ideas proceed along lines without any regard to logic: similarities are treated as identities, negatives are equated with positives. Again, the objects to which the conative trends are attached in the unconscious are extraordinarily changeable – one may be replaced by another along a whole chain of associations that have no rational basis. Freud perceived that the intrusion into conscious thinking of mechanisms that belong properly to the primary process accounts for the oddity not only of dreams but of many other normal and pathological mental events.

It is not much of an exaggeration to say that all the later part of Freud's work lay in an immense extension and elaboration of these early ideas. They were applied to an elucidation of the mechanisms not only of the psychoneuroses and psychoses but also of such normal processes as slips of the tongue, making jokes, artistic creation, political institutions, and religions; they played a part in throwing fresh light on many applied sciences – archaeology, anthropology, criminology, education; they also served to account for the effectiveness of psychoanalytic therapy. Lastly, too, Freud erected on the basis of these elementary observations a theoretical superstructure, what he named a 'metapsychology', of more general concepts. These, however, fascinating as many people will find them, he always insisted were in the nature of provisional hypotheses. Quite late in his life, indeed, influenced by the ambiguity of the term 'unconscious' and its many conflicting uses, he proposed a new structural account of the mind in which the uncoordinated instinctual trends were called the 'id', the organized realistic part the 'ego', and the critical and moralizing function the 'super-ego' – a new account which has certainly made for a clarification of many issues.

This, then, will have given the reader an outline of the external events of Freud's life and some notion of the scope of his discoveries. Is it legitimate to ask for more? to try to penetrate a little further and to inquire what sort of person Freud was? Possibly not. But human curiosity about great men is insatiable, and if it is not gratified with true accounts it will inevitably clutch at mythological ones. In two of Freud's early books (*The Interpretation of Dreams* and *The Psychopathology of Everyday Life*) the presentation of his thesis had forced on him the necessity of bringing up an unusual amount of personal material. Nevertheless, or perhaps for that very reason, he intensely objected to any intrusion into his private life, and he was correspondingly the subject of a wealth of myths. According to the first and most naïve rumours, for instance, he was an abandoned profligate, devoted to the corruption of public morals. Later fantasies have tended in the opposite direction: he has been represented as a harsh moralist, a ruthless disciplinarian, an autocrat, egocentric and unsmiling, and an essentially unhappy man. To anyone who was acquainted with him, even slightly, both these pictures must seem equally preposterous. The second of them was no doubt partly derived from a knowledge of his physical sufferings during his last years; but partly too it may have been due to the unfortunate impression produced by some of his most widespread portraits. He disliked being photographed, at least by professional photographers, and his features on occasion expressed the fact; artists too seem always to have been overwhelmed by the necessity for representing the inventor of psychoanalysis as a ferocious and terrifying figure. Fortunately, however, alternative versions exist of a more amiable and truer kind – snapshots, for instance, taken on a holiday or with his children, such as will be found in his eldest son's memoir of his father (*Glory Reflected*, by Martin Freud [1957]). In many ways, indeed, this delightful and amusing book serves to redress the balance from more official biographies, invaluable as they are, and reveals something of Freud as he was in ordinary life. Some of these portraits show us that in his earlier days he had well-filled features, but in later life, at any rate after the First World War and even before his illness, this was no longer so, and his features, as well as his whole figure (which was of medium height), were chiefly remarkable for the impression they gave of tense energy and alert observation. He was serious but kindly and considerate in his more formal manners, but in other circumstances could be an entertaining talker with a pleasantly ironical sense of humour. It was easy to discover his devoted fondness for his family and to recognize a man who would inspire affection. He had many miscellaneous interests – he was fond of travelling abroad, of country holidays, of mountain walks – and there were other, more engrossing subjects, art, archaeology, literature. Freud was a very well-read man in many languages, not only in German. He read English and French fluently, besides having a fair knowledge of Spanish and Italian. It must be remembered, too, that though the later phases of his education were chiefly scientific (it is true that at the University he studied philosophy for a short time) at school he had learnt the classics and never lost his affection for them. We happen to have a letter written by him at the age of seventeen to a school friend[1]. In it he describes his varying success in the different papers of his school-leaving examination: in Latin a passage from Virgil, and in Greek thirty-three lines from, of all things, *Oedipus Rex*.

In short, we might regard Freud as what in England we should consider the best kind of product of a Victorian upbringing. His tastes in literature and art would obviously differ from ours, his views on ethics, though decidedly liberal, would not belong to the post-Freudian age. But we should see in him a man who lived a life of full emotion and of much suffering without embitterment. Complete honesty and directness were qualities that stood out in him, and so too did his intellectual readiness to take in and consider any fact, however new or extraordinary, that was presented to him. It was perhaps an inevitable corollary and extension of these qualities, combined with a general benevolence which a surface misanthropy failed to disguise, that led to some features of a surprising kind. In spite of his subtlety of mind he was essentially unsophisticated, and there were sometimes unexpected lapses in his critical faculty – a failure, for instance, to perceive an untrustworthy authority in some subject that was off his own beat such as Egyptology or philology, and, strangest of all in someone whose powers of perception had to be experienced to be believed, an occasional blindness to defects in his acquaintances. But though it may flatter our vanity to declare that Freud was a human being of a kind like our own, that satisfaction can easily be carried too far. There must in fact have been something very extraordinary in the

1. [Emil Fluss. The letter is included in the volume of Freud's correspondence (1960a).]

man who was first able to recognize a whole field of mental facts which had hitherto been excluded from normal consciousness, the man who first interpreted dreams, who first accepted the facts of infantile sexuality, who first made the distinction between the primary and secondary processes of thinking – the man who first made the unconscious mind real to us.

JAMES STRACHEY

[Those in search of further information will find it in the three-volume biography of Freud by Ernest Jones, an abridged version of which was published in Pelican in 1964, in the important volume of Freud's letters edited by his son and daughter-in-law, Ernst and Lucie Freud (1960a), in several further volumes of his correspondence, with Wilhelm Fliess (1950a), Karl Abraham (1965a), C. G. Jung (1974a), Oskar Pfister (1963a), Lou Andreas-Salomé (1966a), Edoardo Weiss (1970a) and Arnold Zweig (1968a), and above all in the many volumes of Freud's own works.]

CHRONOLOGICAL TABLE

This table traces very roughly some of the main turning-points in Freud's intellectual development and opinions. A few of the chief events in his external life are also included in it.

1856. 6 May. Birth at Freiberg in Moravia.

1860. Family settles in Vienna.

1865. Enters Gymnasium (secondary school).

1873. Enters Vienna University as medical student.

1876–82. Works under Brücke at the Institute of Physiology in Vienna.

1877. First publications: papers on anatomy and physiology.

1881. Graduates as Doctor of Medicine.

1882. Engagement to Martha Bernays.

1882–5. Works in Vienna General Hospital, concentrating on cerebral anatomy: numerous publications.

1884–7. Researches into the clinical uses of cocaine.

1885. Appointed *Privatdozent* (University Lecturer) in Neuropathology.

1885 (October)–1886 (February). Studies under Charcot at the Salpêtrière (hospital for nervous diseases) in Paris. Interest first turns to hysteria and hypnosis.

1886. Marriage to Martha Bernays. Sets up private practice in nervous diseases in Vienna.

1886–93. Continues work on neurology, especially on the cerebral palsies of children at the Kassowitz Institute in Vienna, with numerous publications. Gradual shift of interest from neurology to psychopathology.

1887. Birth of eldest child (Mathilde).

1887–1902. Friendship and correspondence with Wilhelm Fliess in Berlin. Freud's letters to him during this period, published posthumously in 1950, throw much light on the development of his views.

1887. Begins the use of hypnotic suggestion in his practice.

c. 1888. Begins to follow Breuer in using hypnosis for cathartic treatment of hysteria. Gradually drops hypnosis and substitutes free association.

1889. Visits Bernheim at Nancy to study his suggestion technique.

1889. Birth of eldest son (Martin).

1891. Monograph on Aphasia.

Birth of second son (Oliver).

1892. Birth of youngest son (Ernst).

1893. Publication of Breuer and Freud 'Preliminary Communication': exposition of trauma theory of hysteria and of cathartic treatment.

Birth of second daughter (Sophie).

1893–8. Researches and short papers on hysteria, obsessions, and anxiety.

1895. Jointly with Breuer, *Studies on Hysteria*: case histories and description by Freud of his technique, including first account of transference.

1893–6. Gradual divergence of views between Freud and Breuer. Freud introduces concepts of defence and repression and of neurosis being a result of a conflict between the ego and the libido.

1895. *Project for a Scientific Psychology*: included in Freud's letters to Fliess and first published in 1950. An abortive attempt to state psychology in neurological terms; but foreshadows much of Freud's later theories.

Birth of youngest child (Anna).

1896. Introduces the term 'psychoanalysis'.

Death of father (aged 80).

1897. Freud's self-analysis, leading to the abandonment of the trauma theory and the recognition of infantile sexuality and the Oedipus complex.

1900. *The Interpretation of Dreams*, with final chapter giving first full account of Freud's dynamic view of mental processes, of the unconscious, and of the dominance of the 'pleasure principle'.

1901. *The Psychopathology of Everyday Life*. This, together with the book on dreams, made it plain that Freud's theories applied not only to pathological states but also to normal mental life.

1902. Appointed Professor Extraordinarius.

1905. *Three Essays on the Theory of Sexuality*: tracing for the first time the course of development of the sexual instinct in human beings from infancy to maturity.

c. 1906. Jung becomes an adherent of psychoanalysis.

1908. First international meeting of psychoanalysts (at Salzburg).

1909. Freud and Jung invited to the USA to lecture.

Case history of the first analysis of a child (Little Hans, aged five): confirming inferences previously made from adult analyses, especially as to infantile sexuality and the Oedipus and castration complexes.

c. 1910. First emergence of the theory of 'narcissism'.

1911–15. Papers on the technique of psychoanalysis.

1911. Secession of Adler.

Application of psychoanalytic theories to a psychotic case: the autobiography of Dr Schreber.

1912–13. *Totem and Taboo*: application of psychoanalysis to anthropological material.

1914. Secession of Jung.

'On the History of the Psycho-Analytic Movement'. Includes a polemical section on Adler and Jung.

Writes his last major case history, of the 'Wolf Man' (not published till 1918.)

1915. Writes a series of twelve 'metapsychological' papers on basic theoretical questions, of which only five have survived.

1915–17. *Introductory Lectures*: giving an extensive general account of the state of Freud's views up to the time of the First World War.

1919. Application of the theory of narcissism to the war neuroses.

1920. Death of second daughter.

Beyond the Pleasure Principle: the first explicit introduction of the concept of the 'compulsion to repeat' and of the theory of the 'death instinct'.

1921. *Group Psychology*. Beginnings of a systematic analytic study of the ego.

1923. *The Ego and the Id*. Largely revised account of the structure and functioning of the mind with the division into an id, an ego, and a super-ego.

First onset of cancer.

1925. Revised views on the sexual development of women.

1926. *Inhibitions, Symptoms and Anxiety*. Revised views on the problem of anxiety.

1927. *The Future of an Illusion*. A discussion of religion: the first of a number of sociological works to which Freud devoted most of his remaining years.

1930. *Civilization and its Discontents.* This includes Freud's first extensive study of the destructive instinct (regarded as a manifestation of the 'death instinct').

Freud awarded the Goethe Prize by the City of Frankfurt.

Death of mother (aged 95).

1933. Hitler seizes power in Germany: Freud's books publicly burned in Berlin.

1934-8. *Moses and Monotheism*: the last of Freud's works to appear during his lifetime.

1936. Eightieth birthday. Election as Corresponding Member of Royal Society.

1938. Hitler's invasion of Austria. Freud leaves Vienna for London. *An Outline of Psycho-Analysis.* A final, unfinished, but profound, exposition of psychoanalysis.

1939. 23 September. Death in London.

JAMES STRACHEY

THE PSYCHOPATHOLOGY OF EVERYDAY LIFE

Forgetting, Slips of the Tongue, Bungled Actions, Superstitions and Errors
(1901)

Nun ist die Luft von solchem Spuk so voll,
Dass niemand weiss, wie er ihn meiden soll.
Faust, Part II, Act V, Scene 5

Now fills the air so many a haunting shape,
That no one knows how best he may escape.
(Bayard Taylor's translation)

EDITOR'S INTRODUCTION

ZUR PSYCHOPATHOLOGIE DES ALLTAGSLEBENS

(Über Vergessen, Versprechen, Vergreifen,
Aberglaube und Irrtum)

(A) GERMAN EDITIONS:

1901   *Monatsschrift für Psychiatrie und Neurologie*, **10** (1) [July],
        1–32, and (2) [August], 95–143.

1904   In book form, Berlin: Karger. Pp. 92. (Revised reprint.)

1907   2nd ed. (Enlarged.) Same publishers. Pp. 132.

1910   3rd ed. (Enlarged.) Same publishers. Pp. 149.

1912   4th ed. (Enlarged.) Same publishers. Pp. 198.

1917   5th ed. (Enlarged.) Same publishers. Pp. iv + 232.

1919   6th ed. (Enlarged.) Leipzig and Vienna: Internationaler
        Psychoanalytischer Verlag. Pp. iv + 312.

1920   7th ed. (Enlarged.) Leipzig, Vienna and Zurich: Same
        publishers. Pp. iv + 334.

1922   8th ed. Same publishers. (Reprint of above.)

1923   9th ed. Same publishers. (Reprint of above.)

1924   10th ed. (Enlarged.) Same publishers. Pp. 310.

1924   *Gesammelte Schriften*, **4**, 1–310.

1929   11th ed. Same publishers. (Reprint of 10th ed.)

1941   *Gesammelte Werke*, **4**, Pp. iv + 322.

(B) ENGLISH TRANSLATIONS:
Psychopathology of Everyday Life

1914   London: Fisher Unwin; New York: Macmillan. Pp.
        vii + 342. (Tr. and Introduction A. A. Brill.)

1938   London: Penguin Books. (New York, 1939.) Pp. 218.
         (Same trans.)
1938   In *The Basic Writings of Sigmund Freud*, New York:
         Modern Library. Pp. 35–178. (Same trans.)
1944   London: Ernest Benn. Pp. vii+239. (Same trans.)
1958   London: Collins. Pp. viii+180. (Same trans.)
1960   *Standard Edition*, 6. (Tr. Alan Tyson.)
1966   London: Ernest Benn. (Corrected reprint of above.)

Only one other of Freud's works, the *Introductory Lectures* (1916–17), rivals this one in the number of German editions it has passed through and the number of foreign languages into which it has been translated.[1] In almost every one of its numerous editions fresh material was included in the book, and in this respect it might be thought to resemble *The Interpretation of Dreams* and the *Three Essays on the Theory of Sexuality*, to both of which Freud made constant additions throughout his life. But the cases have in fact no similarity. In these other two books the fresh material consisted for the most part of important enlargements or corrections of clinical findings and theoretical conclusions. In *The Psychopathology of Everyday Life* almost the whole of the basic explanations and theories were already present in the earliest editions;[2] the great mass of what was added later consisted merely in extra examples and illustrations (partly produced by Freud himself but largely by his friends and pupils) to throw further light upon what he had already discussed. No doubt he felt particular pleasure both in the anecdotes themselves and in being presented with such widespread confirmation of his views. But the reader cannot help feeling sometimes that the wealth of new examples inter-

1. Besides the English version of 1914, *The Psychopathology of Everyday Life* was during Freud's lifetime translated into nine other languages, as well as into two further ones at unspecified dates.

2. A few new points of theory were discussed in the later editions of the last chapter of the book.

rupts and even confuses the main stream of the underlying argument. (See, for instance, pp. 109–23 and 250 *n*.)

Here, as in the case of Freud's books on dreams and on jokes but perhaps to a still greater degree, the translator has to face the fact that a large proportion of the material to be dealt with depends on a play upon words which is totally untranslatable. In the previous version the problem was dealt with in a drastic fashion by Brill; he omitted every example which involved terms that could not be rendered into English and inserted a certain number of examples of his own which illustrated similar points to the omitted ones. This was no doubt an entirely justifiable procedure in the circumstances. At the date at which Brill made his version, Freud's work was almost unknown in English-speaking countries, and it was important not to put up unnecessary obstacles to the circulation of this book which had been designed by Freud himself expressly for the general reader (cf. p. 336, footnote). Brill's own examples, too, were for the most part excellent and two or three of them were in fact included by Freud in later editions of the German original. Nevertheless there are obvious objections to perpetuating this situation, especially in any edition intended for more serious students of Freud's writings. In some instances, for example, the omission of a piece of Freud's illustrative material inevitably brought with it the omission of some important or interesting piece of theoretical comment. Moreover, though Brill announced in his preface his intention 'to modify or substitute some of the author's cases', in the text itself these substitutions are not as a rule explicitly indicated and the reader may sometimes be uncertain whether he is reading Freud or Brill. Brill's translation, it must be added, was made from the German edition of 1912 and remained unaltered in all the later reprints. Thus it entirely passes over the very numerous additions to the text made by Freud during the ten or more subsequent years. The total effect of the omissions due to these different causes is a startling one. Of the 305 pages of text of the latest edition, as printed in the *Gesammelte Werke*, between 90 and 100 (almost one third of the book, that is) never appeared in English until 1960, when the *Standard Edition* version was published. The completeness of the present translation must, therefore, be weighed against the undoubted loss of readability caused by the *Standard Edition* policy of dealing with play upon words by the pedestrian method of giving the original German phrases and explaining their point with the help of square brackets and footnotes.

We find the first mention by Freud of a parapraxis[1] in a letter to Fliess of August 26, 1898 (Freud, 1950a, Letter 94). He there speaks of having 'at last grasped a little thing that I have long suspected' – the way in which a name sometimes escapes one and a quite wrong substitute occurs to one in its place. A month later, on September 22 (ibid., Letter 96), he gives Fliess another example, this time the familiar one of 'Signorelli', which he published that same year in a preliminary form in the *Monatsschrift für Psychiatrie und Neurologie* (1898b) and subsequently used for the first chapter of the present work. In the following year the same periodical published a paper by Freud on screen memories (1899a), a subject which he further discussed on rather different lines in Chapter IV below. But his time was fully occupied by the completion of *The Interpretation of Dreams* (1900a) and the preparation of his shorter study *On Dreams* (1901a) and it was not until late in 1900 that he took up *The Psychopathology of Everyday Life* seriously. On January 30, 1901 (Freud, 1950a, Letter 141) he reports to Fliess that it is 'at a standstill, half-finished, but will soon be continued',[2] and on February 15 (Letter 142) announces that he will finish it during the next few days. It actually

---

1. In German '*Fehlleistung*', 'faulty function'. It is a curious fact that before Freud wrote this book the general concept seems not to have existed in psychology, and in English a new word had to be invented to cover it.

2. He had spent January in preparing the 'Dora' case history, though this was not in fact published for another four years (1905e).

appeared in July and August in two issues of the same Berlin periodical as the preliminary studies.

Three years later, in 1904, the work was for the first time issued as a separate volume, with scarcely any alterations, but thereafter additions were made almost continuously over the next twenty years. In 1901 and 1904 it was in ten chapters. Two more (what are now Chapters III and XI) were first added in 1907. An interleaved copy of the 1904 edition was found in Freud's library, in which he had made rough notes of further examples. The majority of these were incorporated in later editions: others, so far as they seem to be of interest, have been included here as footnotes at the appropriate point.

The text of the present edition follows that of *Gesammelte Werke*, itself a reprint of the 10th edition of 1924. Every addition and alteration of substance has been indicated and dated. The only changes which have not been recorded are very small, mainly stylistic variants.

The special affection with which Freud regarded parapraxes was no doubt due to the fact that they, along with dreams, were what enabled him to extend to normal mental life the discoveries he had first made in connection with neuroses. For the same reason he regularly used them as the best preliminary material for introducing non-medical enquirers into the findings of psychoanalysis. This material was both simple and, on the surface at least, unobjectionable, as well as being concerned with phenomena which every normal person had experienced. In his expository writings he sometimes gave parapraxes a preference even over dreams, which involved more complicated mechanisms and tended to lead rapidly into deeper waters. Thus it was that he opened his great series of *Introductory Lectures* of 1916–17 with three devoted to parapraxes – in which, incidentally, a large number (over forty) of the examples in the following pages make their re-appearance; and he gave parapraxes similar priority in his contributions to *Scientia* (1913*j*) and to Marcuse's encyclopaedia (1923*a*). But though these phenomena were simple and easily explained, it was possible for Freud to demonstrate on them what was, after all, the fundamental thesis established in *The Interpretation of Dreams* – the existence of two distinct modes of mental functioning, what he described as the primary and secondary processes. Moreover, there was another fundamental belief of Freud's which could be convincingly supported by the examination of parapraxes – his belief in the universal application of determinism to mental events. This is the truth which he insists upon in the final chapter of the book: it should be possible in theory to discover the psychical determinants of every smallest detail of the processes of the mind. And perhaps the fact that this aim seemed more nearly attainable in the case of parapraxes was another reason why they had a peculiar attraction for Freud.

CHAPTER I

THE FORGETTING OF
PROPER NAMES[1]

IN the 1898 volume of the *Monatsschrift für Psychiatrie und Neurologie* I published under the title of 'The Psychical Mechanism of Forgetfulness' [Freud, 1898b] a short paper the substance of which I shall recapitulate here and take as the starting-point for more extensive discussions. In it I applied psychological analysis to the frequent circumstance of proper names being temporarily forgotten, by exploring a highly suggestive example drawn from my self-observation; and I reached the conclusion that this particular instance (admittedly commonplace and without much practical significance), in which a psychical function – the memory – refuses to operate, admits of an explanation much more far-reaching than that which the phenomenon is ordinarily made to yield.

If a psychologist were asked to explain why it is that on so many occasions a proper name which we think we know perfectly well fails to enter our heads, he would, unless I am much mistaken, be satisfied with answering that proper names succumb more easily to the process of being forgotten than other kinds of memory-content. He would bring forward the plausible reasons why proper names should thus be singled out for special treatment, but would not suspect that any other conditions played their part in such occurrences.

My close preoccupation with the phenomenon of names being temporarily forgotten arose out of my observation of certain characteristics which could be recognized sufficiently clearly in individual cases, though not, it is true, in all of them. These are cases in which a name is in fact not only *forgotten*, but *wrongly remembered*. In the course of our efforts to recover

1. [Apart from the very few alterations recorded below, the whole of this chapter dates back to 1901.]

the name that has dropped out, other ones – *substitute names* – enter our consciousness; we recognize them at once, indeed, as incorrect, but they keep on returning and force themselves on us with great persistence. The process that should lead to the reproduction of the missing name has been so to speak *displaced* and has therefore led to an incorrect substitute. My hypothesis is that this displacement is not left to arbitrary psychical choice but follows paths which can be predicted and which conform to laws. In other words, I suspect that the name or names which are substituted are connected in a discoverable way with the missing name: and I hope, if I am successful in demonstrating this connection, to proceed to throw light on the circumstances in which names are forgotten.

The name that I tried without success to recall in the example I chose for analysis in 1898 was that of the artist who painted the magnificent frescoes of the 'Four Last Things' in Orvieto cathedral.[1] Instead of the name I was looking for – *Signorelli* – the names of two other painters – *Botticelli* and *Boltraffio* – thrust themselves on me, though they were immediately and decisively rejected by my judgement as incorrect. When I learnt the correct name from someone else, I recognized it at once and without hesitation. The investigation into the influences and the associative paths by which the reproducing of the name had been displaced in this way from *Signorelli* to *Botticelli* and *Boltraffio* led to the following results:

(a) The reason why the name *Signorelli* was lost is not to be found in anything special about the name itself or in any psychological characteristic of the context into which it was introduced. The name I had forgotten was just as familiar to me as one of the substitute names – *Botticelli* – and much *more* familiar than the other substitute name – *Boltraffio* – about whose owner I could scarcely produce any information other than that he belonged to the Milanese school. Moreover the context in which the name was forgotten seemed to me harm-

1. [The 'Four Last Things' are Death, Judgement, Hell and Heaven.]

less and did not enlighten me further. I was driving in the company of a stranger from Ragusa in Dalmatia to a place in Herzegovina: our conversation turned to the subject of travel in Italy, and I asked my companion whether he had ever been to Orvieto and looked at the famous frescoes there, painted by . . .

(b) Light was only thrown on the forgetting of the name when I recalled the topic we had been discussing directly before, and it was revealed as a case in which *a topic that has just been raised is disturbed by the preceding topic*. Shortly before I put the question to my travelling companion whether he had ever been to Orvieto, we had been talking about the customs of the Turks living in *Bosnia* and *Herzegovina*. I had told him what I had heard from a colleague practising among those people – that they are accustomed to show great confidence in their doctor and great resignation to fate. If one has to inform them that nothing can be done for a sick person, their reply is: '*Herr* [Sir], what is there to be said? If he could be saved, I know you would have saved him.' In these sentences we for the first time meet with the words and names *Bosnia*, *Herzegovina* and *Herr*, which can be inserted into an associative series between *Signorelli* and *Botticelli – Boltraffio*.

(c) I assume that the series of thoughts about the customs of the Turks in Bosnia, etc., acquired the capacity to disturb the next succeeding thought from the fact that I had withdrawn my attention from that series before it was brought to an end. I recall in fact wanting to tell a second anecdote which lay close to the first in my memory. These Turks place a higher value on sexual enjoyment than on anything else, and in the event of sexual disorders they are plunged in a despair which contrasts strangely with their resignation towards the threat of death. One of my colleague's patients once said to him: '*Herr*, you must know that if *that* comes to an end then life is of no value.' I suppressed my account of this characteristic trait, since I did not want to allude to the topic in a conversation with a stranger. But I did more: I also diverted my attention from pursuing thoughts which might have arisen in my mind from the topic of 'death and sexuality'. On this occasion I was still under the influence of a piece of news which had reached me a few weeks before while I was making a brief stay at *Trafoi*.[1] A patient over whom I had taken a great deal of trouble had put an end to his life on account of an incurable sexual disorder. I know for certain that this melancholy event and everything related to it was not recalled to my conscious memory during my journey to Herzegovina. But the similarity between 'Trafoi' and 'Boltraffio' forces me to assume that this reminiscence, in spite of my attention being deliberately diverted from it, was brought into operation in me at the time [of the conversation].

(*d*) It is no longer possible for me to take the forgetting of the name *Signorelli* as a chance event. I am forced to recognize the influence of a *motive* in the process. It was a motive which caused me to interrupt myself while recounting what was in my mind (concerning the customs of the Turks, etc.), and it was a motive which further influenced me so that I debarred the thoughts connected with them, the thoughts which had led to the news at Trafoi, from becoming conscious in my mind. I wanted, therefore, to forget something; I had *repressed* something. What I wanted to forget was not, it is true, the name of the artist at Orvieto but something else – something, however, which contrived to place itself in an associative connection with his name, so that my act of will missed its target and I forgot *the one thing against my will*, while I wanted to forget *the other thing intentionally*. The disinclination to remember was aimed against one content; the inability to remember emerged in another. It would obviously be a simpler case if disinclination and inability to remember related to the same content. Moreover the substitute names no longer strike me as so entirely unjustified as they did before the matter was elucidated: by a sort of compromise they remind me just as much of what I wanted to forget as of what I wanted to remember; and they

1. [A hamlet in the Tyrol.]

show me that my intention to forget something was neither a complete success nor a complete failure.

(e) The way in which the missing name and the repressed topic (the topic of death and sexuality, etc., in which the names of Bosnia, Herzegovina and Trafoi appeared) became linked is very striking. The schematic diagram which I have inserted at this point, and which is repeated from the 1898 paper [Fig. 1], aims at giving a clear picture of this.

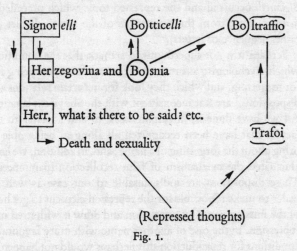

Fig. 1.

The name *Signorelli* has undergone a division into two pieces. One of the pairs of syllables (*elli*) recurs without alteration in one of the substitute names: while the other, by means of the translation of *Signor* into *Herr*, has acquired a numerous and miscellaneous set of relations to the names contained in the repressed topic, but for this reason it is not available for [conscious] reproduction. The substitute for it [for *Signor*] has been arrived at in a way that suggests that a displacement along the connected names of ' *Her*zegovina and *Bo*snia '[1] had taken place,

1. [These two portions of the Austro-Hungarian monarchy used to be habitually spoken of together, almost as though they formed a single word.]

without consideration for the sense or for the acoustic demarcation of the syllables. Thus the names have been treated in this process like the pictograms in a sentence which has had to be converted into a picture-puzzle (or rebus). Of the whole course of events that have in ways like these produced the substitute names instead of the name *Signorelli* no information has been given to consciousness. At first sight it seems impossible to discover any relation between the topic in which the name *Signorelli* occurred and the repressed topic which preceded it in time, apart from this recurrence of the same syllables (or rather sequence of letters).

Perhaps it is not superfluous to remark that the conditions which psychologists assume to be necessary for reproducing and for forgetting, and which they look for in certain relations and dispositions,[1] are not inconsistent with the above explanation. All we have done is, in certain cases, to add a *motive* to the factors that have been recognized all along as being able to bring about the forgetting of a name; and, in addition, we have elucidated the mechanism of false recollection (paramnesia). These dispositions are indispensable to our case as well, in order to make it possible for the repressed element to get hold of the missing name by association and draw it with itself into repression. In the case of another name with more favourable conditions for reproduction this perhaps would not happen. It is probable indeed that a suppressed element always strives to assert itself elsewhere, but is successful in this only when suitable conditions meet it half way. At other times the suppression succeeds without any functional disturbance, or, as we can justly say, without any *symptom*.

The conditions necessary for forgetting a name, when forgetting it is accompanied by paramnesia, may then be summarized as follows: (1) a certain disposition for forgetting the name, (2) a process of suppression carried out shortly before, (3) the possibility of establishing an *external* association between the name in question and the element previously suppressed.

1. [I.e. 'mental traces'. See Stout, 1938, 21.]

The difficulty of fulfilling the last condition need probably not
be rated very high, since, considering the low standards expected of an association of this kind, one could be established
in the great majority of cases. There is, however, the profounder
question whether an external association like this can really be
a sufficient condition for the repressed element's disturbing the
reproduction of the lost name – whether some more intimate
connection between the two topics is not required. On a superficial consideration one would be inclined to reject the latter
demand, and accept as sufficient a temporal contiguity between
the two, even if the contents are completely different. On close
enquiry, however, one finds more and more frequently that
the two elements which are joined by an external association
(the repressed element and the new one) possess in addition
some connection of content; and such a connection is in fact
demonstrable in the *Signorelli* example.[1]

The value of the insight that we have gained in analysing
the *Signorelli* example naturally depends on whether we want to
pronounce that instance as typical or as an isolated occurrence.
I must affirm, then, that the forgetting of names, accompanied
by paramnesia, takes place with uncommon frequency in the
way in which we have explained it in the *Signorelli* case. In
almost every instance in which I could observe this phenomenon in myself, I have also been able to explain it in the way
described above, i.e. as motivated by repression. I must also
draw attention to another consideration which supports the
typical nature of our analysis. I think there is no justification for
making a theoretical separation between those cases in which
the forgetting of names is accompanied by paramnesia and the
sort where incorrect substitute names have not presented
themselves.[2] These substitute names occur spontaneously in
a number of cases; in others, where they have not emerged
spontaneously, it is possible to force them to emerge by an effort

1. [See footnote 1 below, p. 51].
2. [Freud returns to this question in the next chapter, p. 50].

of attention; and they then show the same relation to the repressed element and to the missing name as they would if they had appeared spontaneously. Two factors seem to be decisive in bringing the substitute names to consciousness: first, the effort of attention, and secondly, an inner condition that attaches to the psychical material. We might look for the latter in the greater or lesser facility with which the necessary external association between the two elements establishes itself. A good portion of the cases of name-forgetting *without* paramnesia can thus be added to the cases in which substitute names are formed – to which the mechanism of the *Signorelli* example applies. I shall however certainly not venture to affirm that all cases of name-forgetting are to be classed in the same group. There is no question that instances of it exist which are much simpler. We shall, I think, have stated the facts of the case with sufficient caution if we affirm: *By the side of simple cases where proper names are forgotten there is a type of forgetting which is motivated by repression.*

CHAPTER II

THE FORGETTING OF
FOREIGN WORDS[1]

THE current vocabulary of our own language, when it is confined to the range of normal usage, seems to be protected against being forgotten.[2] With the vocabulary of a foreign language it is notoriously otherwise. The disposition to forget it extends to all parts of speech, and an early stage in functional disturbance is revealed by the fluctuations in the control we have over our stock of foreign words – according to the general condition of our health and to the degree of our tiredness. In a number of cases this kind of forgetting exhibits the same mechanism disclosed to us by the *Signorelli* example. In proof of this I shall give only a single analysis, one which is distinguished, however, by some useful characteristics: it concerns the forgetting of a non-substantival word in a Latin quotation.

1. [Apart from the change recorded in the next footnote, a new footnote on p. 49, and a short addition to the footnote on pp. 50–51, the whole of this chapter dates back to 1901.]

2. [In 1901 and 1904 there was at this point a long footnote. It began: 'I am doubtful whether frequency of use can by itself account for this protection. I have at any rate observed that first names, which do not have the same restricted application that proper names [i.e. surnames] have, are just as liable to be forgotten as the latter.' This was followed by the example now to be found in Chapter III, p. 62 (forgetting the first name of a woman patient's brother). The footnote continued: 'A suppressed thought about oneself or one's own family frequently provides the motive for forgetting a name, as if one were constantly making comparisons between oneself and other people. [Cf. p. 63.] The most curious instance of this sort was reported to me by a Herr Lederer . . .' The example now to be found in Chapter III, p. 63 f., was then cited. In 1907 a new chapter, on the forgetting of names and sets of words, was added to the book (the present Chapter III); these two examples were transferred to it, and the rest of the footnote disappeared.]

Perhaps I may be allowed to present a full and clear account of this small incident.

Last summer – it was once again on a holiday trip – I renewed my acquaintance with a certain young man of academic background. I soon found that he was familiar with some of my psychological publications. We had fallen into conversation – how I have now forgotten – about the social status of the race to which we both belonged; and ambitious feelings prompted him to give vent to a regret that his generation was doomed (as he expressed it) to atrophy, and could not develop its talents or satisfy its needs. He ended a speech of impassioned fervour with the well-known line of Virgil's in which the unhappy Dido commits to posterity her vengeance on Aeneas: '*Exoriare* . . .' Or rather, he *wanted* to end it in this way, for he could not get hold of the quotation and tried to conceal an obvious gap in what he remembered by changing the order of the words: '*Exoriar(e) ex nostris ossibus ultor.*' At last he said irritably: 'Please don't look so scornful: you seem as if you were gloating over my embarrassment. Why not help me? There's something missing in the line; how does the whole thing really go?'

'I'll help you with pleasure,' I replied, and gave the quotation in its correct form: '*Exoriar(e) ALIQUIS nostris ex ossibus ultor.*'[1]

'How stupid to forget a word like that! By the way, you claim that one never forgets a thing without some reason. I should be very curious to learn how I came to forget the indefinite pronoun "*aliquis*" in this case.'

I took up this challenge most readily, for I was hoping for a contribution to my collection. So I said: 'That should not take us long. I must only ask you to tell me, *candidly* and *uncritically*, whatever comes into your mind if you direct your attention to the forgotten word without any definite aim.'[2]

1. [Virgil, *Aeneid*, IV, 625. Literally: 'Let someone (*aliquis*) arise from my bones as an avenger!']
2. This is the general method of introducing concealed ideational

'Good. There springs to my mind, then, the ridiculous notion of dividing up the word like this: *a* and *liquis*.'

'What does that mean?' 'I don't know.' 'And what occurs to you next?' 'What comes next is *Reliquien* [relics], *liquefying*, *fluidity*, *fluid*. Have you discovered anything so far?'

'No. Not by any means yet. But go on.'

'I am thinking', he went on with a scornful laugh, 'of *Simon of Trent*, whose relics I saw two years ago in a church at Trent. I am thinking of the accusation of ritual blood-sacrifice which is being brought against the Jews again just now, and of *Kleinpaul's* book [1892] in which he regards all these supposed victims as incarnations, one might say new editions, of the Saviour.'

'The notion is not entirely unrelated to the subject we were discussing before the Latin word slipped your memory.'

'True. My next thoughts are about an article that I read lately in an Italian newspaper. Its title, I think, was "What St *Augustine* says about Women". What do you make of that?'

'I am waiting.'

'And now comes something that is quite clearly unconnected with our subject.'

'Please refrain from any criticism and –'

'Yes, I understand. I am thinking of a fine old gentleman I met on my travels last week. He was a real *original*, with all the appearance of a huge bird of prey. His name was *Benedict*, if it's of interest to you.'

'Anyhow, here are a row of saints and Fathers of the Church: St *Simon*, St *Augustine*, St *Benedict*. There was, I think, a Church Father called *Origen*. Moreover, three of these names are also first names, like *Paul* in *Kleinpaul*.'

'Now it's St *Januarius* and the miracle of his blood that comes into my mind – my thoughts seem to me to be running on mechanically.'

'Just a moment: St *Januarius* and St *Augustine* both have to

___

elements to consciousness. Cf. my *Interpretation of Dreams* (1900*a*) [Chapter II], *P.F.L.*, 4, 175.]

do with the calendar. But won't you remind me about the miracle of his blood?'

'Surely you must have heard of that? They keep the blood of St Januarius in a phial inside a church at Naples, and on a particular holy day it miraculously *liquefies*. The people attach great importance to this miracle and get very excited if it's delayed, as happened once at a time when the French were occupying the town. So the general in command – or have I got it wrong? was it Garibaldi? – took the reverend gentleman aside and gave him to understand, with an unmistakable gesture towards the soldiers posted outside, that he *hoped* the miracle would take place very soon. And in fact it did take place ...'

'Well, go on. Why do you pause?'

'Well, something *has* come into my mind ... but it's too intimate to pass on ... Besides, I don't see any connection, or any necessity for saying it.'

'You can leave the connection to me. Of course I can't force you to talk about something that you find distasteful; but then you mustn't insist on learning from me how you came to forget your *aliquis*.'

'Really? Is that what you think? Well then, I've suddenly thought of a lady from whom I might easily hear a piece of news that would be very awkward for both of us.'

'That her periods have stopped?'

'How could you guess that?'

'That's not difficult any longer; you've prepared the way sufficiently. Think of *the calendar saints, the blood that starts to flow on a particular day, the disturbance when the event fails to take place, the open threats that the miracle must be vouchsafed, or else* ... In fact you've made use of the miracle of St Januarius to manufacture a brilliant allusion to women's periods.'

'Without being aware of it. And you really mean to say that it was this anxious expectation that made me unable to produce an unimportant word like *aliquis*?'

'It seems to me undeniable. You need only recall the division you made into *a-liquis*, and your associations: *relics, liquefying, fluid*. St Simon was *sacrificed as a child* – shall I go on and show how he comes in? You were led on to him by the subject of relics.'

'No, I'd much rather you didn't. I hope you don't take these thoughts of mine too seriously, if indeed I really had them. In return I will confess to you that the lady is Italian and that I went to Naples with her. But mayn't all this just be a matter of chance?'

'I must leave it to your own judgement to decide whether you can explain all these connections by the assumption that they are matters of chance. I can however tell you that every case like this that you care to analyse will lead you to "matters of chance" that are just as striking.'[1]

I have several reasons for valuing this brief analysis; and my thanks are due to my former travelling-companion who presented me with it. In the first place, this is because I was in this instance allowed to draw on a source that is ordinarily denied to me. For the examples collected here of disturbances of a psychical function in daily life I have to fall back mainly on self-observation. I am anxious to steer clear of the much richer material provided by my neurotic patients, since it might otherwise be objected that the phenomena in question are merely consequences and manifestations of neurosis.[2] My pur-

1. [*Footnote added* 1924:] This short analysis has received much attention in the literature of the subject and has provoked lively discussion. Basing himself directly on it, Bleuler (1919) has attempted to determine mathematically the credibility of psychoanalytic interpretations, and has come to the conclusion that it has a higher probability value than thousands of medical 'truths' which have gone unchallenged, and that it owes its exceptional position only to the fact that we are not yet accustomed to take psychological probabilities into consideration in science.

2. [Cf. Freud's similar remarks on the subject of his choice of dreams for analysis in his preface to the first edition of the *Interpretation of Dreams* (*P.F.L.*, 4, 44–5).]

pose is therefore particularly well served when a person other than myself, not suffering from nervous illness, offers himself as the object of such an investigation. This analysis is significant in a further respect: it throws light on the case of a word being forgotten *without* a substitute for it appearing in the memory. It thus confirms my earlier assertion [p. 43] that the appearance or non-appearance in the memory of incorrect substitutes cannot be made the basis for any radical distinction.[1]

1. Closer scrutiny somewhat diminishes the contrast between the analyses of *Signorelli* and of *aliquis* in regard to substitutive memories. In the latter example too it appears that the forgetting was accompanied by a substitutive formation. When subsequently I asked my companion whether in the course of his efforts to recall the missing word no substitute whatever came into his mind, he reported that at first he had felt a temptation to introduce an *ab* into the line (perhaps the detached portion of *a-liquis*) – *nostris ab ossibus*; and he went on to say that the *exoriare* had thrust itself on him with peculiar clarity and obstinacy, 'evidently', he added with his characteristic scepticism, 'because it was the first word in the line'. When I asked him to attend all the same to the associations starting from *exoriare*, he produced *exorcism*. I can therefore very well believe that the intensification of *exoriare* when it was reproduced actually had the value of a substitutive formation of this sort. This substitute would have been arrived at from the names of the saints *via* the association 'exorcism'. These however are refinements to which one need attach no importance. [The next two sentences were added in 1924:] (On the other hand Wilson, 1922, stresses the fact that the intensification of *exoriare* is of great significance to the understanding of the case, since exorcism would be the best symbolic substitute for repressed thoughts about getting rid of the unwanted child by abortion. I gratefully accept this correction, which does not weaken the validity of the analysis.) It seems possible, however, that the appearance of any kind of substitute memory is a constant sign – even though perhaps only a characteristic and revealing sign – of tendentious forgetfulness which is motivated by repression. It would seem that substitutive formation occurs even in cases not marked by the appearance of incorrect names as substitutes, and that in these it lies in the intensification of an element that is closely related to the forgotten name. For example, in the *Signorelli* case, so long as the painter's name remained inaccessible, the visual memory that I had of the series of frescoes and of the self-portrait which is introduced into the corner of one of the pictures was

The chief importance however of the *aliquis* example lies in another of the ways in which it differs from the *Signorelli* specimen. In the latter, the reproducing of a name was disturbed by the after-effect of a train of thought begun just before and then broken off, whose content, however, had no clear connection with the new topic containing the name of Signorelli. Contiguity in time furnished the only relation between the repressed topic and the topic of the forgotten name; but this was enough to enable the two topics to find a connection in an external association.[1] Nothing on the other hand can be seen in the *aliquis* example of an independent repressed topic of this sort, which had engaged conscious thinking directly before and then left its echoes in a disturbance. The disturbance in reproduction occurred in this instance from the very nature of the topic hit upon in the quotation, since opposition unconsciously arose to the wishful idea expressed in it. The circumstances must be construed as follows. The speaker had been deploring the fact that the present generation of his people was deprived of its full rights; a new generation, he prophesied like Dido, would inflict vengeance on the oppressors. He had in this way expressed his wish for descendants. At this moment a contrary thought intruded. 'Have you really so keen a wish for descendants? That is not so. How embarrassed you would be if you

---

ultra-clear – at any rate much more intense than visual memory-traces normally appear to me. In another case, also described in my 1898 paper, which concerned a visit which I was very reluctant to pay to an address in a strange town, I had forgotten the name of the street beyond all hope of recovery, but my memory of the house number, as if in derision, was ultra-clear, whereas normally I have the greatest difficulty in remembering numbers. [Cf. pp. 81 and 330, below.]

1. I am not entirely convinced of the absence of any internal connection between the two groups of thoughts in the *Signorelli* case. After all, if the repressed thoughts on the topic of death and sexual life are carefully followed up, one will be brought face to face with an idea that is by no means remote from the topic of the frescoes at Orvieto. – [Dr Richard Karpe has suggested that there may be a connection here with the visit to an Etruscan tomb near Orvieto mentioned in *The Interpretation of Dreams* (1900a), *P.F.L.*, 4, 588.]

were to get news just now that you were to expect descendants from the quarter you know of. No: no descendants – however much we need them for vengeance.' This contradiction then asserts itself by exactly the same means as in the *Signorelli* example – by setting up an external association between one of its ideational elements and an element in the wish that has been repudiated; this time, indeed, it does so in a most arbitrary fashion by making use of a roundabout associative path which has every appearance of artificiality. A second essential in which the present case agrees with the *Signorelli* instance is that the contradiction has its roots in repressed sources and derives from thoughts that would lead to a diversion of attention.

So much for the dissimilarity and the inner affinity between these two typical specimens of the forgetting of words. We have got to know a second mechanism of forgetting – the disturbance of a thought by an internal contradiction which arises from the repressed. Of the two processes this is, I think, the easier to understand; and we shall repeatedly come across it again in the course of this discussion.

CHAPTER III

THE FORGETTING OF NAMES AND SETS OF WORDS[1]

OBSERVATIONS such as those mentioned above (Chapter II], of what happens when a portion of a set of words in a foreign tongue is forgotten, may make us curious to know whether the forgetting of sets of words in our own language demands an essentially different explanation. We are not usually surprised, it is true, if a formula learnt by heart, or a poem, can be reproduced only inaccurately some time later, with alterations and omissions. Since, however, this forgetting does not have a uniform effect on what has been learnt as a whole but seems on the contrary to break off isolated portions of it, it may be worth the trouble to submit to analytic investigation a few instances of such faulty reproduction.

A younger colleague of mine told me in conversation that he thought it likely that the forgetting of poetry in one's own language could very well have motives similar to the forgetting of single elements from a set of words in a foreign tongue. At the same time he offered to be the subject of an experiment. I asked him on what poem he would like to make the test, and he chose 'Die Braut von Korinth',[2] a poem of which he was very fond and of which he thought he knew at least some stanzas by heart. At the beginning of his reproduction he was overcome by a rather remarkable uncertainty. 'Does it run "Travelling from Corinth to Athens",' he asked, 'or "Travelling to Corinth from Athens"?' I also had a moment's hesitation, until I laughingly observed that the title of the poem 'The Bride of Corinth' left no doubt which way the young

1. [This chapter was added to the book in 1907. Much new material was included in it later, as will be found specified below. The earlier portion, up to p. 57, dates from 1907.]
2. ['The Bride of Corinth', Goethe's ballad.]

man was travelling. The reproduction of the first stanza then proceeded smoothly or at any rate without any striking falsifications. My colleague seemed to search for a while for the first line of the second stanza; he soon continued, and recited as follows:

> Aber wird er auch willkommen scheinen,
> Jetzt, wo jeder Tag was Neues bringt?
> Denn er ist noch Heide mit den Seinen
> Und sie sind Christen und – getauft.[1]

Before he reached this point I had already pricked up my ears in surprise; and after the end of the last line we were both in agreement that some distortion had occurred here. But as we did not succeed in correcting it, we hurried to the bookcase to get hold of Goethe's poems, and found to our surprise that the second line of the stanza had a completely different wording, which had, as it were, been expelled from my colleague's memory and replaced by something that did not seem to belong. The correct version runs:

> Aber wird er auch willkommen scheinen,
> *Wenn er teuer nicht die Gunst erkauft?*[2]

'*Getauft*' ['baptized', two lines below] rhymes with '*erkauft*', and it struck me as singular that the connected group of

1. [Literally: 'But will he in fact seem welcome,
>   Now, when every day brings something new?
>   For he is still a heathen with his kindred
>   And they are Christians and baptized.'

In addition to the introduction of the completely alien second line, which is discussed in the next paragraph, the third and fourth lines have been slightly misquoted. They should run:

> 'Er ist noch ein Heide mit den Seinen
> Und sie sind schon Christen und getauft.'

> ('He is still a heathen with his kindred
>   And they are already Christians and baptized.')]

2. ['But will he in fact seem welcome *if he does not buy the favour dearly?*']

'heathen', 'Christian' and 'baptized' should have given him so little help in restoring the text.

'Can you explain,' I asked my colleague, 'how you have so completely expunged a line in a poem that you claim you know so well, and have you any notion from what context you can have taken the substitute?'

He was in a position to provide an explanation, though obviously with some reluctance. 'The line "Jetzt, wo jeder Tag was Neues bringt" seems familiar to me; I must have used the words a short time ago in referring to my practice – as you know, I am highly satisfied with its progress at the present time. But how does the sentence fit in here? I could think of a connection. The line "Wenn er teuer nicht die Gunst erkauft" was obviously one which I found disagreeable. It is connected with a proposal of marriage which was turned down on the first occasion, and which, in view of the great improvement in my material position, I am now thinking of repeating. I cannot tell you any more, but if I am accepted now, it certainly cannot be enjoyable for me to reflect that some sort of calculation tipped the scale both then and now.'

This struck me as intelligible, even without my needing to know further particulars. But I continued with my questions: 'How in any case have you and your private affairs become involved in the text of the "Bride of Corinth"? Is yours perhaps a case that involves differences in religious belief like those that play an important part in the poem?'

> (Keimt ein Glaube neu,
> Wird oft Lieb' und Treu
> Wie ein böses Unkraut ausgerauft.)[1]

My guess was wrong; but it was curious to see how a single well-aimed question gave him a sudden perspicacity, so that he was able to bring me as an answer something of which he had certainly been unaware up to that time. He gave me a

1. ['When a faith is newly sprung up, love and troth are often torn out like an evil weed.']

pained, even an indignant look, muttered a later passage from the poem:

> Sieh sie an genau!
> Morgen ist sie grau.[1]

and added shortly: 'She is rather older than I am.' To avoid distressing him further I broke off the enquiry. The explanation struck me as sufficient. But it was certainly surprising that the attempt to trace a harmless failure of memory back to its cause should have had to come up against matters in the subject's private life that were so remote and intimate, and that were cathected with such distressing affect.

Here is another instance, given by Jung (1907, 64), of the forgetting of a set of words in a well-known poem. I shall quote the author's own words.

'A man was trying to recite the well-known poem that begins *"Ein Fichtenbaum steht einsam . . ."*[2] In the line beginning *"Ihn schläfert"*[3] he became hopelessly stuck; he had completely for-

---

1. ['Look on her carefully. Tomorrow she will be grey.'] My colleague has incidentally made changes in this beautiful passage from the poem, somewhat altering both the wording and what the words refer to. The ghostly maiden says to her bridegroom:

> 'Meine Kette hab' ich dir gegeben;
> Deine Locke nehm' ich mit mir fort.
> Sieh sie an genau!
> Morgen bist du grau,
> Und nur braun erscheinst du wieder dort.'

['My necklace I have given thee; your lock of hair I take away with me. Look on it carefully. Tomorrow you will be grey, and you will appear brown again only there.' (The context shows that 'sie' ('it' or 'her') in the third line refers to the lock of hair. In a different context the line could mean: 'Look on her carefully'.)]

2. ['A fir-tree stands alone.' Heine, *Lyrisches Intermezzo*, XXXIII.]

3. [The relevant lines are:

> Ihn schläfert; mit weisser Decke
> Umhüllen ihn Eis und Schnee.

> He slumbers; with a white sheet
> Ice and snow cover him.]

gotten the words "*mit weisser Decke* [with a white sheet]".
Forgetting something in so familiar a verse struck me as surprising, and I therefore made him reproduce what occurred to him in connection with "*mit weisser Decke*". He had the following train of associations: "A white sheet makes one think of a shroud – a linen sheet to cover a dead body" – (a pause) – "now a close friend occurs to me – his brother died recently quite suddenly – he is supposed to have died of a heart attack – he was *also* very stout – my friend is *also* stout, and I have thought before now that it might *also* happen to him – probably he takes too little exercise – when I heard of his brother's death I suddenly became anxious that it might *also* happen to me; for in our family we have in any case a tendency to fatness, and my grandfather, too, died of a heart attack; I have noticed that I too am over-stout and I have therefore begun a course of slimming recently."

'Thus,' comments Jung, 'the man had, unconsciously, identified himself at once with the fir-tree wrapped in the white shroud.'

The following example[1] of the forgetting of a set of words which I owe to my friend Sándor Ferenczi of Budapest, differs from the preceding ones in that it concerns a phrase coined by the subject himself and not a sentence taken from a writer. It may also present us with the somewhat unusual case in which the forgetting ranges itself on the side of our good sense, when the latter threatens to succumb to a momentary desire. The parapraxis thus comes to serve a useful function. When we have sobered down once more we appreciate the rightness of this internal current, which had previously only been able to express itself in a failure to function – a forgetting, a psychical impotence.

'At a social gathering someone quoted " *Tout comprendre c'est tout pardonner* ". I made the comment that the first part of the sentence was enough; "pardoning" was a piece of arrogance:

1. [This paragraph and the four following ones were added in 1910.]

it should be left to God and the priests. One of those present thought this observation very good, and this emboldened me to say – probably with the intention of securing the good opinion of the benevolent critic – that I had recently thought of something better. But when I tried to repeat it I found it had escaped me. I immediately withdrew from the company and wrote down the screen associations [i.e. the substitute ideas]. There first occurred to me the names of the friend and of the street in Budapest that witnessed the birth of the idea I was looking for; next came the name of another friend, Max, whom we usually call Maxi. This led me to the word "maxim" and to the recollection that what we were after was, like my original remark, a variation on a well-known maxim. Strangely enough my next thought was not a maxim but the following sentence: "God created man in His own image" and the same idea in reverse: "Man created God in his." Thereupon the memory of what I was looking for immediately appeared. On that occasion my friend had said to me in Andrássy Street: "Nothing human is foreign to me", whereupon I had answered, in allusion to the discoveries of psychoanalysis: "You ought to have gone further and have admitted that nothing animal is foreign to you."

'But after I had at last remembered what I wanted, I was less than ever able to repeat it in the company I happened to be in. The young wife of the friend whom I had reminded of the animal nature of the unconscious was among those present, and I had to recognize that she was by no means prepared to receive such disagreeable truths. My forgetting spared me a number of unpleasant questions from her and a pointless discussion. This and nothing else must have been the motive for my temporary "amnesia".

'It is interesting that a screen-association was provided by a sentence in which the Deity is debased to the status of a human invention, while in the missing sentence there is an allusion to the animal in man. *Capitis diminutio* [i.e. deprivation of one's status] is therefore the element common to both. The whole subject is clearly only the continuation of the train of thought about understanding and forgiving which the conversation had instigated.

'The fact that what I was looking for in this case was so quick in presenting itself may perhaps be due also to my immediate withdrawal from the company where it was censored to an empty room.'

I have since[1] undertaken numerous other analyses where forgetting or faulty reproduction of a set of words took place, and the consistent result of these investigations has inclined me to assume that the mechanism of forgetting demonstrated above in the instance of '*aliquis*' [p. 46] and 'The Bride of Corinth' [p. 53] has an almost universal validity. It is generally a little awkward to give an account of such analyses since, like those just mentioned, they constantly lead to matters which are of an intimate sort and are distressing to the person analysed. I shall therefore not give any further examples. What is common to all these cases, irrespective of the material, is the fact that the forgotten or distorted matter is brought by some associative path into connection with an unconscious thought-content – a thought-content which is the source of the effect manifested in the form of forgetting.

I now return to the forgetting of names. So far we have not exhaustively considered either the case-material or the motives behind it. As this is exactly the kind of parapraxis that I can from time to time observe abundantly in myself, I am at no loss for examples. The mild attacks of migraine from which I still suffer[2] usually announce themselves hours in advance by my forgetting names, and at the height of these attacks, during which I am not forced to abandon my work, it frequently

1. [What follows from this point until p. 65 dates from 1907, with the exception of the two passages on pp. 62–3 and 63–4.]

2. [Freud suffered from migraine throughout his life. Cf. Jones, 1953, 339.]

happens that all proper names go out of my head. Now it is precisely cases like mine which could furnish the grounds for an objection on principle to our analytic efforts. Should it not necessarily be concluded from such observations that the cause of forgetfulness, and in particular of the forgetting of names, lies in circulatory and general functional disturbances of the cerebrum, and should we not therefore spare ourselves the search for psychological explanations of these phenomena? Not at all, in my view; that would be to confuse the mechanism of a process, which is of the same kind in all cases, with the factors favouring the process, which are variable and not necessarily essential. Instead of a discussion, however, I shall bring forward an analogy to deal with the objection.

Let us suppose that I have been imprudent enough to go for a walk at night in a deserted quarter of the city, and have been attacked and robbed of my watch and purse. I report the matter at the nearest police station in the following words: 'I was in such and such a street, and there *loneliness* and *darkness* took away my watch and purse.' Although I should not have said anything in this statement that was not true, the wording of my report would put me in danger of being thought not quite right in the head. The state of affairs could only be described correctly by saying that *favoured* by the loneliness of the place and under the *shield* of darkness *unknown malefactors* robbed me of my valuables. Now the state of affairs in the forgetting of names need not be any different; favoured by tiredness, circulatory disturbances and intoxication, an unknown psychical force robs me of my access to the proper names belonging to my memory – a force which can in other cases bring about the same failure of memory at a time of perfect health and unimpaired efficiency.

If I analyse the cases of the forgetting of names that I observe in myself, I almost always find that the name which is withheld from me is related to a topic of close personal importance to me, and one which is capable of evoking in me strong and often distressing affects. In accordance with the convenient and commendable practice of the Zurich school (Bleuler, Jung, Riklin) I can also formulate this fact as follows: The lost name has touched on a 'personal complex' in me. The relation of the name to myself is one that I should not have expected and is usually arrived at through superficial associations (such as verbal ambiguity or similarity in sound); it can be characterized quite generally as an oblique relation. Its nature will best be illustrated by some simple examples.

(1) A patient asked me to recommend him a health resort on the Riviera. I knew of such a resort quite close to Genoa, and I also remembered the name of a German colleague of mine who practised there; but the name of the resort itself escaped me, well as I thought I knew that too. There was nothing left for me but to ask the patient to wait while I hurriedly consulted the ladies in my family. 'What on earth is the name of the place near Genoa where Dr N. has his little sanatorium, the one in which so and so was under treatment for so long?' 'Of course you of all people would be the one to forget the name. The place is called *Nervi*.' I must admit I have plenty to do with *nerves*.[1]

(2) Another patient was talking about a neighbouring summer resort, and declared that besides its two well-known inns there was a third one there with which a certain memory of his was connected; he would tell me the name in a moment. I disputed the existence of this third inn, and appealed to the fact that I had spent seven summers at the place and must therefore know it better than he did. But under the provocation of my contradiction he had already got hold of the name. The inn was called the 'Hochwartner'. At this point I was obliged to give in and I even had to confess that I had lived for seven whole summers close by the inn whose existence I had denied. Why in this instance should I have forgotten both the name and the thing? I believe it was because the name was only too similar in sound to that of a colleague, a specialist in Vienna,

1. ['*Nervi*' means 'nerves' in Latin (and in Italian).]

and, once again, had touched upon the 'professional complex' in me.

(3) On another occasion, as I was on the point of booking a ticket at Reichenhall railway station, the name of the next main station would not come into my mind. It was perfectly familiar to me, and I had passed through it very frequently. I had actually to look it up in the time-table. It was '*Rosenheim*'. But I then knew at once owing to what association I had lost it. An hour before, I had paid a visit to my sister at her home close to Reichenhall; as my sister's name is Rosa this was also a '*Rosenheim*' ['Rose-home']. The 'family complex' had robbed me of this name.

(4) I have a whole quantity of examples to illustrate further the positively predatory activities of the 'family complex'.

There came to my consulting-room one day a young man who was the younger brother of a woman patient.[1] I had seen him countless times and used to refer to him by his first name. When I wanted to speak about his visit I found I had forgotten his first name (which was, I knew, not at all an unusual one), and nothing could help me to recover it. I thereupon went out into the street to read the names over the shops, and recognized his name the first time I ran across it. The analysis of the episode showed me that I had drawn a parallel between the visitor and my own brother, a parallel which was trying to come to a head in the repressed question: 'Would my brother in the same circumstances have behaved in a similar way, or would he have done the opposite?' The external link between the thoughts concerned with my own and with the other family was made possible by the chance fact that in both cases the mothers had the same first name of Amalia. Later in retrospect I also understood the substitute names, Daniel and Franz, which had forced themselves on me without making me any wiser. These, like Amalia too, are names from Schiller's [play]

1. [In 1901 and 1904 this example was to be found in a footnote to the first sentence of Chapter II. See above, p. 45, n. 2. It was transferred to its present place in 1907 when Chapter III was added to the book.]

Die Räuber which were the subject of a jest made by *Daniel* Spitzer, the 'Vienna walker'.[1]

(5) Another time I was unable to recall a patient's name; it belonged to associations from my youth. My analysis followed a very devious path before it provided me with the name I was looking for. The patient had expressed a fear of losing his sight; this awoke the memory of a young man who had been blinded by a gunshot; and this in turn was connected with the figure of yet another youth, who had injured himself by shooting. This last person had the same name as the first patient, though he was not related to him. However, I did not find the name until I had become conscious that an anxious expectation was being transferred by me from these two young men who had been injured to a member of my own family.

There thus runs through my thoughts a continuous current of 'personal reference', of which I generally have no inkling, but which betrays itself by such instances of my forgetting names. It is as if I were obliged to compare everything I hear about other people with myself; as if my personal complexes were put on the alert whenever another person is brought to my notice. This cannot possibly be an individual peculiarity of my own: it must rather contain an indication of the way in which we understand 'something other than ourself' in general. I have reasons for supposing that other people are in this respect very similar to me.

The neatest instance of this sort was reported to me by a Herr Lederer, who had experienced it himself.[2] While he was

1. [Daniel Spitzer (1835–1893) was a well-known journalist who made regular contributions to the papers under the title of 'Walks in Vienna'. The reference here is to Spitzer's account of a conversation with a romantic widow, happily under the impression that various characters in Schiller's dramas had been named after members of her family. Cf. Spitzer, 1912, 134 ff.]

2. [In 1901 and 1904 this example was to be found in a footnote to the first sentence of Chapter II. See above, p. 45, *n.* 2. It was transferred to its present position in 1907.]

on his honeymoon in Venice he came across a gentleman with whom he was superficially acquainted and whom he had to introduce to his young wife. Since however he had forgotten the stranger's name, he helped himself out the first time by means of an unintelligible mumble. On meeting the gentleman a second time, as he was bound to do in Venice, he drew him aside and asked him to save him from embarrassment by telling him his name, which he had unfortunately forgotten. The stranger's reply gave evidence of a unusual knowledge of human nature. 'I can readily imagine your failing to remember my name. I have the same name as you – *Lederer*!' – One cannot help having a slightly disagreeable feeling when one comes across one's own name in a stranger. Recently I was very sharply aware of it when a *Herr S. Freud* presented himself to me in my consulting hour. (However, I must record the assurance of one of my critics that in this respect his feelings are the opposite of mine.)[1]

(6) The effects that can be produced by personal reference can also be seen in the following example, reported by Jung (1907, 52):

'A Herr Y. fell in love with a lady; but he met with no success, and shortly afterwards she married a Herr X. There-after, Herr Y., in spite of having known Herr X. for a long time and even having business dealings with him, forgot his name over and over again, so that several times he had to enquire what it was from other people when he wanted to correspond with Herr X.'

The motivation of the forgetting is however more transparent in this case than in the preceding ones that fall within the constellation of personal reference. Here the forgetting seems a direct consequence of Herr Y.'s antipathy to his more fortunate rival; he wants to know nothing about him: 'never thought of shall he be.'[2]

1. [This comment was added in 1907.]

2. ['Nicht gedacht soll seiner werden' – the first line and repeated refrain of a poem of Heine's from the *Nachlese*, 'Aus der Matratzengruft',

(7) The motive for forgetting a name may also be a more refined one; it may consist of what might be called a 'sublimated' grudge against the bearer of it. A Fräulein I. von K. writes from Budapest as follows:

'I have propounded a little theory of my own. I have noticed that people who have a talent for painting have no feeling for music, and vice versa. Some time ago I had a conversation with someone on this point, in which I remarked: "So far my observation has always held good, with the exception of only one person." When I wanted to recall that person's name, I found it had been irretrievably forgotten, even though I knew that the owner of it was one of my closest friends. When I heard the name mentioned quite by chance a few days later, I knew at once, of course, that it was the destroyer of my theory who was being spoken of. The grudge I unconsciously bore against him was expressed by my forgetting his name, which, apart from that, I knew so well.'

(8)[1] The following case, reported by Ferenczi, shows a somewhat different way in which the personal reference led to a name being forgotten. Its analysis is particularly instructive because of the explanation it gives of the substitute associations (like Botticelli and Boltraffio as substitutes for Signorelli [p. 38]).

'A lady, who had heard something about psychoanalysis, could not recall the name of the psychiatrist Jung.[2]

'The following names came to her mind instead: Kl— (a name), Wilde, Nietzsche, Hauptmann.

'I did not tell her the name and invited her to give free associations to each name in turn.

'Starting from Kl— she immediately thought of Frau Kl—, and of how she was a prim and affected person, but

---

No. IV. The phrase is also a traditional Jewish family curse. The following example was added in 1920.]

1. [This example was added in 1910.]

2. ['*Jung*' is also the German for 'young'.]

looked very well for her *age*. "She's *not ageing*." As a common characterization of Wilde and Nietzsche she named "insanity". Then she said chaffingly: "You Freudians will go on looking for the causes of insanity till you're insane yourselves." Then: "I can't bear Wilde and Nietzsche. I don't understand them. I hear they were both homosexuals; Wilde had dealings with *young* people." (In spite of having uttered the correct name – in Hungarian, it is true – in this sentence, she was still unable to recall it.)

'Starting from Hauptmann, first "*Halbe*"[1] and then "*Jugend*" occurred to her; and it was then for the first time, after I had drawn her attention to the word "*Jugend*", that she realized she had been in search of the name *Jung*.

'This lady had lost her husband when she was thirty-nine and had no prospect of marrying again. Thus she had certainly reason enough to avoid recalling anything that reminded her of *youth* or *age*. It is striking that the ideas screening the missing name were associated entirely with its content and that associations with its sound were absent.'

(9)[2] Here is an example of name-forgetting with yet another and a very subtle motivation, which the subject of it has explained himself:

'When I was being examined in philosophy as a subsidiary subject I was questioned by the examiner about the teachings of Epicurus, and after that I was asked if I knew who had taken up his theories in later centuries. I answered with the name of Pierre Gassendi, whom I had heard described as a disciple of Epicurus while I was sitting in a café only a couple of days before. To the surprised question how I knew that, I boldly answered that I had long been interested in Gassendi. The result of this was a certificate *magna cum laude* [with distinction], but also unfortunately a subsequent obstinate tendency to forget the name Gassendi. My guilty conscience is, I

1. [Hauptmann and Halbe were both celebrated German dramatists. One of Halbe's best-known plays was *Jugend* ('Youth').]
2. [This example dates from 1907.]

think, to blame for my inability to remember the name in spite of all my efforts; for I really ought not to have known it on that occasion either.'

In order to appreciate the intensity of our informant's aversion to recalling this examination episode, the reader would have to know the high value he sets on·his doctorate and for how many other things it has to serve as a substitute.

(10)[1] At this point I shall insert another example of the name of a town being forgotten. It is not perhaps as simple as the ones given above [pp. 61 and 62], but it will strike any-one who is fairly well versed in investigations of this nature as authentic and valuable. The name of a town in Italy escaped the subject's memory as a consequence of its great similarity in sound to a woman's first name, with which a number of memories charged with affect were connected, which are doubtless not here reported in full. Sándor Ferenczi of Budapest, who observed this case of forgetting in himself, has treated it in the way in which one analyses a dream or a neurotic idea – a procedure which is fully justified.

'To-day I was with a family that I know, and the conversation turned to cities of North Italy. Someone observed that they still showed traces of Austrian influence. A few of these cities were mentioned, and I wanted to give the name of one too, but it escaped me, although I knew I had spent two very pleasant days there – a fact which did not agree very well with Freud's theory of forgetting. In place of the name I was looking for, the following associations forced themselves on me: *Capua, Brescia, The Lion of Brescia.*

'The picture that I had of this "Lion" took the form of a *marble statue* standing before my eyes like a solid object; I noticed at once, however, that it had less of a resemblance to the lion on the Monument to Freedom at Brescia (of which I have only seen illustrations) than to the other celebrated marble lion which I have seen on the *monument to the dead at Lucerne – the monument to the Swiss guards who fell in the Tuileries,* and of which

1. [This example was added in 1910.]

I have a miniature replica on my bookcase. And now at last the missing name came back to me: it was *Verona*.

'At the same time I knew at once who was to blame for my amnesia. It was no other than a former servant of the family whose guest I was at the time. Her name was *Veronika* (*Verona* in Hungarian), and I had a strong antipathy to her because of her repulsive looks, her *shrill, raucous voice* and her insufferable assertiveness, to which she believed herself entitled by her length of service. At the same time the *tyrannical way* in which she used to treat the children of the house was intolerable to me. I now also understood the meaning of the substitute associations.

'My immediate association to *Capua* was *caput mortuum* [death's head]. I very often compared Veronika's head to a death's head. The Hungarian word "*kapzsi*" (avaricious) doubtless provided an additional determinant for the displacement. I also, of course, found the much more direct associative paths which connect *Capua* and *Verona* as geographical ideas and as Italian words that have the same rhythm.

'The same is true for *Brescia*; but here too there were winding by-paths in the linkage of ideas.

'My antipathy was at one time so violent that I found Veronika positively nauseating, and I had more than once expressed my astonishment that all the same it was possible for her to have an erotic life and be loved by someone. "Why," I said, "to kiss her would make one feel sick!"[1] Nevertheless, she could certainly long since have been brought into connection with the idea of the *fallen* Swiss Guards.

'*Brescia* is very often mentioned, at any rate here in Hungary, in connection not with the lion but with another *wild animal*. The most hated name in this country, and in the north of Italy too, is that of General *Haynau*, commonly known as the "*Hyaena of Brescia*". Thus one thread in my thoughts ran from the hated *tyrant* Haynau *viâ* Brescia to the town of Verona, while the other led, *viâ* the idea of the *animal with the raucous*

---

1. [The first half of the German word for 'nausea' ('*Brechreiz*') has a sound similar to the first syllable of 'Brescia'.]

voice that haunts the graves of the dead (which helped to determine the emergence in my mind of a *monument to the dead*), to the death's head and to the disagreeable voice of Veronika – the victim of such gross abuse by my unconscious – who in her time had acted almost as tyrannically in this house as had the Austrian general after the Hungarian and Italian struggles for freedom.

'*Lucerne* is connected with the thought of the summer which Veronika spent with her employers *in the neighbourhood of the town of Lucerne*, on the lake of that name. The *Swiss Guard* in turn recalls that she knew how to play the tyrant not only to the children but also to the grown-up members of the family, and fancied herself in the part of a "Garde-Dame [duenna, literally, 'guard of ladies']".

'I must expressly remark that this antipathy of mine towards Veronika is – consciously – something that has long been surmounted. Since those times both her appearance and her manner have changed, greatly to her advantage, and I can meet her, though I have in fact little occasion for doing so, with genuinely warm feelings. As usual, my unconscious clings more tenaciously to my [earlier] impressions: it is "retrospective" and resentful.[1]

'The *Tuileries* are an allusion to another person, an elderly French lady, who on many occasions actually "*guarded*" the women of the house; she was respected by everyone, young and old – and no doubt somewhat *feared* as well. For a while I was her *élève* [pupil] for French conversation. The word *élève* further recalls that when I was on a visit to the brother-in-law of my present host, in northern Bohemia, I was very much amused because the local country-people called the *élèves* at the school of forestry there by the name of "Löwen"[2] [lions]. This entertaining memory may also have played a part in the displacement from the hyaena to the lion.'

1. [In German: ' " *nachträglich*" und *nachtragend*.']
2. [The dialect pronunciation of the first syllable of this word would resemble that of the second syllable of '*élèves*'.]

(11)[1] The next example, too, shows how a personal complex which is dominating someone at the time may cause a name to be forgotten in some very remote connection.

'Two men, an older and a younger one, who six months before had made a trip together in Sicily, were exchanging recollections of those pleasant and memorable days. "Let's see," said the younger, "what was the name of the place where we spent the night before making our trip to Selinunte? Wasn't it Calatafimi?" The older one rejected it: "No, it certainly wasn't, but I've forgotten the name too, though I recall most clearly all the details of our stay there. I only need to find someone else has forgotten a name, and it at once makes me forget it too. [Cf. below, p. 81 f.] Let's look for the name. But the only thing that occurs to me is Caltanisetta, which certainly isn't right." "No," said the younger man, "the name begins with a 'w' or has a 'w' in it." "But there's no 'w' in Italian," objected the older. "I really meant a 'v', and I only said 'w' because I'm so used to it in my own language." The older man still opposed the "v". "As a matter of fact," he declared, "I believe I've forgotten a lot of the Sicilian names already; this would be a good time to make some experiments. For example, what was the name of the place on a hill that was called Enna in antiquity? Oh, I know – Castrogiovanni." The next moment the younger man had recalled the lost name as well. "Castelvetrano," he exclaimed, and was pleased at being able to point to the "v" he had insisted on. For a short while the older one had no sense of recognition; but after he had accepted the name it was for him to explain why he had forgotten it. "Obviously," he said, "because the second half, '-vetrano', sounds like 'veteran'. I know I don't much like to think about *growing old*, and I have strange reactions when I'm reminded of it. For instance, I recently charged a very dear friend of mine in the strangest terms with having 'left his youth

1. [This example, first published separately (1911*i*), was added in 1912. The episode is autobiographical, and relates to Freud's visit to Sicily in the autumn of 1910 in the company of Ferenczi.]

far behind him', for the reason that once before, in the middle of the most flattering remarks about me, he had added that I was 'no longer a young man'.[1] Another sign that my resistance was directed against the second half of the name Castelvetrano is that the initial sound recurred in the substitute name Caltanisetta." "What about the name Caltanisetta itself?" asked the younger man. "That," confessed the older one, "has always seemed to me like a pet name for a young woman."

'Some time later he added: "Of course the name for Enna was also a substitute name. And it occurs to me now that Castrogiovanni – a name that forced its way to the front with the help of a rationalization – sounds like '*giovane*' (young) in exactly the same way as the lost name Castelvetrano sounds like '*veteran*' (old)."

'The older man believed that in this way he had accounted for his forgetting the name. No investigation was made of the motive for the similar failure of the younger man's memory.'

Not only the motives, but also the mechanism governing the forgetting of names, deserve our interest.[2] In a large number of cases a name is forgotten not because the name itself arouses such motives, but because – owing to similarity in sound and to assonance – it touches upon *another* name against which these motives do operate. If the determinants are relaxed in this way, the occurrence of the phenomenon will obviously be made very much easier, as the following examples show.

(12) Reported by Dr Eduard Hitschmann (1913*a*): 'Herr N. wanted to give someone the name of the firm of [Vienna] book-sellers Gilhofer and Ranschburg. But however much he thought over it, only the name Ranschburg occurred to him, though he knew the firm perfectly well. He returned home feeling somewhat dissatisfied, and thought it sufficiently im-

---

1. [The friend was J. J. Putnam. The whole episode is discussed in Jones, 1955, 82–3.]

2. [This paragraph and the examples from 12 to 17 inclusive (i.e. down to p. 79) were added in 1917.]

portant to ask his brother (who was apparently already asleep) what the first half of the firm's name was. His brother gave him the name without hesitation. Thereupon the word "Gallhof" immediately sprang to Herr N.'s mind as an association to "Gilhofer". Gallhof was the place where a few months before he had gone for a memorable walk with an attractive young lady. As a memento the lady had given him a present which was inscribed "A souvenir of the happy hours at Gallhof ['*Gallhofer Stunden*', lit. 'Gallhof hours']". In the course of the days just before the name was forgotten, this present had been badly damaged, seemingly by accident, through N.'s shutting a drawer too hastily. He noticed this with a certain sense of guilt, for he was familiar with the meaning of symptomatic acts. [See Chapter IX.] At the time his feelings towards the lady were somewhat ambivalent: he certainly loved her, but he felt hesitation in the face of her desire that they should get married.'

(13) Reported by Dr Hanns Sachs: 'In a conversation about Genoa and its immediate surroundings, a young man wanted to mention the place called *Pegli*, but could only recall the name with an effort after racking his brains. On the way home he thought of the distressing manner in which so familiar a name had slipped away, and in doing so was led to a word sounding very similar: *Peli*. He knew that there was a South Sea island of that name, whose inhabitants still retained a few remarkable customs. He had read about them recently in an ethnological work and had at the time made up his mind to use the information in support of a hypothesis of his own. It then occurred to him that Peli was also the setting of a novel which he had read with interest and enjoyment – namely *Van Zantens glücklichste Zeit* [*Van Zanten's Happiest Time*] by Laurids Bruun. The thoughts that had occupied his mind almost incessantly during the day centred round a letter he had received that same morning from a lady he was very fond of. This letter gave him reason to fear that he would have to forgo a meeting that had been arranged. After being in a very bad mood all day, he had

gone out in the evening resolved not to plague himself any longer with the tiresome thought but to enjoy the social occasion in front of him, on which he in fact set an extremely high value, in as serene a mood as possible. It is clear that his resolution could have been gravely imperilled by the word *Pegli*, as its connection in sound with *Peli* was so close; and Peli in turn, having acquired a personal connection with himself by its ethnological interest, embodied not only Van Zanten's but also his own "happiest time", and therefore the fears and anxieties as well which he had nursed all day long. It is characteristic that this simple explanation only became clear after a second letter from his friend had transformed his doubt into the happy certainty of seeing her again soon.'

This example may recall what might be described as its geographical neighbour, in which the name of the town of Nervi could not be remembered (Example 1 [p. 61]). Thus we see how a pair of words that are similar in sound can have the same effect as a single word that has two meanings.

(14) When war broke out with Italy in 1915 I was able to make the observation upon myself that a whole quantity of Italian place-names which at ordinary times were readily available to me had suddenly been withdrawn from my memory. Like so many other Germans I had made it my habit to spend a part of my holidays on Italian soil, and I could not doubt that this large-scale forgetting of names was the expression of an understandable hostility to Italy which had now replaced my former partiality. In addition to this directly-motivated forgetting of names, however, an indirect amnesia could also be detected, which it was possible to trace back to the same influence. I showed a tendency to forget non-Italian place-names as well; and on investigating the incidents I found that these names were in some way connected by means of remote similarities of sound with the proscribed enemy names. Thus I tormented myself one day in trying to recall the name of the Moravian town of Bisenz. When it finally came to my mind I at once recognized that this act of forgetting was to be

laid to the charge of the Palazzo Bisenzi at Orvieto. The Hotel Belle Arti, where I had stayed on all my visits to Orvieto, is located in this palazzo. The most precious memories had naturally been the most severely damaged by the change in my emotional attitude.

Some examples may also help to remind us of the variety of purposes that can be served by the parapraxis of name-forgetting.

(15) Reported by A. J. Storfer (1914): 'One morning a lady who lived in Basle received news that a friend of her youth, Selma X. of Berlin, who was just then on her honeymoon, was passing through Basle, but staying only one day. The Basle lady hurried straight away to her hotel. When the friends separated, they made an arrangement to meet again in the afternoon and to be with each other up to the time of the Berlin lady's departure.

'In the afternoon the Basle lady *forgot* about the rendezvous. I do not know what determined her forgetting it, yet in this particular situation (a meeting with a *school-friend who has just married*) various typical constellations are possible which could determine an inhibition against the repetition of the meeting. The point of interest in this case lies in a *further* parapraxis, which represents an unconscious safeguarding of the first one. At the time when she was to have met her friend from Berlin the Basle lady happened to be in company at another place. The recent marriage of the Viennese opera singer Kurz[1] came up in conversation; the Basle lady gave vent to some critical remarks (!) about this marriage, but when she wanted to mention the singer by name, she found to her very great embarrassment that she could not think of her first name. (There is, as is well known, a particular tendency to give the first name also, precisely in cases where the surname is a monosyllable.) The Basle lady was all the more put out by her lapse of memory since she had often heard Kurz sing and ordinarily knew her (whole) name perfectly well. Before anyone had

1. [The celebrated coloratura soprano.]

mentioned the missing first name the conversation took another direction.

'In the evening of the same day our Basle lady was among a number of people, some of whom were the same as those she had been with in the afternoon. By a coincidence the conversation again turned to the marriage of the Viennese singer; and without any difficulty the lady produced the name "*Selma* Kurz". "Oh dear!" she at once exclaimed, "it's just struck me – I've completely forgotten I had an appointment with my friend Selma this afternoon." A glance at the clock showed that her friend must have left already.'

We are perhaps not ready yet to appreciate all the aspects of this pretty example. The following is a simpler specimen, though here it was not a name but a foreign word that was forgotten, from a motive arising out of the situation. (We can already see that we are dealing with the same processes, whether they apply to proper names, first names, foreign words or sets of words.) Here it was a case of a young man forgetting the English word for '*Gold*' – which is identical with the German word – so as to find an opportunity for carrying out an action he desired.

(16) Reported by Dr Hanns Sachs: 'A young man became acquainted in a pension with an English lady, whom he took a liking to. On the first evening of their acquaintance he was having a conversation with her in her native language, which he knew fairly well; and in the course of it he wanted to use the English word for "*Gold*". In spite of strenuous efforts the word would not come to him. Instead, the French *or*, the Latin *aurum* and the Greek *chrysos* obstinately forced themselves on him as substitutes, so that it needed quite an effort to reject them, though he knew for certain that they were not related at all to the word he was looking for. In the end the only way he could find of making himself understood was by touching a gold ring on the lady's hand; and he was very much abashed on learning from her that the long-lost word for gold was exactly the same as the German one, namely "gold". The great value

of this touching, for which the forgetting gave an opportunity, did not lie merely in the unobjectionable satisfaction of the instinct for laying hold or touching – for there are other opportunities for this which are eagerly exploited by lovers. It lay much more in the way in which it assisted in clarifying the prospects of the courtship. The lady's unconscious would divine the erotic aim of the forgetting, hidden by its mask of innocence, especially if her unconscious was sympathetically drawn to the man she was talking with. The manner in which she treated his touching of her and accepted its motivation could in this way become a means – unconscious for both of them, yet full of significance – of reaching an understanding on the chances of the flirtation just begun.'

(17) From J. Stärcke (1916) I report another interesting observation that concerns the forgetting and subsequent recovery of a proper name. This case is distinguished by the fact that the forgetting of the name was connected with the misquoting of a set of words from a poem, as in the example of the 'Bride of Corinth' [p. 53].

'Z., an old jurist and philologist, was describing in company how in his student days in Germany he had known a quite exceptionally stupid student, and had some anecdotes to tell of his stupidity. He could not, however, recall the student's name; he believed it began with a "W", but later took back the idea. He recalled that the stupid student later became a *wine merchant*. He then told another anecdote about the student's stupidity, and once again expressed surprise that his name did not come back to him. "He was such an ass," he then remarked, "that I still don't understand how I succeeded in drumming Latin into his head." A moment later he remembered that the name he was looking for ended in "... *man*". At this point we asked him if any other name ending in "man" occurred to him, and he gave "*Erdmann* [Earthman]". "Who is that?" "That was another student of those days." His daughter, however, observed that there was also a Professor Erdmann. Some closer questioning revealed that this Professor

Erdmann, who was the editor of a periodical, had recently refused to accept a piece of work submitted by Z., with which he partly disagreed, except in a shortened form; and Z. had been considerably put out. (In addition, I later discovered that, years before, Z. had very probably expected to become professor in the same department in which Professor Erdmann now lectured. This, then, may have been another reason why the name touched on a sensitive spot.)

'At this point the stupid student's name suddenly came back to him: "Lindeman". Since he had already recalled that the name ended in "man", it was "*Linde* [linden, lime-tree]" that had remained repressed for longer. When he was asked what came to his mind when he thought of "*Linde*", he at first said: "Absolutely nothing." When I urged that something connected with this word would no doubt occur to him, he remarked with an upward gaze and a gesture of his hand in the air: "A linden – well, a linden is a beautiful tree." Nothing further would come to his mind. No one spoke and everyone went on with their reading or other activity, till a few moments later Z. quoted the following passage in a dreamy voice:

> Steht er mit festen
> Gefügigen Knochen
> Auf der *Erde*,
> So reicht er nicht auf,
> Nur mit der *Linde*
> Oder der *Rebe*
> Sich zu vergleichen.[1]

'I gave a cry of triumph. "There's our Erdmann [earth-man]," I said. "The man who 'stands on the earth', that is to say the earthman or Erdmann, cannot reach up far enough to bear comparison with the linden (Lindeman) or the vine (wine merchant). In other words, our Lindeman, the stupid student, who later became a wine merchant, was certainly an ass, but

1. [Literally: 'If he stands with firm, pliant bones on the *earth*, he does not reach up far enough to bear comparison even with the *linden* or the *vine*.']

our Erdmann is a much greater ass than that, and cannot even be compared with this Lindeman." – Such derisive or abusive language in the unconscious is quite usual; so it seemed to me that the chief cause of the name being forgotten had probably now been found.

'I now asked what the poem was from which the lines were quoted. Z. said it was a poem by Goethe, which he thought began:

> Edel sei der Mensch,
> Hilfreich und gut![1]

and which later contained the lines:

> Und hebt er sich aufwärts,
> So spielen mit ihm die Winde.[2]

'The next day I looked up this poem of Goethe's, and it turned out that the case was even prettier (though also more complex) than it had seemed at first.

(*a*) 'The first lines that he quoted run (cf. above):

> Steht er mit festen
> *Markigen* Knochen . . .[3]

'"*Gefügige* Knochen [*pliant* bones]" would be a rather peculiar combination; but I shall not go further into this point.

(*b*) 'The next lines of this stanza run (cf. above):

> . . . Auf der *wohlgegründeten*
> *Dauernden* Erde,
> Reicht er nicht auf,
> Nur mit der *Eiche*
> Oder der Rebe
> Sich zu vergleichen.[4]

So in the whole poem there is no mention of a linden. The change of "oak" into "linden" had taken place (in his un-

1. ['Let Man be noble, helpful and good.']
2. ['And if he raises himself upwards the winds play with him.']
3. ['If he stands with firm, *sturdy* bones . . .']
4. ['. . . on the *firmly-based, enduring* earth, he does not reach up far enough to bear comparison even with the *oak* or the vine.']

conscious) only in order to make the play on the words "earth – linden – vine" possible.

(c) 'This poem is called "Grenzen der Menschheit [The Limits of Mankind]" and compares the omnipotence of the gods with man's puny strength. But the poem beginning:

> Edel sei der Mensch,
> Hilfreich und gut!

is a different one, appearing some pages further on. Its title is "Das Göttliche [The Divine Nature]", and it too contains thoughts about gods and men. As the matter was not gone into further I can at the most offer an opinion that thoughts about life and death, the temporal and the eternal, and the subject's own frail life and future death also played a part in bringing about the occurrence of this case.'

In some of these examples all the subtleties of psycho-analytic technique have to be called upon in order to explain the forgetting of a name. Anyone who wishes to learn more about such work may be referred to a paper by Ernest Jones of London (1911a). It has been translated into German.[1]

(18) Ferenczi has observed that forgetting a name may also make its appearance as a hysterical symptom. In this situation it displays a very different mechanism from that of a para-praxis. The nature of this distinction may be seen from what he says:

'At the moment I am treating a patient, a spinster getting on in years, in whose mind the most familiar and best-known proper names fail to appear, although her memory is otherwise good. In the course of the analysis it has become clear that this symptom is intended by her as a documentation of her ignor-ance. This demonstrative parade of her ignorance is, however, really a reproach against her parents, who did not let her have any higher education. Her tormenting obsession to clean things ("housewife's psychosis") also comes in part from the same

1. [This paragraph was added in 1912. The following example (18) was added in 1920.]

source. What she means by this is something like: "You have turned me into a housemaid."'

I could cite[1] further instances of the forgetting of names and explore the matter much more fully if I were not reluctant to anticipate at this first stage almost all the points of view that will come up for discussion under later topics. But I may perhaps allow myself to summarize in a few sentences the conclusions to be drawn from the analyses that have been reported here:

The mechanism of names being forgotten (or, to be more accurate, the mechanism of names escaping the memory, of being *temporarily* forgotten) consists in the interference with the intended reproduction of the name by an alien train of thought which is not at the time conscious. Between the name interfered with and the interfering complex either a connection exists from the outset, or else such a connection has established itself, often in ways that appear artificial, *viâ* superficial (external) associations.

Among the interfering complexes those of personal reference (i.e. the personal, family and professional complexes) prove to have the greatest effect.

A name which has more than one meaning and consequently belongs to more than one group of thoughts (complexes) is frequently interfered with in its connection with one train of thought owing to its participation in another, stronger complex.

Among the motives for these interferences the purpose of avoiding arousing unpleasure by remembering is conspicuous.

In general two main types of name-forgetting may be distinguished: those cases where the name itself touches on something unpleasant, and those where it is brought into connection with another name which has that effect. Thus names can have their reproduction interfered with on their own account, or because of their closer or remoter associative relations.

A survey of these general propositions shows us why the

1. [What follows up to line 10 on the next page dates back to 1907.]

temporary forgetting of names is the most frequently to be observed of all our parapraxes.

(19) We are however far from having outlined all the characteristics of this phenomenon. There is a further point I wish to make. The forgetting of names is highly contagious. In a conversation between two people it is often sufficient for one of them merely to mention that he has forgotten such and such a name, and the result will be that it slips the other's mind as well. In cases like these, however, where the forgetting is induced, the forgotten name returns more readily.[1] – This 'collective' forgetting, strictly speaking a phenomenon of group psychology, has not yet been made the subject of psychoanalytic study. In a single instance (but an especially neat one) Reik (1920) has been able to offer a good explanation of this curious phenomenon.

'In a small gathering of university people, which included two women students of philosophy, there was a discussion on the numerous questions raised in the fields of religious studies and the history of civilization by the origin of Christianity. One of the young ladies who took part in the conversation recalled that in an English novel she had read recently she had found an interesting picture of the many religious currents by which that age had been stirred. She added that the novel portrayed the whole of Christ's life from his birth up to his death; but the name of the work refused to come to her mind. (The visual memory she had of the cover of the book and the appearance of the lettering in the title was ultra-clear [cf. p. 50 f. n.].) Three of the men who were present also said that they knew the novel, and they remarked that – strange to relate – they too were unable to produce the name.'

The young lady was the only one to subject herself to analysis in order to discover why this name was forgotten. The title of the book was *Ben Hur*, by Lewis Wallace. The ideas

---

1. [Cf. pp. 70 and 104. – The rest of the chapter, with the exception of the last paragraph, was added in 1920.]

that had occurred to her as substitutes for it had been: '*Ecce homo*' – '*Homo sum*' – '*Quo vadis?*' The girl herself realized that she had forgotten the name 'because it contains an expression that I (like any other girl) do not care to use – especially in the company of young men'.[1] In the light of the very interesting analysis, this explanation took on a profounder significance. In the context already alluded to, the translation of '*homo*' (man) also has a disreputable meaning. Reik's conclusion is as follows: 'The young lady treated the word as though by uttering the questionable title in front of young men she would have been acknowledging the wishes which she had rejected as out of keeping with her character and distressing to her. More briefly: saying the words "Ben Hur"[2] was unconsciously equated by her with a sexual offer, and her forgetting accordingly corresponded to the fending-off of an unconscious temptation of that kind. We have reason for supposing that similarly unconscious processes had determined the young men's forgetting. Their unconscious understood the real significance of the girl's forgetting and, so to speak, interpreted it. The men's forgetting shows respect for this modest behaviour ... It is as if the girl who was talking with them had by her sudden lapse of memory given a clear sign, which the men had unconsciously understood well enough.'

A type of continued forgetting of names occurs also, in which whole chains of names are withdrawn from the memory.[3] If in the attempt to recover a lost name other names closely connected with it are pursued, it frequently happens that these new names, which were to serve as stepping stones to the other one, disappear in just the same way. The forgetting thus jumps from one name to another, as if to prove the existence of an obstacle which cannot easily be surmounted.

1. ['*Hure*' is the German for 'whore'.]
2. [The German words '*bin Hure*' ('I am a whore') sound not unlike 'Ben Hur'.]
3. [This paragraph dates from 1907.]

CHAPTER IV

CHILDHOOD MEMORIES AND SCREEN MEMORIES[1]

In a second paper, which was published in the *Monatsschrift für Psychiatrie und Neurologie* (1899a), I was in a position to demonstrate at an unexpected point the tendentious nature of the workings of our memory. I started from the striking fact that a person's earliest childhood memories seem frequently to have preserved what is indifferent and unimportant, whereas (frequently, though certainly not universally) no trace is found in an adult's memory of impressions dating from that time which are important, impressive and rich in affect. It might be assumed from this – since it is known that the memory makes a selection from among the impressions offered to it – that in childhood the selection is conducted on entirely different principles from those which apply at the time of intellectual maturity. Careful investigation nevertheless shows that such an assumption is unnecessary. The indifferent memories of childhood owe their existence to a process of displacement: they are substitutes, in [mnemic] reproduction, for other impressions which are really significant. The memory of these significant impressions can be developed out of indifferent ones by means of psychical analysis, but a resistance prevents them from being directly reproduced. As the indifferent memories owe their preservation not to their own content but to an associative relation between their content and another which is repressed, they have some claim to be called 'screen memories', the name by which I have described them.

1. [In 1901 and 1904 the title of this chapter was simply 'Screen Memories' and it consisted of the first four paragraphs only. The whole of the remainder was added in 1907, except for one paragraph (on p. 89 f.) which dates from 1920, and the final footnote.]

In the paper which I have mentioned I only touched on and in no way exhausted the multiplicity of the relations and meanings of screen memories. In the example quoted there, of which I gave a detailed analysis,[1] I laid special stress on a peculiarity of the *chronological* relation between the screen memory and the content which is screened off by it. In that example the content of the screen memory belonged to one of the earliest years of childhood, while the mental experiences which were replaced by it in the memory and which had remained almost unconscious occurred in the subject's later life. I described this sort of displacement as a *retro-active* or *retrogressive* one. The opposite relation is found perhaps still more frequently: an indifferent impression of recent date establishes itself in the memory as a screen memory, although it owes that privilege merely to its connection with an earlier experience which resistances prevent from being reproduced directly. These would be screen memories that have *pushed ahead* or been *displaced forward*.[2] Here the essential thing with which the memory is occupied *precedes* the screen memory in time. Finally, we find yet a third possibility, in which the screen memory is connected with the impression that it screens not only by its content but also by contiguity in time: these are *contemporary* or *contiguous* screen memories.

How large a part of our store of memory falls into the category of screen memories, and what role they play in various neurotic thought-processes, are problems whose significance I neither discussed in my earlier paper nor shall enter into here. My only concern is to emphasize the similarity between the forgetting of proper names accompanied by paramnesia, and the formation of screen memories.

At first sight the differences between the two phenomena are much more striking than any analogies that may be found.

1. [This example, like the one at the end of the present chapter, was in fact derived from Freud's own experience.]

2. [I.e. the *displacement* in their case would have been in a forward direction.]

The former phenomenon relates to proper names; the latter to whole impressions, things experienced either in reality or in thought. In the former we have a manifest failure of the function of memory; in the latter, an act of memory that strikes us as strange. In the former it is a case of momentary disturbance – for the name that has just been forgotten may have been produced correctly a hundred times before, and from tomorrow may be produced once again; in the latter it is a case of a permanent and constant memory, since the indifferent childhood memories seem to have the power of staying with us through a large part of our life. The problem in these two cases appears to be quite differently focused. In the former it is the forgetting, in the latter the retention which arouses our scientific curiosity. Closer study reveals that in spite of the dissimilarity between the two phenomena in regard to their psychical material and their duration, the points at which they agree far outbalance it. Both have to do with mistakes in remembering: what the memory reproduces is not what it should correctly have reproduced, but something else as a substitute. In the case of the forgetting of names the act of memory occurs, though in the form of substitute names; the case of the formation of screen memories has as its basis a forgetting of other more important impressions. In both instances an intellectual feeling gives us information of interference by some disturbing factor; but it takes two different forms. With the forgetting of names we *know* that the substitute names are *false*: with screen memories we are *surprised* that we possess them at all. If, now, psychological analysis establishes that the substitutive formation has come about in the same way in both cases, by means of displacement along a superficial association, it is precisely the dissimilarities between the two phenomena, in regard to their material, their duration and their focal point, which serve to heighten our expectation that we have discovered something of importance and of general validity. This general principle would assert that when the reproducing function fails or goes astray, the occurrence points, far more frequently than we suspect, to interference by a tendentious factor – that is, by a *purpose* which favours one memory while striving to work against another.[1]

The subject of childhood memories seems to me to be of such significance and interest that I should like to devote to it a few additional observations which go beyond the views that I have so far expressed.

How far back into childhood do our memories extend? I am familiar with a few investigations into this question, such as those by V. and C. Henri (1897) and by Potwin (1901). They show that great individual differences exist among the persons examined: a few assign their earliest memories to the sixth month of life, while others remember nothing of their lives up to the end of their sixth or even eighth year. But with what are these differences in retaining childhood memories connected, and what significance attaches to them? Clearly it is not sufficient to assemble the material for answering these points by means of a questionnaire; what is required in addition is that it should be worked over – a process in which the person supplying the information must participate.

In my opinion we take the fact of infantile amnesia – the loss, that is, of the memories of the first years of our life – much too easily; and we fail to look upon it as a strange riddle. We forget how high are the intellectual achievements and how complicated the emotional impulses of which a child of some four years is capable, and we ought to be positively astonished that the memory of later years has as a rule preserved so little of these mental processes, especially as we have every reason to suppose that these same forgotten childhood achievements have not, as might be thought, slipped away without leaving their mark on the subject's development, but have exercised a determining influence for the whole of his later life. And in spite of this unique efficacy they have been forgotten! This suggests that

1. [In the 1901 and 1904 editions the chapter ended at this point. See footnote, p. 83.]

there are conditions for remembering (in the sense of conscious reproducing) of a quite special kind, which have evaded recognition by us up to now. It may very well be that the forgetting of childhood can supply us with the key to the understanding of those amnesias which lie, according to our more recent discoveries, at the basis of the formation of all neurotic symptoms.[1]

Of the childhood memories that have been retained a few strike us as perfectly understandable, while others seem odd or unintelligible. It is not difficult to correct certain errors regarding both sorts. If the memories that a person has retained are subjected to an analytic enquiry, it is easy to establish that there is no guarantee of their accuracy. Some of the mnemic images are certainly falsified, incomplete or displaced in time and place. Any such statement by the subjects of the enquiry as that their first recollection comes from about their second year is clearly not to be trusted. Moreover, motives can soon be discovered which make the distortion and displacement of the experience intelligible, but which show at the same time that these mistakes in recollection cannot be caused simply by a treacherous memory. Strong forces from later life have been at work on the capacity of childhood experiences for being remembered – probably the same forces which are responsible for our having become so far removed in general from understanding our years of childhood.

Remembering in adults, as is well known, makes use of a variety of psychical material. Some people remember in visual images; their memories have a visual character. Other people can scarcely reproduce in their memory even the scantiest [visual] outlines of what they have experienced. Following Charcot's proposal, such people are called *auditifs* and *moteurs* in contrast to the *visuels*. In dreams these distinctions disappear: we all dream predominantly in visual images. But

1. [Freud had discussed the connection between infantile amnesia and the psychoneuroses more fully near the beginning of the second of his *Three Essays* (1905d), *P.F.L.*, 7, 89–91.]

this development[1] is similarly reversed in the case of child-hood memories: they are plastically visual even in people whose later function of memory has to do without any visual element. Visual memory accordingly preserves the type of infantile memory. In my own case the earliest childhood memories are the only ones of a visual character; they are regular scenes worked out in plastic form, comparable only to representations on the stage. In these scenes of childhood, whether in fact they prove to be true or falsified, what one sees invariably includes oneself as a child, with a child's shape and clothes. This circumstance must cause surprise: in their recollections of later experiences adult *visuels* no longer see themselves.[2] Furthermore it contradicts all that we have learnt to suppose that in his experiences a child's attention is directed to himself instead of exclusively to impressions from outside. One is thus forced by various considerations to suspect that in the so-called earliest childhood memories we possess not the genuine memory-trace but a later revision of it, a revision which may have been subjected to the influences of a variety of later psychical forces. Thus the 'childhood memories' of individuals come in general to acquire the significance of 'screen memories' and in doing so offer a remarkable analogy with the childhood memories that a nation preserves in its store of legends and myths.[3]

Anyone who has investigated a number of people psycho-logically by the method of psychoanalysis will in the course of his work have collected numerous examples of every kind of screen memory. However, the reporting of these examples is made extraordinarily difficult owing to the nature of the relations, which I have just discussed, between childhood memories

1. [I.e. the development of the distinctions proposed by Charcot.]

2. This statement is based on a number of enquiries I have made.

3. [This analogy between the childhood memories of an individual and the myths and legends of a nation relating to its prehistoric past is developed by Freud in Chapter II of his essay on Leonardo da Vinci (1910c). See also below, p. 199.]

and later life. In order to show that a childhood memory is to be regarded as a screen memory, it would often be necessary to present the complete life history of the person in question. Only rarely is it possible to lift a single screen memory out of its context in order to give an account of it, as in the following good example.

A man of twenty-four has preserved the following picture from his fifth year. He is sitting in the garden of a summer villa, on a small chair beside his aunt, who is trying to teach him the letters of the alphabet. He is in difficulties over the difference between *m* and *n* and he asks his aunt to tell him how to know one from the other. His aunt points out to him that the *m* has a whole piece more than the *n* – the third stroke. There appeared to be no reason for challenging the trustworthiness of this childhood memory: it had, however, only acquired its meaning at a later date, when it showed itself suited to represent symbolically another of the boy's curiosities. For just as at that time he wanted to know the difference between *m* and *n*, so later he was anxious to find out the difference between boys and girls, and would have been very willing for this particular aunt to be the one to teach him. He also discovered then that the difference was a similar one – that a boy, too, has a whole piece more than a girl; and at the time when he acquired this piece of knowledge he called up the recollection of the parallel curiosity of his childhood.

Here is another example, from the later years of childhood.[1] A man who is severely inhibited in his erotic life, and who is now over forty, is the eldest of nine children. At the time that the youngest of his brothers and sisters was born he was fifteen, yet he maintains firmly and obstinately that he had never noticed any of his mother's pregnancies. Under pressure from my scepticism a memory presented itself to him: once at the age of eleven or twelve he had seen his mother hurriedly *unfasten* her skirt in front of the mirror. He now added of his own accord that she had come in from the street and had been overcome

1. [This paragraph was added in 1920.]

by unexpected labour pains. The unfastening ['*Aufbinden*'] of the skirt was a screen memory for the confinement ['*Entbindung*']. We shall come across the use of 'verbal bridges' of this kind in further cases.[1]

I should like now to give a single example of the way in which a childhood memory, which previously appeared to have no meaning, can acquire one as a result of being worked over by analysis. When I began in my forty-third year to direct my interest to what was left of my memory of my own childhood there came to my mind a scene which had for a long while back (from the remotest past, as it seemed to me) come into consciousness from time to time, and which I had good evidence for assigning to a date before the end of my third year.[2] I saw myself standing in front of a cupboard ['*Kasten*'] demanding something and screaming, while my half-brother, my senior by twenty years, held it open. Then suddenly my mother, looking beautiful and slim, walked into the room, as if she had come in from the street. These were the words in which I described

1. [See below, pp. 156 and 338. – In Freud's interleaved copy of the 1904 edition (cf. Editor's Introduction, p. 35) the following notes on screen memories are to be found. 'Dr B— showed very neatly one Wednesday [i.e. at a meeting of the "Vienna Psycho-Analytical Society" (cf. Jones, 1955, 9)] that fairy tales can be made use of as screen memories in the same kind of way that empty shells are used as a home by the hermit crab. These fairy tales then become favourites, without the reason being known.' – 'From a dream of P.'s it appears that ice is in fact a symbol by antithesis for an erection: i.e. something that becomes hard in the cold instead of – like a penis – in heat (in excitation). The two antithetical concepts of sexuality and death are frequently linked through the idea that death makes things stiff. One of the Henris' informants instanced a piece of ice as a screen memory for his grandmother's death. See my paper on "Screen Memories" [1899*a*, where the paper by V. and C. Henri (1897) is more fully discussed].']

2. [The important part played by this screen memory in Freud's self-analysis, and the progressive stages in its elucidation, can be followed in two letters which he wrote to Fliess on October 3–4 and October 15, 1897 (Freud, 1950*a*, Letters 70 and 71). At that date Freud was, in fact, in his forty-*second* year.]

the scene, of which I had a plastic picture, but I did not know what more I could make of it. Whether my brother wanted to open or shut the cupboard – in my first translation of the picture I called it a 'wardrobe' ['*Schrank*'] – why I was crying, and what the arrival of my mother had to do with it – all this was obscure to me. The explanation I was tempted to give myself was that what was in question was a memory of being teased by my elder brother and of my mother putting a stop to it. Such misunderstandings of a childhood scene which is preserved in the memory are by no means rare: a situation is recalled, but it is not clear what its central point is, and one does not know on which of its elements the psychical accent is to be placed. Analytic effort led me to take a quite unexpected view of the picture. I had missed my mother, and had come to suspect that she was shut up in this wardrobe or cupboard; and it was for that reason that I was demanding that my brother should open the cupboard. When he did what I asked and I had made certain that my mother was not in the cupboard, I began to scream. This is the moment that my memory has held fast; and it was followed at once by the appearance of my mother, which allayed my anxiety or longing. But how did the child get the idea of looking for his absent mother in the cupboard? Dreams which I had at the same time [as the analysis of this memory] contained obscure allusions to a nurse of whom I had other recollections, such as, for example, that she used to insist on my dutifully handing over to her the small coins I received as presents – a detail which can itself claim to have the value of a screen memory for later experiences.[1] I accordingly resolved that this time I would make the problem of interpretation easier for myself and would ask my mother, who was by then grown old, about the nurse. I learned a variety of details, among them that this clever but dishonest person had carried out considerable thefts in the house during my mother's confinement and

---

1. [More details about this will be found in the two letters to Fliess referred to in the last footnote.]

had been taken to court on a charge preferred by my half-brother. This information threw a flood of light on the child-hood scene, and so enabled me to understand it. The sudden disappearance of the nurse had not been a matter of indifference to me: the reason why I had turned in particular to this brother, and had asked him where she was, was probably because I had noticed that he played a part in her disappearance; and he had answered in the elusive and punning fashion that was charac-teristic of him: 'She's "boxed up" ["*eingekastelt*"].' At the time, I understood this answer in a child's way [i.e. literally], but I stopped asking any more questions as there was nothing more to learn. When my mother left me a short while later, I suspected that my naughty brother had done the same thing to her that he had done to the nurse and I forced him to open the cupboard ['*Kasten*'] for me. I now understand, too, why in the translation of this visual childhood scene my mother's slimness was emphasized: it must have struck me as having just been restored to her. I am two and a half years older than the sister who was born at that time, and when I was three years old my half-brother and I ceased living in the same place.[1]

1. [*Footnote added* 1924:] Anyone who is interested in the mental life of these years of childhood will find it easy to guess the deeper determinant of the demand made on the big brother. The child of not yet three had understood that the little sister who had recently arrived had grown inside his mother. He was very far from approving of this addition to the family, and was full of mistrust and anxiety that his mother's inside might conceal still more children. The wardrobe or cupboard was a symbol for him of his mother's inside. So he insisted on looking into this cupboard, and turned for this to his big brother, who (as is clear from other material) had taken his father's place as the child's rival. Besides the well-founded suspicion that this brother had had the lost nurse 'boxed up', there was a further suspicion against him – namely that he had in some way introduced the recently born baby into his mother's inside. The affect of disappointment when the cupboard was found to be empty derived, therefore, from the superficial motivation for the child's demand. As regards the *deeper* trend of thought, the affect was in the wrong place. On the other hand, his great satisfaction over his

mother's slimness on her return can only be fully understood in the light of this deeper layer. – [Freud returned repeatedly to the subject of childhood memories. In his study on Leonardo da Vinci (1910*c*) and his paper on a memory of Goethe's (1917*b*) he applied his clinical observations to historical characters. – Some discussion of the processes of 'normal' forgetting will be found on pp. 184–5 and in a footnote on p. 339 below.]

CHAPTER V

SLIPS OF THE TONGUE[1]

THE ordinary [linguistic] material which we use for talking in our native language appears to be protected against being forgotten; but it succumbs all the more frequently to another disturbance, which is known as a 'slip of the tongue'. The slips of the tongue that we observe in normal people give an impression of being the preliminary stages of the so-called 'paraphasias' that appear under pathological conditions.[2]

This is a subject on which I find myself in the exceptional position of being able to acknowledge the value of a previous work. In 1895 Meringer and C. Mayer published a study on 'Slips in Speaking and Reading'. Their lines of approach differ widely from my own. One of the authors, who acts as spokesman in the text, is in fact a philologist, and it was his linguistic interests which led him to attempt to discover the rules that govern the making of slips of the tongue. He hoped to be able to conclude from these rules that there exists 'a certain mental mechanism, in which the sounds of a word, or of a sentence, and the [whole] words as well, are mutually linked and connected in a quite peculiar way' (10).[3]

The examples of slips of the tongue collected by the authors

1. [With the exception of two paragraphs on p. 96 f., and Example 8 on p. 106 f., the whole of the earlier portion of this chapter (up to p. 109) dates back to 1901.]

2. [Freud had discussed 'paraphasia' as a symptom of organic brain disorders in his book on aphasia (1891*b*, English translation, 1953, 13 ff.); but he had also pointed out there that the *symptom* of paraphasia in such disorders 'does not differ from the incorrect use and the distortion of words which the healthy person can observe in himself in states of fatigue or divided attention or under the influence of disturbing affects'.]

3. [Page references in this chapter without a preceding 'p.', unless otherwise specified, are to Meringer and Mayer (1895).]

are first grouped by them in purely descriptive categories. They are classed as *transpositions* (e.g. 'the Milo of Venus' instead of 'the Venus of Milo'); *pre-sonances* or *anticipations* (e.g. 'es war mir auf der Schwest . . . auf der Brust so schwer'[1]); *post-sonances* or *perseverations* (e.g. 'ich fordere Sie *auf, auf* das Wohl unseres Chefs *auf*zustossen' instead of '*anzustossen*');[2] *contaminations* (e.g. 'er setzt sich auf den Hinterkopf', combined from 'er setzt sich einen Kopf auf' and 'er stellt sich auf die Hinterbeine');[3] and *substitutions* (e.g. 'ich gebe die Präparate in den Briefkasten' instead of 'Brütkasten').[4] There are in addition to these main categories a few others which are less important (or less significant from our own point of view). In the above arrangement into groups it makes no difference whether the transposition, distortion, amalgamation, etc., is concerned with single sounds in a word, with syllables, or with complete words forming part of the intended sentence.

To explain the various kinds of slips of the tongue he had observed, Meringer postulates that different spoken sounds have a different psychical valency. When we innervate the first sound in a word or the first word in a sentence, the excitatory process already extends to the later sounds and the following words, and in so far as these innervations are simultaneous with one another they can exercise a modifying influence on one another. The excitation of the sound that is psychically more intense anticipates other excitations or perseverates after them, and in this way disturbs the less valent process of innervation. The question has therefore to be decided which sounds in a word

1. [The intended phrase was: 'it lay so heavily on my breast (*Brust*).' The substituted '*Schwest*' is a non-existent word. This instance is further discussed and explained below, p. 125.]

2. ['I call on you to *hiccough to* the health of our Principal' instead of '*drink to*'. This instance is referred to again below, pp. 126-7.]

3. ['He stands on the back of his head' (a meaningless phrase) combined from 'He is obstinate' (literally, 'he puts on a head') and 'He gets on his hind legs'.]

4. ['I put the preparation into the letter-box' instead of 'incubator', literally 'hatching-box'.]

have the highest valency. Here is Meringer's view: 'If we want to know which sound in a word has the highest intensity, we must observe ourselves when we are searching for a forgotten word, e.g. for a name. Whichever [sound] is the first to come back into consciousness is in every case the one that had the greatest intensity before the word was forgotten' (160). 'The sounds which are of high valency are the initial sound in the root syllable, and the initial sound in the word, and the accentuated vowel or vowels' (162).

I cannot help contradicting him here. Whether the initial sound of the name is one of the elements of highest valency in a word or not, it is certainly untrue that in a forgotten word it is the first to return to consciousness. The rule stated above is therefore inapplicable. If we observe ourselves while searching for a forgotten name, we are comparatively often obliged to express a conviction that it begins with a particular letter. This conviction proves to be unfounded just as often as not. Indeed, I should like to assert that in the majority of cases the initial sound which we announce is a wrong one. In our example of 'Signorelli' [p. 38], in fact, the substitute names had lost the initial sound and the essential syllables: it was precisely the less valent pair of syllables – *elli* – which returned to memory in the substitute name Botticelli.

How little attention[1] is paid by the substitute names to the initial sound of the missing name may be learned, for instance, from the following case:

One day I found it impossible to recall the name of the small country of which *Monte Carlo* is the chief town. The substitute names for it ran: *Piedmont, Albania, Montevideo, Colico. Albania* was soon replaced in my mind by *Montenegro*; and it then occurred to me that the syllable 'Mont' (pronounced 'Mon') was found in all the substitute names except the last. Thus it was easy for me, starting from the name of Prince Albert [the ruling Prince], to find the forgotten name *Monaco. Colico* gives a

---

1. [This paragraph and the next were added in 1907.]

pretty close imitation of the sequence of syllables and the rhythm of the forgotten name.[1]

If we allow ourselves to suppose that a mechanism similar to that which has been demonstrated for the forgetting of names could also play a part in the phenomena of slips of the tongue, we are led to form a more deeply based judgement of instances of the latter. The disturbance in speaking which is manifested in a slip of the tongue can in the first place be caused by the influence of another component of the same speech – by an anticipatory sound, that is, or by a perseveration – or by another formulation of the ideas contained within the sentence or context that it is one's intention to utter. This is the type to which all the above examples borrowed from Meringer and Mayer belong. The disturbance could, however, be of a second kind, analogous to the process in the Signorelli case; it could result from influences *outside* this word, sentence or context, and arise out of elements which are not intended to be uttered and of whose excitation we only learn precisely through the actual disturbance. What these two ways in which slips of the tongue arise have in common would be the simultaneity of the interfering excitation; what differentiates them would be the position of the excitation inside or outside the sentence or context. The difference does not at first appear great in so far as it concerns certain deductions that can be made from the symptomatology of slips of the tongue. It is clear, however, that only in the former case is there any prospect of drawing conclusions from the phenomena of slips of the tongue about a mechanism which links sounds and words with one another so that they mutually influence their articulation – conclusions, that is, such as the

---

1. [This example was used later by Freud in the sixth of his *Introductory Lectures* (1916–17). He states there (in a slightly different and perhaps more lucid account of the episode) that the replacement of *Albania* by *Montenegro* was probably due to the contrast between black and white; and that it was thoughts connected with *Munich* – which is also *Monaco* in Italian – which had caused him to forget the name. (Cf. *P.F.L.*, 1, 141.)]

philologist hoped to arrive at from studying slips of the tongue. In the case of interference from influences *outside* the same sentence or context of what is being said, it would be above all a matter of getting to know what the interfering elements are – after which the question would arise whether the mechanism of this disturbance, too, can reveal the supposed laws of speech formation.

Meringer and Mayer cannot be said to have overlooked the possibility that disturbances of speech may be the result of 'complicated psychical influences', of elements outside the same word, sentence or sequence of spoken words. They were bound to observe that the theory which asserts that sounds are of unequal psychical valency is strictly speaking only adequate for explaining sound-disturbances, together with sound-anticipations and perseverations. Where word-disturbances cannot be reduced to sound-disturbances (as, for instance, in substitutions and contaminations of words), they have not hesitated to look *outside* the intended context for the cause of the slip – a procedure which they justify by some good examples. I quote the following passages:

'Ru. was speaking of occurrences which, within himself, he pronounced to be "*Schweinereien* [disgusting, literally, piggish]". He tried, however, to express himself mildly, and began: "But then facts came to '*Vorschwein*' . . ."[1] Mayer and I were present and Ru. confirmed his having thought "*Schweinereien*". The fact that this word which entered his thoughts was betrayed in "Vorschwein" and suddenly became operative is sufficiently explained by the similarity of the words.' (62)

'Just as in contaminations, so also – and probably to a much higher degree – in substitutions an important role is played by "floating" or "wandering" speech images. Even if they are beneath the threshold of consciousness they are still near enough to be operative, and can easily be brought into play by any resemblance they may have to the complex that is to be spoken.

1. [Ru. intended to say 'came to "*light*"' and should have used the word 'Vor*schein*'. Instead he used the meaningless word 'Vor*schwein*'.]

When this is so they cause a deviation in the train of words or cut across it. "Floating" or "wandering" speech images are often, as we have said, stragglers following after speech processes which have recently terminated (perseverations).' (73)

'Resemblance can also cause a deviation when another, similar word lies a short way below the threshold of consciousness, *without a decision to speak it having been reached*. This is the case with substitutions. – Thus I hope that my rules will of necessity be confirmed when they are tested. But for this it is necessary (if the speaker is someone else) *that we should obtain a clear notion of everything that was in the speaker's thoughts*.[1] Here is an instructive case. Li., a schoolmaster, said in our presence: "Die Frau würde mir Furcht ein*l*agen."[2] I was taken aback, for the *l* struck me as inexplicable. I ventured to draw the speaker's attention to his slip in saying "ein*l*agen" for "ein*j*agen", upon which he at once replied: "Yes, the reason was that I thought: I should not be 'in der *Lage* [in a position]', etc."

'Here is another case. I asked R. von Schid. how his sick horse was getting on. He replied: "Ja, das *draut* ... dauert vielleicht noch einen Monat."[3] I could not understand the "*draut*", with an *r*, for the *r* in "*dauert*" could not possibly have had this result. So I drew his attention to it, whereupon he explained that his thought had been: "das ist eine *traurige* Geschichte [it's a *sad* story]." Thus the speaker had two answers in his mind and they had been intermixed.' (97)

It is pretty obvious that the consideration of 'wandering' speech images which lie below the threshold of consciousness and are not intended to be spoken, and the demand for information about everything that had been in the speaker's mind, are procedures which constitute a very close approach to the state

1. My italics.

2. [He intended to say: 'The lady would strike (*einjagen*) terror into me.' But instead of '*einjagen*' he said '*einlagen*', which is a non-existent verb – though '*Lage*' is a familiar noun meaning 'position'.]

3. [What he intended to say was: 'Well, it will last (*dauert*) another month perhaps.' Instead of '*dauert*' he used the meaningless word '*draut*'.]

of affairs in our 'analyses'. We too are looking for unconscious material; and we even look for it along the same path, except that, in proceeding from the ideas that enter the mind of the person who is being questioned to the discovery of the disturbing element, we have to follow a longer path, through a complicated series of associations.

I shall dwell for a moment on another interesting process, to which Meringer's examples bear witness. The author himself holds that it is some sort of similarity between a word in the sentence intended to be spoken and another word not so intended which permits the latter to make itself felt in consciousness by bringing about a distortion, a composite figure or a compromise-formation (contamination):

| jagen, | dauert, | Vorschein |
| lagen, | traurig, | . . . schwein. |

Now in my *Interpretation of Dreams* (1900a) I have demonstrated the part played by the work of *condensation* in forming what is called the manifest dream-content out of the latent dream-thoughts. A similarity of any sort between two elements of the unconscious material – a similarity between the things themselves or between their verbal presentations – is taken as an opportunity for creating a third, which is a composite or compromise idea. In the dream-content this third element represents both its components; and it is as a consequence of its originating in this way that it so frequently has various contradictory characteristics. The formation of substitutions and contaminations which occurs in slips of the tongue is accordingly a beginning of the work of condensation which we find taking a most vigorous share in the construction of dreams.[1]

In a short essay designed for a wider circle of readers Meringer (1900) has claimed that a special practical significance attaches to particular cases in which one word is put for another – viz. to those cases in which a word is replaced by

1. [Cf. *The Interpretation of Dreams* (1900a), *P.F.L.*, 4, 383 ff.]

another that has the opposite meaning. 'You probably still recall', he writes, 'the way in which the President of the Lower House of the Austrian Parliament *opened* the sitting a short while ago: "Gentlemen: I take notice that a full quorum of members is present and herewith declare the sitting *closed*!" His attention was only drawn by the general merriment and he corrected his mistake. In this particular case the explanation no doubt was that the President secretly *wished* he was already in a position to close the sitting, from which little good was to be expected. But this accompanying idea, as frequently hapens, broke through, at least partially, and the result was "closed" instead of "open" – the opposite, that is, of what was intended to be expressed. Now extensive observations have taught me that words with opposite meanings are, quite generally, very often interchanged; they are already associated in our linguistic consciousness, they lie very close to each other and it is easy for the wrong one to be evoked.'[1]

It cannot be said that in all cases where words are replaced by their opposites it is as easy as in this instance of the President to show the probability of the slip being a consequence of a contradiction arising in the speaker's mind against the uttered sentence. We found an analogous mechanism in our analysis of the *aliquis* example [p. 46]. There the internal contradiction expressed itself in a word being forgotten, instead of its being replaced by its opposite. But in order to soften the distinction we may note that the word *aliquis* is in fact incapable of having an opposite like 'to close' and 'to open', and that 'to open' is a word that cannot be forgotten as it is too familiar a part of our vocabulary.

If the last examples of Meringer and Mayer show that the disturbance of speech can arise on the one hand from the influence of anticipatory or perseverating sounds and words of the same sentence which are intended to be spoken, and on the other hand from the effect of words outside the intended sen-

1. [Freud quotes philological evidence in support of this view in the eleventh of his *Introductory Lectures* (1916–17), *P.F.L.*, I, 213–14.]

tence *whose excitation would not otherwise have been revealed*, the first thing we shall want to know is whether the two classes of slips of the tongue can be sharply divided, and how an example of one class can be distinguished from a case of the other. At this point in the discussion one must however bear in mind the views expressed by Wundt, who deals with the phenomena of slips of the tongue in the course of his comprehensive discussion of the laws of the development of speech.

According to him, a feature that is never missing from these and other related phenomena is the activity of certain psychical influences. 'First of all they have a positive determinant in the form of the uninhibited stream of *sound-associations* and *word-associations* evoked by the spoken sounds. In addition there is a negative factor in the form of the suppression or relaxation of the inhibitory effects of the will on this current, and of the attention which is also active here as a function of the will. Whether this play of association manifests itself by a coming sound being anticipated, or by the preceding sounds being reproduced, or by a habitually practised sound being intercalated between others, or finally by quite different words, which stand in an associative relation to the sounds that are spoken, having an effect upon them – all these indicate only differences in the direction and at the most in the scope of the associations taking place, and not differences in their general nature. In some cases, too, it may be doubtful to which form a certain disturbance is to be assigned, or whether it would not be more justifiable, *in accordance with the principle of the complication of causes*,[1] to trace it back to a concurrence of several motive forces.' (Wundt, 1900, 380–81.) [Cf. below, p. 125.]

I consider these observations of Wundt's fully justified and very instructive. Perhaps it would be possible to emphasize more definitely than Wundt does that the positive factor favouring the slip of the tongue (the uninhibited stream of

1. My italics. [Freud was no doubt regarding this as equivalent to his own concept of 'overdetermination'. Cf. *Studies on Hysteria* (1895*d*), *P.F.L.*, **3**, 289–90 *n*.]

associations) and the negative factor (the relaxation of the inhibiting attention) invariably achieve their effect in combination, so that the two factors become merely different ways of regarding the same process. What happens is that, with the relaxation of the inhibiting attention – in still plainer terms, *as a result of* this relaxation – the uninhibited stream of associations comes into action.

Among the slips of the tongue that I have collected myself, I can find hardly one in which I should be obliged to trace the disturbance of speech simply and solely to what Wundt [1900, 392] calls the 'contact effect of sounds'. I almost invariably discover a disturbing influence in addition which comes from something *outside* the intended utterance; and the disturbing element is either a single thought that has remained unconscious, which manifests itself in the slip of the tongue and which can often be brought to consciousness only by means of searching analysis, or it is a more general psychical motive force which is directed against the entire utterance.

(1) My daughter had made an ugly face when she took a bite at an apple, and I wanted to quote to her:

> Der Affe gar possierlich ist,
> Zumal wenn er vom Apfel frisst.[1]

But I began: 'Der Apfe...' [a non-existent word]. This looks like a contamination of '*Affe* [ape]' and '*Apfel* [apple]' (a compromise-formation), or it might be regarded as an anticipation of the word 'Apfel' that was in preparation. The circumstances were, however, more precisely as follows. I had already begun the quotation once before and had not made a slip of the tongue the first time. I only made a slip when I repeated it. The repetition was necessary because the person I was addressing had had her attention distracted from another quarter and she had not been listening to me. I must include the fact of the repetition, together with my impatience to have done with my sentence,

1. [The ape's a very comic sight
   When from an apple he takes a bite.]

among the motives of the slip which made its appearance as a product of condensation.

(2) My daughter said: 'I am writing to Frau Schresinger . . .' The lady's name is Sch*l*esinger. This slip of the tongue is probably connected with a trend towards making articulation easier, for an *l* is difficult to pronounce after a repeated *r*. I must add, however, that my daughter made this slip a few minutes after I had said '*Apfe*' for '*Affe*'. Now slips of the tongue are in a high degree contagious, like the forgetting of names [p. 81 f.] – a peculiar fact which Meringer and Mayer have noticed in the case of the latter. I cannot suggest any reason for this psychical contagiousness.

(3) 'I shut up like a *Tassenmescher* [a non-existent word] – I mean *Taschenmesser* [pocket-knife]', said a woman patient at the start of the hour of treatment. Here again a difficulty in articulation (cf. 'Wiener Weiber Wäscherinnen waschen weisse Wäsche' [Viennese washer-women wash white washing], 'Fischflosse' [fish-fin] and similar tongue-twisters) could serve as an excuse for her interchanging the sounds. When her attention was drawn to her slip, she promptly replied: 'Yes, that's only because you said "*Ernscht*" to-day.' I had in fact received her with the remark: 'To-day we shall really be in earnest ["*Ernst*"]' (because it was going to be the last session before the holidays), and had jokingly broadened '*Ernst*' into '*Ernscht*'.[1] In the course of the hour she repeatedly made further slips of the tongue, and I finally observed that she was not merely imitating me but had a special reason for dwelling in her unconscious on the word '*Ernst*' in its capacity as a name ['Ernest'].[2]

1. [An uneducated way of pronouncing the word.]
2. In fact she turned out to be under the influence of unconscious thoughts about pregnancy and contraception. By the words 'shut up like a pocket-knife', which she uttered consciously as a complaint, she wanted to describe the position of a child in the womb. The word '*Ernst*' in my opening remark had reminded her of the name (S. Ernst) of a well known Viennese firm in the Kärntnerstrasse which used to advertise the sale of contraceptives.

(4) 'I've got such a cold, I can't *durch die Ase natmen* – I mean, *Nase atmen*',[1] the same patient happened to say another time. She knew immediately how she had come to make the slip. 'Every day I get on the tram in Hasenauer Street, and while I was waiting for one to come along this morning it struck me that if I was French I should say "*Asenauer*", as the French always drop their aitches at the beginning of a word.' She then brought a series of reminiscences about French people of her acquaintance, and came in a very roundabout manner to a memory of having played the part of Picarde in the short play *Kurmärker und Picarde*[2] when she was a girl of fourteen, and of having spoken broken German in the part. The chance arrival at her boarding house of a guest from Paris had awoken the whole series of memories. The interchanging of the sounds was therefore the result of a disturbance by an unconscious thought from an entirely different context.

(5) A slip of the tongue had a similar mechanism in the case of another woman patient, whose memory failed her in the middle of reproducing a long-lost recollection of childhood. Her memory would not tell her what part of her body had been grasped by a prying and lascivious hand. Immediately afterwards she called on a friend with whom she discussed summer residences. When she was asked where her cottage at M. was situated she answered: 'on the *Berglende* [hill-thigh]' instead of *Berglehne* [hill-side].

(6) When I asked another woman patient at the end of the session how her uncle was, she answered: 'I don't know, nowadays I only see him *in flagranti*.' Next day she began: 'I am really ashamed of myself for having given you such a stupid answer. You must of course have thought me a very uneducated person who is always getting foreign words mixed up. I meant to say: *en passant*.' We did not as yet know the source of the foreign phrase which she had wrongly applied. In the same session,

1. [She meant to say: 'I can't breathe through my nose.' Her actual last two words, '*Ase natmen*', have no meaning.]
2. [A *Singspiel* by the Berlin dramatist, Louis Schneider (1805–78).]

however, while continuing the previous day's topic, she brought up a reminiscence in which the chief role was played by being caught *in flagranti*. The slip of the tongue of the day before had therefore anticipated the memory which at the time had not yet become conscious.

(7) At a certain point in the analysis of another woman patient I had to tell her that I suspected her of having been ashamed of her family during the period we were just then concerned with, and of having reproached her father with something we did not yet know about. She remembered nothing of the kind and moreover declared it was unlikely. However, she continued the conversation with some remarks about her family: 'One thing must be granted them: they are certainly unusual people, they all possess *Geiz* [greed] – I meant to say "*Geist* [cleverness]".' And this was in fact the reproach which she had repressed from her memory. It is a frequent occurrence for the idea one wants to withhold to be precisely the one which forces its way through in the form of a slip of the tongue. We may compare Meringer's case of 'zum Vorschwein gekommen' [p. 98]. The only difference is that Meringer's speaker wanted to keep back something that was in his consciousness, whereas my patient did not know what was being kept back, or, to put it in another way, did not know she was keeping something back and what that something was.

(8) ¹The next example of a slip of the tongue is also to be traced back to something intentionally withheld. I once met two ladies in the Dolomites who were dressed up in walking clothes. I accompanied them part of the way, and we discussed the pleasures and also the trials of spending a holiday in that way. One of the ladies admitted that spending the day like that entailed a good deal of discomfort. 'It is certainly not at all pleasant', she said, 'if one has been tramping all day in the sun and has perspired right through one's blouse and chemise.' In

1. [This example was added in 1917.]

this sentence she had to overcome a slight hesitation at one point. Then she continued: 'But then when one gets "nach *Hose*" and can change . . .' No interpellation, I fancy, was necessary in order to explain this slip. The lady's intention had obviously been to give a more complete list of her clothes: blouse, chemise and *Hose* [drawers]. Reasons of propriety led her to suppress any mention of the third article of linen. But in the next sentence, with its different subject-matter, the suppressed word emerged against her will, in the form of a distortion of the similar word 'nach *Hause* [home]'.

(9) 'If you want to buy carpets,' a lady said to me, 'you must go to Kaufmann [a proper name, also meaning 'merchant'] in the Matthäusgasse [Matthew Street]. I think I can give you a recommendation there.' 'At Matthäus . . .,' I repeated, 'I mean Kaufmann's.' My repeating one name in the other's place looks like a result of my thoughts being distracted. They really were distracted by what the woman said, for she diverted my attention to something much more important to me than carpets. As a matter of fact, the house in which my wife lived when she was my fiancée was in the Matthäusgasse. The entrance to the house was in another street, and I now noticed that I had forgotten its name and could only make it conscious in a roundabout way. The name Matthäus, which I was lingering over, was therefore a substitute name for the forgotten street-name. It was more suitable for this purpose than the name Kaufmann, for Matthäus is exclusively a personal name, while Kaufmann is not, and the forgotten street also bears the name of a person: Radetzky.

(10) The following case could just as appropriately be included in the chapter below on 'Errors' [Chapter X], but I quote it here since the phonetic relations, which were the basis of one word being put in place of another, are quite unusually clear. A woman patient told me a dream: A child had resolved to kill itself by means of a snake-bite. It carried out its resolution. She watched it writhing in convulsions, and so on. She had now to find the impressions of the previous day

which the dream had taken as its starting point. She immediately recalled that on the previous evening she had listened to a public lecture on first aid for snake-bites. If an adult and a child were bitten at the same time, the child's injury should be attended to first. She also remembered what the lecturer had prescribed by way of treatment. It would very much depend, he had said, on what kind of snake caused the bite. I interrupted at this point and asked: Surely he must have said that we have very few poisonous kinds in these parts and he must have told you which are the dangerous ones? 'Yes, he particularly mentioned the "*Klapperschlange* [rattlesnake]".' My laughter drew her attention to her having said something wrong. She did not correct the *name*, but took back her statement: 'Yes, of course, they aren't found here; he was talking of the viper. How can I have got the idea of the rattlesnake?' I suspected it was due to interference by the thoughts which had hidden behind her dream. Suicide by means of a snake-bite could hardly be anything other than an allusion to the beautiful Cleopatra [in German: '*Kleopatra*']. The great similarity between the sound of the two words, the occurrence in both of the same letters 'Kl...p...r' in the same order, and of the same stressed 'a', was unmistakable. The close connection between the names '*Klapper*schlange' and '*Kleopatra*' resulted in her judgement being momentarily restricted, so that she saw no objection to asserting that the lecturer had given his audience in Vienna instructions on how to treat rattlesnake bites. In the ordinary way she knew as well as I did that that species of snake is not among the fauna of our country. We will not blame her for her equal lack of hesitation in transferring the rattlesnake to Egypt, for it is usual for us to lump together everything which is non-European and exotic, and I had myself to reflect for a moment before declaring that the rattlesnake is confined to the New World.

The continuation of the analysis brought further confirmation. On the previous day the dreamer had for the first time inspected the Mark *Antony* monument by Strasser, which stood in the vicinity of her home.[1] This then was the second exciting cause of the dream (the first having been the lecture on snake-bites). In the continuation of the dream she was rocking a child in her arms. This scene reminded her of Gretchen.[2] Further ideas which occurred to her brought reminiscences of *Arria und Messalina*.[3] From the fact that the names of so many plays made their appearance in the dream-thoughts we may already have a suspicion that in her earlier years the dreamer had cherished a secret passion for the profession of actress. The beginning of the dream – 'A child had resolved to put an end to its life by means of a snake-bite' – had in fact no other meaning than that when she was a child she had made up her mind to become a famous actress one day. Finally, from the name 'Messalina' the path of thoughts branched off which led to the essential content of the dream. Certain recent events had made her apprehensive that her only brother might make a socially unsuitable marriage, a *mésalliance* with a non-*Aryan*.

(11)[4] I will reproduce here an entirely innocent example (or perhaps one whose motives were insufficiently elucidated), because it displays a transparent mechanism.

A German who was travelling in Italy needed a strap to tie up his damaged trunk. For 'strap' ['*Riemen*'] the dictionary gave him the Italian word '*correggia*'. It will be easy, he thought, to remember the word by thinking of the painter *Correggio*. After that he went into a shop and asked for '*una ribera*'.

He had apparently not been successful in replacing the German word by the Italian one in his memory, but his efforts were nevertheless not entirely unsuccessful. He knew he had to keep in mind the name of a painter, and in this way he hit upon the name not of the painter who sounded much the same

---

1. [A bronze group in Vienna representing the Triumph of Mark Antony by the Austrian sculptor Artur Strasser (1854–1927).]

2. [In Goethe's *Faust*.]

3. [A tragedy by the Viennese playwright Adolf Wilbrandt (1837–1911).]

4. [This example and the following one (No. 12) were added in 1907.]

as the Italian word, but of another one who resembled the German word '*Riemen*'.[1] I could of course have quoted the present case just as appropriately as an example of the forgetting of a name rather than of a slip of the tongue.

When I was collecting slips of the tongue for the first edition of this book I proceeded by subjecting to analysis every case I was able to observe, and accordingly included the less impressive ones. Since then a number of other people have undertaken the amusing task of collecting and analysing slips of the tongue, and have thus enabled me to select from a richer material.

(12) A young man said to his sister: 'I've completely fallen out with the D.'s now. We're not on speaking terms any longer.' 'Yes indeed!' she answered, 'they're a fine *Lippschaft*.'[2] She meant to say '*Sippschaft* [lot, crew]', but in the slip she compressed two ideas: viz. that her brother had himself once begun a flirtation with the daughter of this family, and that this daughter was said to have recently become involved in a serious and irregular *Liebschaft* [love-affair].

(13)[3] A young man addressed a lady in the street in the following words: 'If you will permit me, madam, I should like to "*begleit-digen*" you.' It was obvious what his thoughts were: he would like to '*begleiten* [accompany]' her, but was afraid his offer would '*beleidigen* [insult]' her. That these two conflicting emotional impulses found expression in one word – in the slip of the tongue, in fact – indicates that the young man's real intentions were at any rate not of the purest, and were bound to seem, even to himself, insulting to the lady. But while he attempted to conceal this from her, his unconscious played a trick on him by betraying his real intentions. But on the other hand he in this way, as it were, anticipated the lady's conventional retort: 'Really! What do you take me for? How dare you *insult* me!' (Reported by O. Rank.)

1. [Ribera, the well-known seventeenth century Spanish painter.]
2. [A non-existent word.]
3. [This example was added in 1912.]

I will next quote a number of examples[1] from an article by Stekel, entitled 'Unconscious Admissions', in the *Berliner Tageblatt* of January 4, 1904.

(14) 'An unpleasant part of my unconscious thoughts is disclosed by the following example. I may start by stating that in my capacity as a doctor I never consider my remuneration but only have the patient's interest in mind: that goes without saying. I was with a woman patient to whom I was giving medical attention in a period of convalescence after a serious illness. We had been through hard days and nights together. I was happy to find her improved; I painted a picture for her benefit of the delights of a stay in Abbazia, and concluded by saying: "If, as I hope, you will *not* leave your bed soon . . ." This obviously owed its origin to an egoistic motive in the unconscious, namely that I should be able to continue treating this well-to-do patient some time longer – a wish that is entirely foreign to my waking consciousness and which I would indignantly repudiate.'

(15) Here is another example from Stekel. 'My wife was engaging a French governess for the afternoons, and after agreement had been reached on the terms, wanted to retain her testimonials. The Frenchwoman asked to be allowed to keep them, giving as her reason: *Je cherche encore pour les après-midis, pardon, pour les avant-midis* [I am still looking for work in the afternoons – I mean, in the forenoons]. She obviously had the intention of looking round elsewhere and perhaps finding better terms – an intention which she in fact carried out.'

(16) From Stekel: 'I had to give a stiff lecture to a wife; and her husband, at whose request I did it, stood outside the door listening. At the end of my sermon, which had made a visible impression, I said: "Good-bye, sir." To any well-informed person I was thus betraying the fact that my words were addressed to the husband and that I had spoken them for his benefit.'

(17) Stekel reports of himself that at one time he had two patients from Trieste in treatment whom he always used to

1. [These examples (Nos. 14–20) were added in 1907.]

address the wrong way round. 'Good morning, Herr Peloni', he would say to Askoli, and 'Good morning, Herr Askoli' to Peloni. He was at first inclined not to attribute any deeper motive to this confusion but to explain it as being due to the numerous points of resemblance between the two gentlemen. However it was easy for him to convince himself that the inter-changing of the names corresponded in this case to a kind of boastfulness: he was able in this way to let each of his Italian patients know that he was not the only visitor from Trieste who had come to Vienna in search of his medical advice.

(18) Stekel reports that during a stormy General Meeting he said: 'We shall now *streiten* [quarrel]' (instead of '*schreiten* [proceed]') 'to point four on the agenda.'

(19) A professor declared in his inaugural lecture: 'I am not *geneigt* [inclined]' (instead of '*geeignet* [qualified]') 'to describe the services of my most esteemed predecessor.'

(20) To a lady whom he suspected of having Graves' disease Stekel said: 'You are about a *Kropf* [goitre]' (instead of '*Kopf* [head]') 'taller than your sister.'

(21) [1] Stekel reports: 'Someone wanted to describe the rela-tionship of two friends and to bring out the fact that one of them was Jewish. He said: "They lived together like Castor and Pollak."[2] This was certainly not said as a joke; the speaker did not notice the slip himself until I drew his attention to it.'

(22) Occasionally a slip of the tongue takes the place of a detailed characterization. A young woman who wore the breeches in her home told me that her sick husband had been to the doctor to ask what diet he ought to follow for his health. The doctor, however, had said that a special diet was not important. She added: 'He can eat and drink what *I* want.'

The following[3] two examples given by Reik (1915) have their origin in situations where slips of the tongue occur

1. [This and the following example (No. 22) were added in 1910.]

2. [Castor and Pollux were the 'heavenly twins' of Greek mythology. Pollak is a common Jewish name in Vienna.]

3. [This paragraph and Nos. 23–6 were added in 1917.]

especially easily – situations in which more must be kept back than can be said.

(23) A gentleman was offering his condolences to a young lady whose husband had recently died, and he intended to add: 'You will find consolation in *devoting* [*widmen*] yourself entirely to your children.' Instead he said '*widwen*'.[1] The suppressed thought referred to consolation of another kind: a young and pretty widow [*Witwe*] will soon enjoy fresh sexual pleasures.

(24) At an evening party the same gentleman was having a conversation with the same lady about the extensive preparations being made in Berlin for Easter, and asked: 'Have you seen today's display [*Auslage*] at Wertheim's?[2] The place is completely *decollated*.' He had not dared to express his admiration for the beautiful lady's *décolletage*, while the word '*Auslage*' ['display'] was used unconciously in two senses.

The same condition applies to another case, observed by Dr Hanns Sachs, of which he has tried to give an exhaustive account:

(25) 'A lady was telling me about a common acquaintance. The last time she saw him, he was, she said, as elegantly dressed as ever: in particular he was wearing strikingly beautiful brown *Halbschuhe* [low shoes]. When I asked where she had met him she replied: "He rang at the door of my house and I saw him through the blinds, which were down. But I didn't open the door or give any other sign of life, as I didn't want him to know I was already back in town." While I was listening to her I had an idea that she was concealing something from me, most probably the fact that her reason for not opening the door was that she was not alone and not properly dressed to receive visitors; and I asked her somewhat ironically: "So you were able to admire his *Hausschuhe* [house shoes] – *Halbschuhe* [low shoes], I mean – through the blinds when they were drawn?" In *Hausschuhe* I was giving expression to the thought of her *Hauskleid* [lit. house dress, i.e. *négligée*] which I had refrained

1. [A non-existent word.]
2. [A well-known department store.]

from uttering. There was on the other hand a temptation to get rid of the word "*Halb* [half]" for the reason that it was precisely this word which contained the core of the forbidden answer: "You are only telling me *half* the truth and are hiding the fact that you were *half* dressed." The slip of the tongue was encouraged by the additional circumstance that we had been talking directly before about this particular gentleman's married life, about his *häuslich* [domestic] happiness; this no doubt helped to determine the displacement [of "*Haus*"] on to him. Finally, I must confess that envy on my part may perhaps have contributed to my placing this elegant gentleman in the street in house shoes; only recently I myself bought a pair of brown low shoes, which are certainly not "strikingly beautiful" any longer.'

Times of war like the present produce numerous slips of the tongue which there is not much difficulty in understanding.

(26) 'What regiment is your son with?' a lady was asked. She replied: 'With the 42nd Murderers' ['*Mörder*' – instead of '*Mörser*', 'Mortars'].

(27)[1] Lieutenant Henrik Haiman writes from the front (1917): 'While I was reading an absorbing book, I was torn away to act temporarily as reconnaissance telephone operator. When the artillery post gave the signal to test the line I reacted with: "Duly tested and in order; *Ruhe*."[2] According to regulations the message should have run: "Duly tested and in order; *Schluss* [end (of message)]." My aberration is to be explained by my annoyance at being interrupted while I was reading.'

(28)[3] A sergeant instructed his men to give their people at home their correct addresses, so that '*Gespeckstücke*' should not go astray.[4]

1. [This example was added in 1919.]

2. ['Quiet'; often used as an exclamation: 'Silence!']

3. [This example, and Nos. 30 and 31, were added in 1920; No. 29 was added in 1919.]

4. [He meant to say '*Gepäckstücke*' ('parcels'). '*Gespeckstücke*' is a non-existent word; but '*Speckstücke*' would mean 'bits of bacon'. The vowel after the 'p' has practically the same sound in each case (whether written 'e' or 'ä').]

(29) The following exceedingly fine example, which is also significant in view of its most unhappy background, I owe to Dr L. Czeszer, who observed it while he was living in neutral Switzerland during the war and who analysed it exhaustively. I quote his letter verbatim with some inessential omissions:

'I am taking the liberty of sending you an account of a slip of the tongue of which Professor M. N. of O. University wsa the victim in one of the lectures that he gave on the psychology of feelings during the summer term which has just ended. I must start by saying that these lectures took place in the Aula of the University before a great crowd of interned French prisoners-of-war as well as of students, most of whom were French-Swiss whose sympathies lay strongly on the side of the *Entente*. In the town of O., as in France itself, "*boche*" is the name in universal and exclusive use for the Germans. But in public announcements, and in lectures and the like, senior public servants, professors and other persons in responsible positions make an effort, for the sake of neutrality, to avoid the ominous word.

'Professor N. was in the middle of discussing the practical significance of affects, and intended to quote an example illustrating how an affect can be deliberately exploited in such a way that a muscular activity which is uninteresting in itself becomes charged with pleasurable feelings, and so made more intense. He accordingly told a story – he was, of course, speaking in French – which had just then been reproduced in the local papers from a German one. It concerned a German schoolmaster who had put his pupils to work in the garden, and in order to encourage them to work with greater intensity invited them to imagine that with every clod of earth that they broke up they were breaking a French skull. Every time the word for "German" came up in the course of his story N. of course said "*allemand*" quite correctly and not "*boche*". But when he came to the point of the story he gave the school-master's words in the following form: *Imaginez-vous qu'en chaque moche vous écrasez le crâne d'un Français*. That is to say, instead of *motte* [the French word for 'clod'] – *moche*!

'One can see very clearly how this scrupulous scholar took a firm grip on himself at the beginning of his story, to prevent himself from yielding to habit – perhaps even to temptation – and from permitting a word that had actually been expressly proscribed by a federal decree to fall from the rostrum of the University Aula! And at the precise moment at which he had successfully said "*instituteur allemand* [German schoolmaster]" with perfect correctness for what was the last time, and was hurrying with an inward sigh of relief to the conclusion, which seemed to offer no pitfalls – the word which had been suppressed with so much effort caught hold of the similar-sounding "*motte*", and the damage was done. Anxiety about committing a political indiscretion, perhaps a suppressed desire to employ the usual word in spite of everything – the word that everyone expected – and the resentment of one who was born a re-publican and a democrat at every restriction on the free expression of opinion – all these interfered with his main inten-tion of giving a punctilious rendering of the illustration. The interfering trend was known to the speaker and he had, as we cannot but suppose, thought of it directly before he made the slip of the tongue.

'Professor N. did not notice his slip: at least he did not correct it, which is something one usually does quite automatically. On the other hand the slip was received by the mainly French audience with real satisfaction and its effect was exactly as though it had been an intentional play upon words. I myself followed this seemingly innocent occurrence with real inner excitement. For although I had for obvious reasons to forgo asking the professor the questions prompted by the psycho-analytic method, I nevertheless took his slip of the tongue as conclusive evidence of the correctness of your theory about the determining of parapraxes and the deep-lying analogies and connections between slips of the tongue and jokes.'

(30) The following slip of the tongue, which was reported by an Austrian officer, Lieutenant T., on his return home, also had its origin among the melancholy impressions of war-time:

'For several months of the time that I was a prisoner-of-war in Italy I was one of two hundred officers accommodated in a small villa. During this time one of our number died of influenza. The impression made by this event was naturally a deep one, for the circumstances in which we found ourselves, the lack of medical assistance and the helplessness of our condition at the time made it more than probable that an epidemic would break out. – We had laid out the dead man in a cellar-room. In the evening, after I had taken a walk around our house with a friend, we both expressed a wish to see the dead body. The sight which greeted me on entering the cellar (I was the one in front) startled me violently, for I had not expected to find the bier so near the entrance and to be confronted at such close quarters with a face transformed by the play of the candle-light into something set in movement. While the effects of this scene were still on us we continued our walk around the house. When we came to a place from where there was a view of the park bathed in the light of a full moon, a brightly-lit meadow and beyond it a thin veil of mist, I described the picture that it conjured up; it was as if I saw a ring of elves dancing under the fringe of the neighbouring pine trees.

'The next afternoon we buried our dead comrade. The course of our walk from our prison to the cemetery of the small neighbouring village was both bitter and humiliating for us; for a mocking, jeering crowd made up of shouting half-grown lads and rough, noisy villagers took advantage of the occasion to give open vent to their emotions, which were a mixture of curiosity and hatred. My feeling that even in this defenceless condition we could not escape insults and my disgust at the demonstration of coarseness overwhelmed me with bitterness until the evening. At the same hour as on the previous day and with the same companion, I began to walk along the gravel path around our house, just as I had done before; and as we passed by the grating of the cellar behind which the dead body had lain I was seized by the memory of the impression which the sight of it had made on me. At the place where the brightly-lit park once more lay before me, in the light of the same full moon, I stopped and said to my companion: "We could sit down here in the *grave* ['*Grab*'] – grass ['*Gras*'] – and *sink* ['*sinken*'] a serenade." My attention was not caught until I made the second slip; I had corrected the first one without having become conscious of the meaning it contained. I now reflected on them and put them together: "in the grave – to sink!" The following pictures flashed through my mind with lightning rapidity: elves dancing and hovering in the moonlight; our comrade lying on his bier, the impression of movement; some scenes from the burial, the sensation of the disgust I had felt and of the disturbance of our mourning; the memory of some conversations about the infectious illness that had appeared, and the forebodings expressed by several of the officers. Later I remembered that it was the date of my father's death; in view of my usually very poor memory for dates I found this striking.

'Subsequent reflection brought home to me the sameness of the external circumstances on the two evenings: the same time of day and lighting conditions, the identical place and companion. I recalled my uneasy feelings when there had been an anxious discussion of the possibility of the influenza spreading; and I remembered at the same time my inner prohibition against letting myself be overcome by fear. I also became conscious of the significance attaching to the order of the words "we could – in the grave – sink",[1] and I realized that only the initial correction of "grave" into "grass", which had taken place unobtrusively, had led to the second slip ("sink" for "sing") in order to ensure that the suppressed complex should have its full expression.

'I may add that I suffered at the time from alarming dreams about a very close relative. I repeatedly saw her ill and once actually dead. Just before I was taken prisoner I had received

1. ['*Wir könnten ins Grab sinken*' – 'we could sink in the grave'. The order of the words, on which the present point turns, is different in English and in German.]

news that the influenza was raging with particular virulence in her part of the world, and I had expressed my lively fears to her about it. Since then I had been out of touch with her. Some months later I received news that she had fallen a victim to the epidemic a fortnight before the episode I have described!'

(31) The next example of a slip of the tongue throws a flash of light on one of those painful conflicts which fall to the lot of a doctor. A man whose illness was in all probability a fatal one, though the diagnosis had not as yet been confirmed, had come to Vienna to await the solution of his problem, and had begged a friend whom he had known since his youth, and who had become a well-known physician, to undertake his treatment. This the friend had with some reluctance finally agreed to do. It was intended that the sick man should stay in a nursing home and the doctor proposed that it should be the 'Hera' sanatorium. 'Surely', objected the patient, 'that is a home for a special type of case only (a maternity home).' 'Oh no!' replied the doctor hastily, 'in the "Hera" they can *umbringen* [put an end to] – I mean, *unterbringen* [take in] – every type of patient.' He then violently disputed the interpretation of his slip. 'Surely you won't believe I have hostile impulses against you?' A quarter of an hour later, as the doctor was going out with the lady who had undertaken to nurse the invalid, he said: 'I can't find anything, and I still don't believe in it. But if it should be so, I am in favour of a strong dose of morphia and a peaceful finish.' It emerged that his friend had stipulated that he (the doctor) should shorten his sufferings by means of a drug as soon as it was confirmed that he was past helping. Thus the doctor had in fact undertaken to put an end to his friend.

(32)[1] Here is a quite especially instructive slip of the tongue which I should not like to omit, although according to my authority it is some twenty years old. 'A lady once advanced the following opinion at a social gathering – and the words show that they were uttered with fervour and under the pressure of a host of secret impulses: "Yes, a woman must be pretty if

1. [This example was added in 1910.]

she is to please men. A man is much better off; as long as he has his *five* straight [*fünf gerade*] limbs he needs nothing more!" This example allows us a good view of the intimate mechanism of a slip of the tongue that results from *condensation* or from a *contamination* (cf. p. 95). It is plausible to suppose that we have here a fusion of two turns of phrase with similar meanings:

> as long as he has his *four straight limbs*
> as long as he has his *five wits* about him.

Or the element *straight* ['*gerade*'] may have been common to two intended expressions which ran:

> as long as he has his *straight* limbs
> to treat all *five(s)* as *even numbers*[1]

'There is nothing in fact to prevent us from assuming that *both* turns of phrase, the one about his five wits and the one about 'the even number five', played their separate parts in causing first a number, and the then mysterious five instead of the simple four, to be introduced into the sentence dealing with the straight limbs. But this fusion would certainly not have come about if, in the form that appeared in the slip of the tongue, it had not had a good meaning of its own – one expressing a cynical truth which could not of course be admitted to undisguised, coming as it did from a woman. – Finally we should not omit to draw attention to the fact that the lady's remark, as worded, could pass just as well for a capital joke as for an amusing slip of the tongue. It is simply a question of whether she spoke the words with a conscious or an unconscious intention. In our case the way the speaker behaved certainly ruled out any notion of conscious intention and excluded the idea of its being a joke.'

How closely[2] a slip of the tongue can approximate to a joke

1. ['Alle *fünf gerade* sein lassen.' The German '*gerade*' means both 'straight' and 'even'. The meaning of the phrase, literally translated in the text, is: 'To close one's eyes to irregularities.']

2. [This paragraph and Example 33 were added in 1917.]

is shown in the following case, reported by Rank (1913), in which the woman responsible for the slip actually ended by herself treating it as a joke and laughing at it.

(33) 'A recently married man, whose wife was concerned about preserving her girlish appearance and only with reluctance allowed him to have frequent sexual intercourse, told me the following story which in retrospect both he and his wife found extremely funny. After a night in which he had once again disobeyed his wife's rule of abstinence, he was shaving in the morning in the bedroom which they shared, while his wife was still in bed; and, as he had often done to save trouble, he made use of his wife's powder-puff which was lying on the bedside table. His wife, who was extremely concerned about her complexion, had several times told him not to, and therefore called out angrily: "There you go again, powdering *me* [*mich*] with *your* [*deiner*] puff!' Her husband's laughter drew her attention to her slip (she had meant to say: "you are powdering *yourself* [*dich*] again with *my* [*meiner*] puff") and she herself ended by joining in his laughter. "To powder" ["*pudern*"] is an expression familiar to every Viennese for "to copulate"; and a powder-puff is an obvious phallic symbol.'

(34)[1] In the following example, too – supplied by Storfer – it might be thought that a joke was intended:

Frau B., who was suffering from an affection of obviously psychogenic origin, was repeatedly recommended to consult a psychoanalyst, Dr X. She persistently declined to do so, saying that such treatment could never be of any value, as the doctor would wrongly trace everything back to sexual things. A day finally came, however, when she was ready to follow the advice, and she asked: 'Nun gut, wann *ordinärt* also dieser Dr X.?'[2]

1. [Added in 1924.]
2. [What she meant to say was: 'All right, then, when does this Dr X. have his consulting hours?' She should have used the word '*ordiniert*' for 'has his consulting hours'. Instead she said '*ordinärt*', which is a non-existent word. '*Ordinär*', however, means 'common', 'vulgar'.]

(35)[1] The connection between jokes and slips of the tongue is also shown in the fact that in many cases a slip of the tongue is nothing other than an abbreviation:

On leaving school, a girl had followed the ruling fashion of the time by taking up the study of medicine. After a few terms she had changed over from medicine to chemistry. Some years later she described her change of mind in the following words: 'I was not on the whole squeamish about dissecting, but when I once had to pull the finger-nails off a dead body, I lost my pleasure in the whole of – *chemistry*.'

(36)[2] At this point I insert another slip of the tongue which it needs little skill to interpret. 'In an anatomy lesson the professor was endeavouring to explain the nasal cavities, which are notoriously a very difficult department of enterology. When he asked whether his audience had understood his presentation of the subject, he received a general reply in the affirmative. Thereupon the professor, who was known for his high opinion of himself, commented: 'I can hardly believe that, since, even in Vienna with its millions of inhabitants, those who understand the nasal cavities can be counted *on one finger*, I mean on the fingers of one hand.'

(37) On another occasion the same professor said: 'In the case of the female genitals, in spite of many *Versuchungen* [temptations] – I beg your pardon, *Versuche* [experiments] . . .'

(38)[3] I am indebted to Dr Alfred Robitsek of Vienna for drawing my attention to two slips of the tongue which were recorded by an old French writer. I reproduce them without translating them:

Brantôme (1527–1614), *Vies des Dames galantes*, 'Discours second': 'Si ay-je cogneu une très-belle et honneste dame de par le monde, qui, devisant avec un honneste gentilhomme de la cour des affaires de la guerre durant ces civiles, elle luy dit: "J'ay ouy dire que le roy a faict rompre tous les c . . . de ce

1. [Added in 1920.]
2. [This example and the following one (No. 37) were added in 1912.]
3. [Added in 1910.]

pays là." Elle vouloit dire *les ponts*. Pensez que, venant de coucher d'avec son mary, ou songeant à son amant, elle avoit encor ce nom frais en la bouche; et le gentilhomme s'en eschauffa en amours d'elle pour ce mot.

'Une autre dame que j'ai cogneue, entretenant une autre grand' dame plus qu'elle, et luy louant et exaltant ses beautez, elle luy dit après: "Non, madame, ce que je vous en dis, ce n'est point pour vous *adultérer*"; voulant dire *adulater*, comme elle le rhabilla ainsi: pensez qu'elle songeoit à [l'adultère et à] adultérer.'[1]

(39)[2] There are of course more modern examples as well of sexual *doubles entendres* originating in a slip of the tongue. Frau F. was describing her first hour in a language course. 'It is very interesting; the teacher is a nice young Englishman. In the very first hour he gave me to understand *"durch die Bluse"* [through the blouse] – I mean, *"durch die Blume"* [literally, 'through flowers', i.e. 'indirectly'] – that he would rather take me for individual tuition.' (From Storfer.)

In the psychotherapeutic procedure[3] which I employ for resolving and removing neurotic symptoms I am very often faced with the task of discovering, from the patient's apparently casual utterances and associations, a thought-content which is

1. ['Thus I knew a very beautiful and virtuous lady of the world who, discoursing with a virtuous gentleman of the court on the affairs of the war during those civil disturbances, said to him: "I have heard tell that the king had a breach made in all the c . . . of that region." She meant to say *the "bridges"* ["*ponts*", which rhymes with the missing French word]. One may suppose that, having just lain with her husband, or thinking of her lover, she had this word freshly on her tongue; and the gentleman was fired with love of her on account of this word.

'Another lady whom I knew, entertaining another lady of higher rank than herself, and praising her and extolling her beauties, she said after to her: "No, madame, what I say to you is not in order to *adulterate* you"; meaning to say *adulate*, as she clad the word thus anew, one may suppose that she was thinking of [adultery and of] adulteration.']

2. [Added in 1924.]

3. [Except where otherwise indicated, the whole of what follows down to p. 129 dates back to 1901.]

at pains to remain concealed but which cannot nevertheless avoid unintentionally betraying its existence in a whole variety of ways. Slips of the tongue often perform a most valuable service here, as I could show by some highly convincing and at the same time very singular examples. Thus, for instance, a patient will be speaking of his aunt and, without noticing the slip, will consistently call her 'my mother'; or another will refer to her husband as her 'brother'. In this way they draw my attention to the fact that they have 'identified' these persons with one another – that they have put them into a series which implies a recurrence of the same type in their emotional life. – To give another example:[1] a young man of twenty introduced himself to me during my consulting hours in these words: 'I am the father of So-and-so who came to you for treatment. I beg your pardon, I meant to say I am his brother: he is four years older than I am.' I inferred that he intended this slip to express the view that, like his brother, he had fallen ill through the fault of his father; that, like his brother, he wished to be cured; but that his father was the one who most needed to be cured. – At other times an arrangement of words that sounds unusual, or an expression that seems forced, is enough to reveal that a repressed thought is participating in the patient's remarks, which had a different end in view.

What I find, therefore, both in grosser disturbances of speech and in those more subtle ones which can still be subsumed under the heading of 'slips of the tongue', is that it is not the influence of the 'contact effects of sounds' [p. 103] but the influence of thoughts that lie outside the intended speech which determines the occurrence of the slip and provides an adequate explanation of the mistake. It is not my wish to throw doubt on the laws governing the way in which sounds modify one another; but by themselves these laws do not seem to me to be sufficiently effective to disturb the process of correct speaking. In the cases that I have studied and explored in some

1. [This example was inserted in 1907.]

detail these laws represent no more than the preformed mechanism which a more remote psychical motive makes use of for its convenience, though without becoming subject to the sphere of influence of these [phonetic] relations. *In a large number of substitutions* [p. 95] *resulting from slips of the tongue such phonetic laws are completely disregarded.* In this respect I find myself in full agreement with Wundt, who assumes as I do that the conditions governing slips of the tongue are complex and extend far beyond the contact effects of the sounds.

If I accept these 'remoter psychical influences' (as Wundt calls them [cf. above, p. 102]) as established, there is nothing, on the other hand, to prevent me at the same time from allowing that, in situations where speaking is hurried and attention is to some extent diverted, the conditions governing slips of the tongue may easily be confined within the limits defined by Meringer and Mayer.[1] For some of the examples collected by these authors a more complicated explanation nevertheless seems more plausible. Take, for instance, one of those quoted above [p. 95]: 'Es war mir auf der *Schwest* . . .

Brust so schwer.'

Was what happened here simply that the sound '*schwe*' forced back the equally valent sound '*bru*' by 'anticipating' it? The idea can hardly be dismissed that the sounds making up '*schwe*' were further enabled to obtrude in this manner because of a special relation. That could only be the association *Schwester* [sister] – *Bruder* [brother]; perhaps also *Brust der Schwester* [sister's breast], which leads one on to other groups of thoughts. It is this invisible helper behind the scenes which lends the otherwise innocent '*schwe*' the strength to produce a mistake in speaking.

There are other slips of the tongue where we may assume that the true disturbing factor is some similarity in sound to obscene words and meanings. Deliberate distortion and deformation of

1. [I.e. may be confined to phonetic factors. Cf. p. 94.]

words and expressions, which is so dear to vulgar minds, has
the sole purpose of exploiting innocent occasions for hinting at
forbidden topics; and this playing with words is so frequent
that there would be nothing remarkable in its occurring even
when not intended and against one's wishes. To this category
no doubt belong such examples as *Eischeissweibchen* (for *Eiweiss-
scheibchen*),[1] *Apopos Fritz* (for *apropos*),[2] *Lokuskapität* (for *Lotus-
kapität*),[3] etc.; and perhaps also the *Alabüsterbachse* (*Alabaster-
büchse*)[4] of St Mary Magdalen.[5] – 'Ich fordere Sie auf, auf das

1. [A meaningless term (literally: 'egg-shit-female'), for 'small slices
of white of egg'.]

2. ['Apopos' is a non-existent word; but 'Popo' is the nursery word
for 'buttocks'.]

3. [A meaningless word, literally: 'W.C. capital', for 'lotus capital',
an architectural term.]

4. [A non-existent word (though the middle part of it, 'Büste', means
'breast'), for 'alabaster box'.]

5. Making slips of the tongue was a symptom of a woman patient
of mine which persisted until it was traced back to the childhood joke
of replacing '*ruinieren* [ruin]' by '*urinieren* [urinate]'. – [*Added* 1924:] The
temptation to employ the artifice of a slip of the tongue for enabling
improper and forbidden words to be freely used forms the basis of
Abraham's observations on parapraxes 'with an overcompensating purpose' (Abraham, 1922*a*). A woman patient was very liable to duplicate
the first syllable of proper names by stammering. She changed the name
'Protagoras' to 'Protragoras', shortly after having said 'A-alexander'
instead of 'Alexander'. Inquiry revealed that in childhood she had been
especially fond of the vulgar joke of repeating the syllables 'a' and 'po'
when they occurred at the beginnings of words, a form of amusement
which quite commonly leads to stammering in children. ['*A-a*' and
'*Popo*' are the German nursery words for 'faeces' and 'buttocks'.] On
approaching the name 'Protagoras' she became aware of the risk that
she might omit the 'r' in the first syllable and say 'Po-potagoras'. As a
protection against this danger she held on firmly to this 'r', and inserted
another 'r' in the second syllable. She acted in the same way on other
occasions, distorting the words '*Parterre* [ground floor]' and '*Kondolenz*
[condolence]' so as to avoid '*Pater* (father)' and '*Kondom* [condom]'
which were closely linked to them in her associations. Another of
Abraham's patients confessed to an inclination to say 'Angora' every
time for 'angina' – very probably because of a fear of being tempted to

Wohl unseres Chefs *auf*zustossen' [see p. 95] can hardly be anything other than an unintentional parody which is a perseveration of an intended one. If I were the Principal who was being honoured at the ceremony to which the speaker contributed this slip, I should probably reflect on the cleverness of the Romans in permitting the soldiers of a general who was enjoying a Triumph openly to express in the form of satirical songs their inner criticisms of the man who was being honoured. – Meringer relates that he himself once said to someone, who by reason of being the eldest member of the company was addressed familiarly by the honorific title of '*Senexl*'[1] or '*altes* [old] *Senexl*': '*Prost* [Your health!], *Senex altesl!*' He was himself shocked at this mistake (Meringer and Mayer, 1895, 50). We can perhaps interpret his emotion if we reflect how close '*Altesl*' comes to the insulting phrase 'alter Esel' ['old ass']. There are powerful internal punishments for any breach of the respect due to age (that is, reduced to childhood terms, of the respect due to the father).

I hope that readers will not overlook the difference in value between these interpretations, of which no proof is possible, and the examples that I have myself collected and explained by means of an analysis. But if I still secretly cling to my expectation that even apparently simple slips of the tongue could be traced to interference by a half-suppressed idea that lies *outside* the intended context, I am tempted to do so by an observation of Meringer's which is highly deserving of attention. This author says that it is a curious fact that no one is ready to admit having made a slip of the tongue. There are some very sensible and honest people who are offended if they are told they have

---

replace 'angina' by 'vagina'. These slips of the tongue owed their existence therefore to the fact that a defensive trend had retained the upper hand instead of the distorting one; and Abraham justly draws attention to the analogy between this process and the formation of symptoms in obsessional neurosis.

1. [This is the affectionate Austrian form of diminutive applied to the Latin 'senex', 'old man'.]

made one. I would not venture to put it so generally as does Meringer in saying 'no one'. But the trace of affect which follows the revelation of the slip, and which is clearly in the nature of shame, has a definite significance. It may be compared to the annoyance we feel when we cannot recall a forgotten name [p. 46], and to our surprise at the tenacity of an apparently indifferent memory [p. 85]; and it invariably indicates that some motive has contributed to the occurrence of the interference.

The twisting round of a name when it is intentional amounts to an insult; and it might well have the same significance in a whole number of cases where it appears in the form of an unintentional slip of the tongue. The person who, as Mayer reports, said 'Freuder' on one occasion instead of 'Freud' because he had shortly before mentioned Breuer's name (Meringer and Mayer, 1895, 38), and who another time spoke of the 'Freuer-Breudian' method of treatment (ibid., 28), was probably a professional colleague – and one who was not particularly enthusiastic about that method. In the chapter below on slips of the pen I shall report an instance of the distortion of a name which certainly cannot be explained in any other way [p. 165 f.].[1]

1. [*Footnote added* 1907:] It can in fact be observed that members of the aristocracy in particular are prone to distort the names of the doctors they consult. We may conclude from this that inwardly they despise them, in spite of the courtesy they habitually show them. – [*Added* 1912:] I quote here some pertinent observations on the forgetting of names which come from an account of our subject written in English by Dr Ernest Jones, at that time in Toronto (Jones, 1911*b* [488]):

'Few people can avoid feeling a twinge of resentment when they find that their name has been forgotten, particularly if it is by some one with whom they had hoped or expected it would be remembered. They instinctively realize that if they had made a greater impression on the person's mind he would certainly have remembered them again, for the name is an integral part of the personality. Similarly, few things are more flattering to most people than to find themselves addressed by name by a great personage where they could hardly have anticipated it. Napoleon, like most leaders of men, was a master of this art. In the

In these cases the disturbing factor which intervenes is a criticism which has to be set aside since at the moment it does not correspond to the speaker's intention.

Conversely,[1] replacing one name by another assuming someone else's name, identification by means of a slip over a name, must signify an appreciative feeling which has for some reason to remain in the background for the time being. An experience of this kind from his schooldays is described by Sándor Ferenczi:

'When I was in the first form at the *Gymnasium* [Secondary School] I had, for the first time in my life, to recite a poem in public (i.e. in front of the whole class). I was well prepared and was dismayed at being interrupted at the very start by a burst of laughter. The teacher subsequently told me why I had met with this strange reception. I gave the title of the poem "Aus der Ferne [From Afar]" quite correctly, but instead of attributing it to its real author I gave my own name. The poet's name

---

midst of the disastrous Campaign of France, in 1814, he gave an amazing proof of his memory in this direction. When in a town near Craonne he recollected that he had met the mayor, De Bussy, over twenty years ago in the La Fère regiment; the delighted De Bussy at once threw himself into his service with extraordinary zeal. Conversely there is no surer way of affronting some one than by pretending to forget his name; the insinuation is thus conveyed that the person is so unimportant in our eyes that we cannot be bothered to remember his name. This device is often exploited in literature. In Turgenev's *Smoke* the following passage occurs. "'So you still find Baden entertaining, M'sieu – Litvinov.' Ratmirov always uttered Litvinov's surname with hesitation, every time, as though he had forgotten it, and could not at once recall it. In this way, as well as by the lofty flourish of his hat in saluting him, he meant to insult his pride." The same author in his *Fathers and Sons* writes: "The Governor invited Kirsanov and Bazarov to his ball, and within a few minutes invited them a second time, regarding them as brothers, and calling them Kisarov." Here the forgetting that he had spoken to them, the mistake in the names, and the inability to distinguish between the two young men, constitute a culmination of disparagement. Falsification of a name has the same significance as forgetting it; it is only a step towards complete amnesia.' [Quoted by Freud in German; here given in the original English.]

1. [The next four paragraphs were added in 1910.]

is Alexander (Sándor [in Hungarian]) Petöfi. The exchange of names was helped by our having the same first name; but the real cause was undoubtedly the fact that at that time I identified myself in my secret wishes with the celebrated hero-poet. Even consciously my love and admiration for him bordered on idolatry. The whole wretched ambition-complex is of course to be found as well behind this parapraxis.'

A similar identification by means of an exchange of names was reported to me by a young doctor. He had timidly and reverently introduced himself to the famous Virchow[1] as 'Dr Virchow'. The professor turned to him in surprise and asked: 'Ah! is your name Virchow too?' I do not know how the ambitious young man justified the slip of the tongue he had made – whether he relied upon the flattering excuse that he felt himself so small beside the great name that his own could not fail to slip away from him, or whether he had the courage to admit that he hoped one day to become as great a man as Virchow, and to beg the Professor not to treat him so contemptuously on that account. One of these two thoughts – or perhaps both of them simultaneously – may have confused the young man while he was introducing himself.

From motives of an extremely personal nature I must leave it open whether a similar interpretation is applicable to the following case as well. At the International Congress at Amsterdam in 1907 my theory of hysteria was the subject of lively discussion.[2] In a diatribe against me one of my most vigorous opponents repeatedly made slips of the tongue which took the form of putting himself in my place and speaking in my name. For example, he said: 'It is well known that Breuer and *I* have proved . . .' where he could only have meant '. . . Breuer and *Freud* . . .' My opponent's name bears not the least resemblance to my own. This example, together with many other cases

1. [The celebrated pathologist (1821–1902).]
2. [The First International Congress of Psychiatry and Neurology, Amsterdam, September, 1907. The 'opponent' was Aschaffenburg. See Jones (1955, 126).]

where a slip of the tongue results in one name replacing another, may serve to remind us that such slips can entirely dispense with the assistance afforded by similarity in sound [cf. p. 125] and can come about with no more support than is provided by hidden factors in the subject-matter.

In other, far more significant, cases[1] it is self-criticism, internal opposition to one's own utterance, that obliges one to make a slip of the tongue and even to substitute the opposite of what one had intended. One then observes in astonishment how the wording of an assertion cancels outs its own intention, and how the slip has exposed an inner insincerity.[2] The slip of the tongue here becomes a mode of mimetic expression – often, indeed, for the expression of something one did not wish to say: it becomes a mode of self-betrayal. This was the case, for instance, when a man who did not care for what is called normal sexual intercourse in his relations with women broke into a conversation about a girl who was said to be a flirt, [kokett] with the words: 'If she had to do with me, she'd soon give up her koëttieren [a non-existent word].' There is no doubt that it can only have been another word, namely 'koitieren' [to have coitus], whose influence was responsible for making this change in the word that was intended, 'kokettieren' [to flirt, coquette]. – Or take the following case: 'We have an uncle who for months past had been very much offended because we never visited him. We took his move to a new house as an occasion for paying him a long overdue visit. He seemed very glad to see us, and as we were leaving he said with much feeling: "I hope from now on I shall see you still *more seldom* than in the past."'

1. [The first part of this paragraph, down to the words 'mode of mimetic expression', dates back to 1901. The next two and a half sentences were added in 1907, and the final section (beginning: 'Or take the following case') in 1920.]

2. Slips of the tongue of this type are used, for instance, by Anzengruber [the Viennese dramatist (1839–89)] in his *Der G'wissenswurm* to expose the character of the hypocritical legacy-hunter.

When the linguistic material happens to be favourable,[1] it often causes slips of the tongue to occur which have the positively shattering result of a revelation, or which produce the full comic effect of a joke. – This is the case in the following example observed and reported by Dr Reitler:

'"That smart new hat – I suppose you '*aufgepatzt*' [instead of '*aufgeputzt*' (trimmed)] it yourself?" said one lady in a voice of admiration to another. She could proceed no further with her intended praise; for the criticism she had silently felt that the hat's trimmings ["*Hutaufputz*"] were a "*Patzerei* [botch]" had been indicated much too clearly by the unfriendly slip of the tongue for any further phrases of conventional admiration to sound convincing.'[2]

The criticism contained in the following example[3] is milder but none the less unambiguous:

'A lady who was visiting an acquaintance became very impatient and weary at her tedious and long-winded conversation. When at last she succeeded in tearing herself away and taking her leave she was detained by a fresh deluge of words from her companion, who had meanwhile accompanied her into the front hall and now forced her, as she was on the very point of departing, to stand at the door and listen once more. At last she interrupted her hostess with the question: "Are you at home in the front hall [*Vorzimmer*]?" It was not till she saw the

1. [This and the following paragraph were added in 1907.]
2. [In the editions of 1910 and 1912 only, the following paragraphs appeared in the text at this point.

'The same is to be found in a case reported by Dr Ferenczi:

'"'Come *geschminkt* [painted, i.e., with make-up on]' (instead of '*geschwind* [quickly]'), said one of my [Hungarian] women patients to her German-speaking mother-in-law. By this slip she gave away precisely what she wanted to conceal from her: namely, her irritation at the old lady's vanity."

'It is by no means rare for someone who is not speaking his mother tongue to exploit his clumsiness for the purpose of making highly significant slips of the tongue in the language that is foreign to him.']
3. [Added in 1920.]

other's astonished face that she noticed her slip of the tongue. Weary of being kept standing so long in the front hall she had meant to break off the conversation by asking: "Are you at home in the mornings [*Vormittag*]?", and her slip betrayed her impatience at the further delay.'

The next example,[1] which was witnessed by Dr Max Graf, is a warning that one should keep a watch on oneself.

'At the General Meeting of the "Concordia", the Society of Journalists, a young member who was invariably hard-up made a violently aggressive speech, and in his excitement spoke of the "*Vorschussmitglieder* [lending members]" (instead of "*Vorstandsmitglieder* [officers]" or "*Ausschussmitglieder* [committee members]'). The latter have the authority to sanction loans, and the young speaker had in fact put in an application for a loan.'

We have seen[2] from the example of '*Vorschwein*' [p. 98] that a slip of the tongue can easily occur if an effort has been made to suppress insulting words. In this way one gives vent to one's feelings:

A photographer who had made a resolution to refrain from zoological terms in dealing with his clumsy employees, addressed an apprentice – who tried to empty out a large dish that was full to the brim and in doing so naturally spilt half the contents on the floor – in the following words: 'But, man, *schöpsen Sie*[3] some of it off first.' And soon after this, in the course of a tirade against a female assistant who had nearly spoilt a dozen valuable plates by her carelessness, he said: 'Are you so *hornverbrannt . . .?*[4]

1. [This was added in 1907.]
2. [This and the following paragraph were added in 1920.]
3. [He meant to say 'draw', which would have been '*schöpfen Sie*'. Instead he used '*schöpsen Sie*', which is meaningless. The word '*Schöps*', however, means 'sheep' or 'silly fellow'.]
4. [Here he meant to say '*hirnverbrannt*', 'idiotic', literally 'with your brain (*Hirn*) burnt up'. The word he used instead, a non-existent term, would mean 'with your horn (*Horn*) burnt up'. The word '*Hornvieh*', literally 'horned cattle', is used in the sense of 'fool'.]

The next example[1] shows how a slip of the tongue resulted in a serious self-betrayal. Certain details in it justify its repetition in full from the account given by Brill in the *Zentralblatt für Psychoanalyse*, Volume II.[2]

'I went for a walk one evening with Dr Frink, and we discussed some of the business of the New York Psychoanalytic Society. We met a colleague, Dr R., whom I had not seen for years and of whose private life I knew nothing. We were very pleased to meet again, and on my invitation he accompanied us to a café, where we spent two hours in lively conversation. He seemed to know some details about me, for after the usual greetings he asked after my small child and told me that he heard about me from time to time from a mutual friend and had been interested in my work ever since he had read about it in the medical press. To my question as to whether he was married he gave a negative answer, and added: "Why should a man like me marry?"'

'On leaving the café, he suddenly turned to me and said: "I should like to know what you would do in a case like this: I know a nurse who was named as co-respondent in a divorce case. The wife sued the husband and named her as co-respondent, and *he* got the divorce."[3] I interrupted him, saying: "You mean *she* got the divorce." He immediately corrected himself, saying: "Yes, of course, *she* got the divorce", and continued to tell how the nurse had been so affected by the divorce proceedings and the scandal that she had taken to drink, had become very nervous, and so on; and he wanted me to advise him how to treat her.'

'As soon as I had corrected his mistake I asked him to explain

1. [Added in 1912.]
2. In the *Zentralblatt* the paper was ascribed in error to Ernest Jones. [The version given here is the one to be found in Brill (1912), slightly modified.]
3. [In the German version of Brill's paper the following footnote appeared at this point:] 'By our laws a divorce cannot be obtained unless it is proved that one party has committed adultery; and in fact the divorce is granted only to the innocent party.'

it, but I received the usual surprised answers: had not everyone a right to make a slip of the tongue? it was only an accident, there was nothing behind it, and so on. I replied that there must be a reason for every mistake in speaking, and that, had he not told me earlier that he was unmarried, I would be tempted to suppose he himself was the hero of the story; for in that case the slip could be explained by his wish that he had obtained the divorce rather than his wife, so that he should not have (by our matrimonial laws) to pay alimony, and so that he could marry again in New York State. He stoutly denied my conjecture, but the exaggerated emotional reaction which accompanied it, in which he showed marked signs of agitation followed by laughter, only strengthened my suspicions. To my appeal that he should tell the truth in the interests of science, he answered: "Unless you wish me to lie you must believe that I was never married, and hence your psychoanalytic interpretation is all wrong." He added that someone who paid attention to every triviality was positively dangerous. Then he suddenly remembered that he had another appointment and left us.

'Both Dr Frink and I were still convinced that my interpretation of his slip of the tongue was correct, and I decided to corroborate or disprove it by further investigation. Some days later I visited a neighbour, an old friend of Dr R., who was able to confirm my explanation in every particular. The divorce proceedings had taken place some weeks before, and the nurse was cited as co-respondent. Dr R. is to-day thoroughly convinced of the correctness of the Freudian mechanisms.'

The self-betrayal is equally unmistakable in the following case,[1] reported by Otto Rank:

'A father who was without any patriotic feelings, and who wished to educate his children so that they too should be free from what he regarded as a superfluous sentiment, was criticizing his sons for taking part in a patriotic demonstration; when they protested that their uncle had also taken part in it, he replied: "*He* is the one person you should not imitate: he is an

1. [Added in 1912.]

idiot." On seeing his children's look of astonishment at their father's unusual tone, he realized that he had made a slip of the tongue, and added apologetically: "I meant to say '*patriot*', of course."'

Here is a slip of the tongue[1] which was interpreted as a self-betrayal by the other party to the conversation. It is reported by Stärcke, who adds a pertinent comment, though it goes beyond the task of interpreting the slip.

'A woman dentist promised her sister that she would have a look some time to see if there was *Kontakt* [contact] between two of her molars (that is, to see if the lateral surfaces of the molars were touching each other so that no fragments of food could lodge in between). Her sister finally complained about having to wait so long for this inspection, and jokingly said: "She's probably treating a colleague at the moment, but her sister has to go on waiting." The dentist eventually examined her, found there was in fact a small cavity in one of the molars, and said: "I didn't think it was in such a bad way – I thought it was merely that you had no *Kontant* [ready money] – I mean *Kontakt*." "You see?" laughed her sister; "your greed is the only reason why you made me wait so much longer than your paying patients!"

'(Obviously I should not add my own associations to hers or base any conclusions on them, but when I heard of this slip of the tongue it at once sprang to my mind that these two pleasant and gifted young ladies are unmarried and have in fact very little to do with young men, and I asked myself whether they would have more *contact* with young people if they had more *ready money*.)' [Cf. Stärcke, 1916.]

In the following example, too, reported by Reik (1915), the slip of the tongue amounts to a self-betrayal:

'A girl was to become engaged to a young man whom she did not care for. To bring the two young people closer together, their parents arranged a meeting which was attended by the

1. [This example and the two following ones (i.e. down to the bottom of the next page) were added in 1917.]

parties to the intended match. The young girl possessed sufficient self-control to prevent her suitor, who behaved in a very
on-coming manner towards her, from detecting her antipathy
to him. But when her mother asked her how she liked the young
man, she answered politely: "Well enough. He's most *liebenswidrig!*"[1]

Equally self-revealing is the following, which Rank (1913)
describes as a 'witty slip of the tongue'.

'A married woman, who enjoyed hearing anecdotes and who
was said not to be altogether averse to extra-marital affairs if
they were reinforced by adequate gifts, was told the following
time-honoured story, not without design on his part, by a young
man who was eager to obtain her favours. One of two business
friends was trying to obtain the favours of his partner's somewhat prudish wife. In the end she consented to grant them to
him in exchange for a present of a thousand gulden.[2] When,
therefore, her husband was about to start on a journey, his
partner borrowed a thousand gulden from him and promised
to pay them back next day to his wife. He then, of course, paid
the sum to the wife, implying that it was the reward for her
favours; and she supposed she had been caught at last when her
husband on his return asked for the thousand gulden and thus
found insult added to injury. When the young man reached
the point in his story at which the seducer says: "I'll *repay* the
money to your wife tomorrow", his listener interrupted with
the highly revealing words: "Let me see, haven't you *repaid* me
that – I'm sorry – I mean *told*[3] me that already?" She could
hardly have given a clearer indication, without actually putting
it into words, of her willingness to offer herself on the same
terms.'

  1. [She intended to say '*liebenswürdig*', 'agreeable' (literally 'worthy
of love'). The word she actually used, '*liebenswidrig*', would mean
literally 'repelling to love'.]
  2. [Worth at the time about £80 or $400.]
  3. [There is no resemblance between the two German words used
here for 'repaid' and 'told'.]

A good example[1] of this kind of self-betrayal, which did not lead to serious consequences, is reported by Tausk (1917) under the title of 'The Faith of our Fathers'. 'As my fiancée was a Christian', Herr A. related, 'and was unwilling to adopt the Jewish faith, I myself was obliged to be converted from Judaism to Christianity so that we could marry. I did not change my religion without some internal resistance, but I felt it was justified by the purpose behind it, the more so because it involved abandoning no more than an outward adherence to Judaism, not a religious conviction (which I had never had). Notwithstanding this, I always continued later on to acknowledge the fact of my being a Jew, and few of my acquaintances know I am baptized. I have two sons by this marriage, who were given Christian baptism. When the boys were sufficiently old they were told of their Jewish background, so as to prevent them from being influenced by anti-semitic views at their school and from turning against their father for such a superfluous reason. Some years ago I and my children, who were then at their primary school, were staying with the family of a teacher at the summer resort in D. One day while we were sitting at tea with our otherwise friendly hosts, the lady of the house, who had no inkling of her summer guests' Jewish ancestry, launched some very sharp attacks on the Jews. I ought to have made a bold declaration of the facts in order to set my sons the example of "having the courage of one's convictions", but I was afraid of the unpleasant exchanges that usually follow an avowal of this sort. Besides, I was alarmed at the possibility of having to leave the good lodgings we had found and of thus spoiling my own and my children's in any case limited holiday period, should our hosts' behaviour towards us take an unfriendly turn because of the fact that we were Jews. As however I had reason to expect that my sons, in their candid and ingenuous way, would betray the momentous truth if they heard any more of the conversation, I tried to get them to leave the company by sending them into the garden. I said: "Go into

1. [Added in 1919.]

the garden, *Juden* [Jews]", quickly correcting it to "*Jungen* [youngsters]". In this way I enabled the "courage of my convictions" to be expressed in a parapraxis. The others did not in fact draw any conclusions from my slip of the tongue, since they attached no significance to it; but I was obliged to learn the lesson that the "faith of our fathers" cannot be disavowed with impunity if one is a son and has sons of one's own.'

The effect produced by the following slip of the tongue,[1] which I would not report had not the magistrate himself made a note of it for this collection during the court proceedings, is anything but innocent:

A soldier charged with housebreaking stated in evidence: 'Up to now I've not been discharged from military *Diebsstellung*;[2] so at the moment I'm still in the army.'

A slip of the tongue[3] has a more cheering effect during psychoanalytic work, when it serves as a means of providing the doctor with a confirmation that may be very welcome to him if he is engaged in a dispute with the patient. I once had to interpret a patient's dream in which the name 'Jauner' occurred. The dreamer knew someone of that name, but it was impossible to discover the reason for his appearing in the context of the dream; I therefore ventured to suggest that it might be merely because of his name, which sounds like the term of abuse '*Gauner*' [swindler]. My patient hastily and vigorously contested this; but in doing so he made a slip of the tongue which confirmed my guess, since he confused the same letters once more. His answer was: 'That seems to me too *jewagt* [instead of "*gewagt* (far-fetched)"].'[4] When I had drawn his attention to his slip, he accepted my interpretation.

1. [Added in 1920.]
2. [He meant to say '*Dienststellung*', 'service', literally 'service [*Dienst*] position [*Stellung*]'. Instead he said '*Diebsstellung*', which would mean literally 'thief position'.]
3. [This paragraph and the following one were added in 1907.]
4. [In vulgar speech, particularly in North Germany, 'g' at the beginning of a word is often pronounced like the German 'j' (English 'y') instead of like the hard English 'g'.]

If one of the parties involved in a serious argument makes a slip of the tongue which reverses the meaning of what he intended to say, it immediately puts him at a disadvantage with his opponent, who seldom fails to make the most of his improved position.

This makes it clear[1] that people give slips of the tongue and other parapraxes the same interpretation that I advocate in this book, even if they do not endorse theoretically the view I put forward, and even if they are disinclined, so far as it applies to themselves, to renounce the convenience that goes along with tolerating parapraxes. The amusement and derision which such oral slips are certain to evoke at the crucial moment can be taken as evidence against what purports to be the generally accepted convention that a mistake in speaking is a *lapsus linguae* and of no psychological significance. It was no less a person than the German Imperial Chancellor Prince Bülow who protested on these lines in an effort to save the situation, when the wording of his speech in defence of his Emperor (in November, 1907) was given the opposite meaning by a slip of the tongue. 'As for the present, the new epoch of the Emperor Wilhelm II, I can only repeat what I said a year ago, namely that *it would be unfair and unjust to speak of a coterie of responsible advisers round our Emperor . . .*' (loud cries of 'irresponsible') '. . . *irresponsible advisers.* Forgive the *lapsus linguae.*' (Laughter.)

In this case, as a result of the accumulation of negatives, Prince Bülow's sentence was somewhat obscure; sympathy for the speaker and consideration for his difficult position prevented this slip from being put to any further use against him. A year later another speaker in the same place was not so fortunate. He wished to appeal for a demonstration *with no reserves* [*rückhaltlos*] in support of the Emperor, and in doing so was warned by a bad slip of the tongue that other emotions were to be found within his loyal breast. 'Lattmann (German National

1. [This paragraph and the two following ones were added in 1910.]

Party): On the question of the Address our position is based on the standing orders of the Reichstag. According to them the Reichstag is entitled to tender such an address to the Emperor. It is our belief that the united thoughts and wishes of the German people are bent on achieving a *united demonstration* in this matter as well, and if we can do so in a form that takes the Emperor's feelings fully into account, then we should do so *spinelessly* [*"rückgratlos"*] as well.' (Loud laughter which continued for some minutes.) 'Gentlemen, I should have said not *"rückgratlos"* but *"ruckhaltlos* [unreservedly]"' (laughter), 'and at this difficult time even our Emperor accepts a manifestation by the people – one made without reserve – such as we should like to see.'

The [social-democratic paper] *Vorwärts* of November 12, 1908, did not miss the opportunity of pointing to the psychological significance of this slip of the tongue: 'Probably never before in any parliament has a member, through an involuntary self-accusation, characterized his own attitude and that of the parliamentary majority towards the Emperor so exactly as did the anti-Semitic Lattmann, when, speaking with solemn emotion on the second day of the debate, he slipped into an admission that he and his friends wished to express their opinion to the Emperor *spinelessly*. Loud laughter from all sides drowned the remaining words of this unhappy man, who thought it necessary explicitly to stammer out by way of apology that he really meant *"unreservedly"*.'

I will add a further instance,[1] in which the slip of the tongue assumed the positively uncanny characteristics of a prophecy. Early in 1923 there was a great stir in the world of finance when the very young banker X. – probably one of the newest of the '*nouveaux riches*' in W., and at any rate the richest and youngest – obtained possession, after a short struggle, of a majority of the shares of the — Bank; and as a further consequence, a remarkable General Meeting took place at which

1. [Added in 1924.]

the old directors of the bank, financiers of the old type, were not re-elected, and young X. became president of the bank. In the valedictory speech which the managing director Dr Y. went on to deliver in honour of the old president, who had not been re-elected, a number of the audience noticed a distressing slip of the tongue which occurred again and again. He continually spoke of the *expiring* [*dahinscheidend*] president instead of the *outgoing* [*ausscheidend*] president. As it turned out, the old president who was not re-elected died a few days after this meeting. He was, however, over eighty years old! (From Storfer.)

A good example of a slip of the tongue[1] whose purpose is not so much to betray the speaker as to give the listener in the theatre his bearings, is to be found in [Schiller's] *Wallenstein* (*Piccolomini*, Act I, Scene 5); and it shows us that the dramatist, who here availed himself of this device, was familiar with the mechanism and meaning of slips of the tongue. In the preceding scene Max Piccolomini has ardently espoused the Duke's [Wallenstein's] cause, and has been passionately describing the blessings of peace, of which he has become aware on the course of a journey while escorting Wallenstein's daughter to the camp. As he leaves the stage, his father [Octavio] and Questenberg, the emissary from the court, are plunged in consternation. Scene 5 continues:

QUESTENBERG: Alas, alas! and stands it so?
                What friend! and do we let him go away
                In this delusion – let him go away?
                Not call him back immediately, not open
                His eyes upon the spot?

OCTAVIO (*recovering himself out of a deep study*):
                              He has now open'd mine,
                And I see more than pleases me.

QUEST: What is it?

OCT: Curse on this journey!

---

1. [Added in 1907.]

QUEST: But why so? What is it?

OCT: Come, come along, friend! I must follow up
                       The ominous track immediately. Mine eyes
                       Are open'd now, and I must use them. Come!
                           (*Draws Q. on with him*)

QUEST: What now? *Where* go you then?

OCT: To her herself.

QUEST: To –

OCT: (*correcting himself*): To the Duke. Come let us go.
                                         [Coleridge's translation.]

The small slip of saying 'to her' instead of 'to him' is meant
to reveal to us that the father has seen through his son's motive
for espousing the Duke's cause, while the courtier complains
that he is 'talking absolute riddles' to him.[1]

Another example[2] in which a dramatist makes use of a slip
of the tongue has been discovered by Otto Rank (1910) in
Shakespeare. I quote Rank's account.

'A slip of the tongue occurs in Shakespeare's *Merchant of
Venice* (Act III, Scene 2), which is from the dramatic point of
view extremely subtly motivated and which is put to brilliant
technical use. Like the slip in *Wallenstein* to which Freud has
drawn attention, it shows that dramatists have a clear understanding of the mechanism and meaning of this kind of parapraxis and assume that the same is true of their audience.
Portia, who by her father's will has been bound to the choice
of a husband by lot, has so far escaped all her unwelcome
suitors by a fortunate chance. Having at last found in Bassanio
the suitor who is to her liking, she has cause to fear that he too
will choose the wrong casket. She would very much like to tell
him that even so he could rest assured of her love; but she is
prevented by her vow. In this internal conflict the poet makes
her say to the suitor she favours:

1. [Octavio realizes that his son's motive springs from love of the
Duke's daughter.]
2. [Added in 1912].

> I pray you tarry; pause a day or two,
> Before you hazard: for, in choosing wrong,
> I lose your company; therefore, forbear awhile:
> There's something tells me (*but it is not love*)
> I would not lose you . . .
>
>   . . . I could teach you
> How to choose right, but then I am forsworn;
> So will I never be; so may you miss me;
> But if you do you'll make me wish a sin,
> That I have been forsworn. Beshrew your eyes,
> They have o'erlooked me, and divided me;
> *One half of me is yours, the other half yours, –*
> *Mine own, I would say*; but if mine, then yours,
> And so all yours.

'The thing of which she wanted to give him only a very subtle hint, because she should really have concealed it from him altogether, namely, that even before he made his choice she was *wholly* his and loved him – it is precisely this that the poet, with a wonderful psychological sensitivity, causes to break through openly in her slip of the tongue; and by this artistic device he succeeds in relieving both the lover's unbearable uncertainty and the suspense of the sympathetic audience over the outcome of his choice.'[1]

In view of the interest that is lent to our theory of slips of the tongue by support of this nature from great writers, I feel justified in citing a third such instance which has been reported by Ernest Jones[2] (1911*b*, 496):

'In a recently published article Otto Rank drew our attention to a pretty instance of how Shakespeare caused one of his characters, Portia, to make a slip of the tongue which revealed

1. [Freud reproduced this example in the second of his *Introductory Lectures* (1916–17), where he added a further comment of his own. Cf. *P.F.L.*, 1, 64–5.]

2. [This example – also added in 1912 – appears in Freud's book in a German translation. We here give the original English.]

her secret thoughts to an attentive member of the audience. I propose to relate a similar example from *The Egoist*, the masterpiece of the greatest English novelist, George Meredith. The plot of the novel is, shortly, as follows: Sir Willoughby Patterne, an aristocrat greatly admired by his circle, becomes engaged to a Miss Constantia Durham. She discovers in him an intense egoism, which he skilfully conceals from the world, and to escape the marriage she elopes with a Captain Oxford. Some years later Patterne becomes engaged to a Miss Clara Middleton, and most of the book is taken up with a detailed description of the conflict that arises in her mind on also discovering his egoism. External circumstances, and her conception of honour, hold her to her pledge, while he becomes more and more distasteful in her eyes. She partly confides in his cousin and secretary, Vernon Whitford, the man whom she ultimately marries; but from loyalty to Patterne and other motives he stands aloof.

'In a soliloquy about her sorrow Clara speaks as follows: "'If some noble gentleman could see me as I am and not disdain to aid me! Oh! to be caught out of this prison of thorns and brambles. I cannot tear my own way out. I am a coward. A beckoning of a finger[1] would change me, I believe. I could fly bleeding and through hootings to a comrade ... Constantia met a soldier. Perhaps she prayed and her prayer was answered. She did ill. But, oh, how I love her for it! His name was Harry Oxford ... She did not waver, she cut the links, she signed herself over. Oh, brave girl, what do you think of me? But I have no Harry Whitford; I am alone ...' The sudden consciousness that she had put another name for Oxford struck her a buffet, drowning her in crimson."

1. Note by the [German] translator [J. Theodor von Kalmár]: I had originally proposed to translate the English words 'beckoning of a finger' by '*leiser Wink*' ['slight hint'] till I realized that by suppressing the word 'finger' I was robbing the sentence of a psychological subtlety.

'The fact that both men's names end in "ford" evidently renders the confounding of them more easy, and would by many be regarded as an adequate cause for this, but the real underlying motive for it is plainly indicated by the author. In another passage the same *lapsus* occurs, and is followed by the spontaneous hesitation and sudden change of subject that one is familiar with in psychoanalysis and in Jung's association experiments when a half-conscious complex is touched. Sir Willoughby patronisingly says of Whitford: "'False alarm. The resolution to do anything unaccustomed is quite beyond poor old Vernon.'" Clara replies: "'But if Mr Oxford – Whitford... your swans, coming sailing up the lake, how beautiful they look when they are indignant! I was going to ask you, surely men witnessing a marked admiration for someone else will naturally be discouraged?' Sir Willoughby stiffened with sudden enlightenment."

'In still another passage, Clara by another *lapsus* betrays her secret wish that she was on a more intimate footing with Vernon Whitford. Speaking to a boy friend, she says: "'Tell Mr Vernon – tell Mr Whitford.'"'[1]

The view[2] of slips of the tongue which is advocated here can meet the test even in the most trivial examples. I have repeatedly been able to show that the most insignificant and obvious errors in speaking have their meaning and can be explained in the same way as the more striking instances. A woman patient who was acting entirely against my wishes in planning a short trip to Budapest, but who was determined to have her own way, justified herself by telling me that she was going for only three days; but she made a slip of the tongue and

1. [*Footnote added* 1920:] Other instances of slips of the tongue which the writer intends to be taken as having a meaning and usually as being self-revealing can be found in Shakespeare's Richard II (Act II, Scene 2), and in Schiller's *Don Carlos* (Act II, Scene 8; a slip made by Princess Eboli). There would doubtless be no difficulty in extending this list.

2. [This paragraph was added in 1907; the one which follows dates back to 1901.]

actually said 'only three *weeks*'. She was betraying the fact that, to spite me, she would rather spend three weeks than three days there in the company which I considered unsuitable for her. – One evening I wanted to excuse myself for not having fetched my wife home from the theatre, and said: 'I was at the theatre at ten past ten.' I was corrected: 'You mean ten *to* ten.' Of course I meant ten *to* ten. *After* ten o'clock would have been no excuse. I had been told that the theatre bills said the performance ended before ten. When I reached the theatre I found the entrance-hall in darkness and the theatre empty. The performance had in fact ended earlier and my wife had not waited for me. When I looked at the clock it was only five to ten. But I decided to make my case out more favourably when I got home and to say it had been ten to ten. Unfortunately, my slip of the tongue spoilt my plan and revealed my disingenuousness, by making me confess more than there was to confess.

This leads on to those speech-disturbances which cannot any longer be described as slips of the tongue because what they affect is not the individual word but the rhythm and execution of a whole speech: disturbances like, for instance, stammering and stuttering caused by embarrassment. But here too, as in the former cases, it is a question of an internal conflict, which is betrayed to us by the disturbance in speech. I really do not think that anyone would make a slip of the tongue in an audience with his Sovereign, in a serious declaration of love or in defending his honour and name before a jury – in short, on all those occasions in which a person is heart and soul engaged. Even in forming an appreciation of an author's style we are permitted and accustomed to apply the same elucidatory principle which we cannot dispense with in tracing the origins of individual mistakes in speech. A clear and unambiguous manner of writing shows us that here the author is at one with himself; where we find a forced and involved expression which (to use an apt phrase) is aimed at more than one target, we may recognize the intervention of an insufficiently worked-out, complicating thought, or we may hear the stifled voice of the author's self-criticism.[1]

Since this book first appeared[2] friends and colleagues who speak other languages have begun to turn their attention to slips of the tongue which they have been able to observe in countries where their language is spoken. As was to be expected they have found that the laws governing parapraxes are independent of the linguistic material; and they have made the same interpretations that have been exemplified here in instances coming from speakers of the German language. Of countless examples I include only one:

Brill (1909) reports of himself: 'A friend described to me a nervous patient and wished to know whether I could benefit him. I remarked: "I believe that in time I could remove all his symptoms by psychoanalysis because it is a *durable* case" – wishing to say "*curable*"!'[3]

1. [*Footnote added* 1910:] Ce qu'on conçoit bien
          S'annonce clairement
          Et les mots pour le dire
          Arrivent aisément.

          [What is well thought out
          Presents itself with clarity,
          And the words to express it
          Come easily.]

                    Boileau: *Art poétique.*

[In a letter to Fliess of September 21, 1899 (Freud, 1950*a*, Letter 119), Freud applied a criticism of this precise kind to what he felt was his own unsatisfactory style in *The Interpretation of Dreams*. The passage will be found quoted at the end of the Editor's Introduction, *P.F.L.*, 4, 42.]

2. [This paragraph and the example that follows were added in 1912.]

3. [This example is given in English in the original. – In the 1912 edition only, the following passage appeared in the text at this point: 'An extremely instructive instance of the way in which a simple slip of the tongue may be made use of in a psychoanalysis has been reported by Stekel (1910):

"'A patient suffering from agoraphobia said during the analysis: 'If I start on a subject I keep "*dablei*" [for "*dabei*", "at it"] with some obstinacy.' When his attention had been drawn to his slip, he went on:

In conclusion,[1] for the benefit of readers who are prepared to make a certain effort and to whom psychoanalysis is not unfamiliar, I will add an example which will enable them to form some picture of the mental depths into which the pursuit even of a slip of the tongue can lead. It has been reported by Jekels (1913).

'On December 11, a lady of my acquaintance addressed me (in Polish) in a somewhat challenging and overbearing manner, as follows: "Why did I say to-day that I have twelve fingers?" At my request she gave an account of the scene in which the remark was made. She had got ready to go out with her daughter to pay a visit, and had asked her daughter – a case of dementia praecox then in remission – to change her blouse; and this she in fact did, in the adjoining room. On re-entering, the daughter found her mother busy cleaning her nails, and the following conversation ensued:

'Daughter: "There! I'm ready now and you're not!"

'Mother: "Yes, but you have only one blouse and I have *twelve nails*."

'Daughter: "What?"

'Mother (impatiently): "Well, of course I have; after all, I have *twelve fingers*."

'A colleague who heard the story at the same time as I did asked what occurred to her in connection with *twelve*. She answered equally quickly and definitely: "Twelve means nothing to me – it is not the date of anything (of importance)."

'To *finger* she gave the following association after a little hesitation: "Some of my husband's family were born with six fingers on their feet (Polish has no specific word for 'toe'). When

---

'I have done what children do and said "l" instead of "r" – "blei" instead of "brei"', so making a second slip of the tongue.

' "This slip was obviously of great significance. The syllables 'bei – brei – blei' [in German: 'at', 'broth', 'lead'] carried important associations." ']

1. [The rest of the chapter was added in 1917.]

our children were born they were immediately examined to see if they had six fingers." For external reasons the analysis was not continued that evening.

'Next morning, December 12, the lady visited me and told me with visible excitement: "What do you suppose has happened? For about the last twenty years I have been sending congratulations to my husband's elderly uncle on his birthday, which is to-day, and I have always written him a letter on the 11th. This time I forgot about it and had to send a telegram just now."

'I myself remembered, and I reminded the lady, how positive she had been the evening before in dismissing my colleague's question about the number twelve – which was in fact very fitted to remind her of the birthday – by remarking that the twelfth was not a date of importance to her.

'She then admitted that this uncle of her husband's was a wealthy man from whom she had in fact always expected to inherit something, quite especially in her present straitened financial circumstances. Thus, for instance, it was he, or rather his death, that had immediately sprung to her mind a few days before when an acquaintance of hers had predicted from cards that she would receive a large sum of money. It flashed through her mind at once that the uncle was the only person from whom money could possibly come to her or her children; and this same scene also instantly reminded her of the fact that this uncle's wife had once promised to remember the lady's children in her will. But in the meanwhile she had died intestate; had she perhaps given her husband appropriate instructions?

'The death-wish against the uncle must clearly have emerged with very great intensity, for she said to the friend who made the prophecy: "You encourage people to make away with others." In the four or five days that elapsed between the prophecy and the uncle's birthday she was constantly looking at the obituary columns in the newspapers from the town where the uncle lived. Not suprisingly, therefore, in view of the intensity of her wish for his death, the event and the date of the birthday he was about to celebrate were so strongly suppressed that not only was a resolution which had been carried out for years forgotten in consequence, but even my colleague's question failed to bring them to consciousness.

'In the slip "twelve fingers" the suppressed "twelve" had broken through and had helped to determine the parapraxis. I say "*helped* to determine"; for the striking association to "finger" leads us to suspect the existence of some further motivations. It also explains why the "twelve" had falsified precisely this most innocent phrase, "ten fingers". The association ran: "Some members of my husband's family were born with six fingers on their feet." Six toes are a sign of a particular abnormality. Thus six fingers mean *one* abnormal child and twelve fingers *two* abnormal children. And that was really the fact in this case. The lady had married at a very early age; and the only legacy left her by her husband, a highly eccentric and abnormal person who took his own life shortly after their marriage, were two children whom the doctors repeatedly pronounced to be abnormal and victims of a grave hereditary taint derived from their father. The elder daughter recently returned home after a severe catatonic attack; soon afterwards, the younger daughter, now at the age of puberty, also fell ill from a serious neurosis.

'The fact that the children's abnormality is here linked with the death-wish against the uncle, and is condensed with this far more strongly suppressed and psychically more powerful element, enables us to assume the existence of a second determinant for the slip of the tongue, namely a *death-wish against the abnormal children*.

'But the special significance of twelve as a death wish is already indicated by the fact that the uncle's birthday was very intimately associated in the lady's mind with the idea of his death. For her husband had taken his life on the 13th – one day, that is, after the uncle's birthday; and the uncle's wife had said to the young widow: "Yesterday he was sending his congratulations, so full of warmth and kindness – and to-day... !"

'I may add that the lady had real enough reasons as well for wishing her children dead; for they brought her no pleasure at all, only grief and severe restrictions on her independence, and she had for their sake renounced all the happiness that love might have brought her. On this occasion she had in fact gone to exceptional lengths to avoid putting the daughter with whom she was going to pay the visit in a bad mood; and it may be imagined what demands this makes on anyone's patience and self-denial where the case is one of dementia praecox, and how many angry impulses have to be suppressed in the process.

'The meaning of the parapraxis would accordingly be:

'"The uncle shall die, these abnormal children shall die (the whole of this abnormal family, as it were), and I will get their money."

'This parapraxis bears, in my view, several indications of an unusual structure:

'(a) Two determinants were present in it, condensed in a single element.

'(b) The presence of the two determinants was reflected in the doubling of the slip of the tongue (twelve nails, twelve fingers).

'(c) It is a striking point that one of the meanings of "twelve", viz., the twelve fingers which expressed the children's abnormality, stood for an indirect form of representation; the psychical abnormality was here represented by the physical abnormality, and the highest part of the body by the lowest.'

CHAPTER VI

MISREADINGS AND SLIPS OF THE PEN[1]

WHEN we come to mistakes in reading and writing, we find that our general approach and our observations in regard to mistakes in speaking hold good here too – not surprisingly, in view of the close kinship between these functions. I shall confine myself here to reporting a few carefully analysed examples, and shall make no attempt to cover every aspect of the phenomena.

(A) MISREADINGS

(1) I was sitting in a café, turning over the pages of a copy of the *Leipziger Illustrierte* [an illustrated weekly] (which I was holding up at an angle), when I read the following legend under a picture that stretched across the page: 'A Wedding Celebration in the *Odyssee* [Odyssey].' It caught my attention; in surprise I took hold of the paper in the proper way and then corrected my error: 'A Wedding Celebration on the *Ostsee* [Baltic].' How did I come to make this absurd mistake in reading? My thoughts at once turned to a book by Ruths (1898), *Experimentaluntersuchungen über Musikphantome*[2] . . . , which had occupied me a good deal recently since it trenches on the psychological problems that I have been concerned with. The author promised that he would shortly be bringing out a book to be called 'Analysis and Principles of Dream Phen-

1. [The earlier portion of this chapter, up to p. 158, dates back to 1901.]
2. ['Experimental investigations of music phantoms.' These 'music phantoms' are, according to Ruths, a 'group of psychical phenomena which make an [involuntary] appearance in the brains of many people while they are listening to music'.]

omena'. Seeing that I have just published an *Interpretation of Dreams* it is not surprising that I should await this book with the keenest interest. In Ruths' work on music phantoms I found at the beginning of the list of contents an announcement of a detailed inductive proof that the ancient Greek myths and legends have their main source of origin in phantoms of sleep and music, in the phenomena of dreams and also in deliria. Thereupon I at once plunged into the text to find out whether he also realized that the scene in which Odysseus appears before Nausicaä was derived from the common dream of being naked. A friend had drawn my attention to the fine passage in Gottfried Keller's *Der Grüne Heinrich* which explains this episode in the Odyssey as an objective representation of the dreams of a sailor wandering far from home; and I had pointed out the connection with exhibitionist dreams of being naked.[1] I found nothing on the subject in Ruths' book. In this instance it is obvious that my thoughts were occupied with questions of priority.

(2) How did I come to read in a newspaper one day: '*Im Fass* [in a tub] across Europe', instead of '*Zu Fuss* [on foot]'? Solving this problem caused me prolonged difficulties. The first associations, it is true, indicated that it must have been the tub of Diogenes that I had in mind; and I had recently been reading about the art of the age of Alexander in a history of art. From there it was easy to recall Alexander's celebrated remark: 'If I were not Alexander I should like to be Diogenes.' I also had some dim recollection of a certain Hermann Zeitung[2] who had set out on his travels packed in a trunk. But the train of associations declined to run on further, and I did not succeed in rediscovering the page in the history of art on which the remark had caught my eye. It was not till months later that the problem, which I had meanwhile set aside, suddenly sprang to my mind once more; and this time it brought

1. *The Interpretation of Dreams* (1900a), *P.F.L.*, 4, 345-6 [Chapter V (D), near the end of Section *a*].
2. ['*Zeitung*', here a proper name, is also the German for 'newspaper'.]

its solution with it. I recalled the comment of a newspaper article on the strange means of *transport* [*Beförderung*] that people were then choosing in order to go to Paris for the International Exhibition [of 1900]; and the passage, I believe, went on with a joking account of how one gentleman intended to get himself rolled in a tub to Paris by another gentleman. Needless to say the only motive of these people would be to draw attention to themselves by such folly. Hermann Zeitung was in fact the name of the man who had provided the first instance of such extraordinary methods of transport. It then struck me that I once treated a patient whose pathological anxiety about reading newspapers was to be explained as a reaction against his pathological *ambition* to see himself in print and to read of his fame in the newspapers. Alexander of Macedon was undoubtedly one of the most ambitious men that ever lived. He even complained that he would find no Homer to sing of his exploits. But how could I possibly have *failed to recall* that there is another Alexander who is closer to me, that Alexander is the name of my younger brother? I now immediately found the objectionable thought about this other Alexander that had had to be repressed, and what it was that had given rise to it at the present time. My brother is an authority on matters connected with tariffs and *transport*, and at a certain date he was due to receive the title of professor for his work in teaching at a commercial college. Several years ago my own name had been suggested at the University for the same *promotion* [*Beförderung*], without my having obtained it.[1] At the time, our mother expressed her surprise that her younger son was to become a professor before her elder. This had been the situation when I was unable to solve my mistake in reading. Subsequently my brother too met with

1. [This question is repeatedly discussed in connection with Freud's dreams in *The Interpretation of Dreams* (1900a). See, for instance, the first example in Chapter IV, *P.F.L.*, 4, 217 ff. He received the appointment ultimately, in 1902, the year following the first publication of this paragraph.]

difficulties; his prospects of becoming professor sank even lower than my own. But at that point the meaning of the misreading suddenly became clear to me; it was as though the fading of my brother's prospects had removed an obstacle. I had behaved as if I was reading of my brother's appointment in the newspaper and was saying to myself: 'How curious that a person can appear in the newspaper (i.e. can be appointed professor) on account of such stupidities (which is what his profession amounts to)!' Afterwards I had no difficulty in finding the passage about Hellenistic art in the age of Alexander, and to my astonishment convinced myself that in my previous search I had repeatedly read parts of the same page and had each time passed over the relevant sentence as if I was under the dominance of a negative hallucination. However, this sentence did not contain anything at all to enlighten me – anything that would have deserved to be forgotten. I suspect that the symptom consisting of my failure to find the passage in the book was only formed with the purpose of leading me astray. I was intended to search for a continuation of the train of thought in the place where my enquiries encountered an obstacle – that is, in some idea connected with Alexander of Macedon; in this way I was to be more effectively diverted from my brother of the same name. In fact the device was entirely successful; all my efforts were directed towards rediscovering the lost passage in the history of art.

In this case the ambiguity of the word '*Beförderung*' ['transport' and 'promotion'] forms the associative bridge between the two complexes,[1] the unimportant one which was aroused by the newspaper article, and the more interesting but objectionable one which asserted itself here in the form of a disturb-

---

1. [In 1901 and 1904: 'circles of thoughts'. The word 'complexes' replacing this in the 1907 edition, marks the beginning of Jung's influence on Freud. – For the similar use of verbal bridges in the construction of dreams, jokes and neurotic symptoms see *The Interpretation of Dreams*, near the opening of Chapter VI (D), *P.F.L.*, 4, 456 *n.* 1. See also p. 338, *n.* 2, below.]

ance of what was to be read. It can be seen from this example that it is not always easy to explain occurrences such as this mistake in reading. At times one is even forced to postpone solving the problem to a more favourable time. But the harder the work of solving it proves to be, the more certainly can one anticipate that the disturbing thought which is finally disclosed will be judged by our conscious thinking as something alien and opposed to it.

(3) One day I received a letter from the neighbourhood of Vienna which brought me a piece of news that shocked me. I immediately called my wife and broke the news to her that '*die* arme [the poor][1] Wilhelm M.' had fallen very seriously ill and been given up by the doctors. There must, however, have been a false ring about the words I chose to express my sorrow, for my wife grew suspicious, asked to see the letter and declared she was certain it could not read as I had said it did, since no one called a wife by her husband's first name, and in any case the lady who wrote the letter knew the wife's first name perfectly well. I obstinately defended my assertion and referred to the very common use of visiting cards on which a woman styles herself by her husband's first name. I was finally compelled to pick up the letter, and what we in fact read in it was '*der*[2] arme W.M.', or rather something even plainer: 'der arme *Dr* W. M.', which I had entirely overlooked. My mistake in reading therefore amounted to a kind of convulsive attempt to shift the sad news from the husband to the wife. The title that stood between the article, adjective and name did not fit in well with my requirement that the wife should be the one referred to. For this reason it was simply done away with in the process of reading. My motive for falsifying the message was not, however, that my feelings for the wife were less warm than those I had for her husband, but that the poor man's fate had excited my fears for another person in close contact with me. This

1. [The use of '*die*', the feminine form of the definite article, implied that the person concerned was a woman.]
2. [The masculine form of the definite article.]

person shared with him what I knew to be one of the determinants of the illness.

(4)[1] There is one misreading which I find irritating and laughable and to which I am prone whenever I walk through the
streets of a strange town on my holidays. On these occasions
I read every shop sign that resembles the word in any way as
'Antiquities'. This betrays the questing spirit of the collector.

(5)[2] Bleuler relates in his important book, *Affektivität,
Suggestibilität, Paranoia* (1906, 121): 'Once while I was reading
I had an intellectual feeling that I saw my name two lines further
down. To my astonishment I only found the word "*Blut-
körperchen* [blood-corpuscles]".I have analysed many thousands
of misreadings in the peripheral as well as the central visual
field; but this is the grossest instance. Whenever I imagined I
saw my name, the word that gave rise to the notion usually
resembled my name much more, and in most cases every single
letter of my name had to be found close together before I could
make such an error. In this case, however, the delusion of
reference and the illusion could be explained very easily: what
I had just read was the end of a comment on a type of bad
style found in scientific words, from which I did not feel free.'

(6)[3] Hanns Sachs reports having read: 'The things that strike
other people are passed over by him in his "*Steif leinenheit*
[pedantry]".' 'This last word', Sachs proceeds, 'surprised me,
and on looking more closely I discovered that it was "*Stilfeinheit*
[elegance of style]". The passage occurred in the course of some
remarks by an author whom I admired, which were in ex-
travagant praise of a historian whom I do not find sympathetic
because he exhibits the "German professorial manner" in too
marked a degree.'

(7)[4] Dr Marcell Eibenschütz (1911) describes an instance
of misreading in the course of his philological studies. 'I was
engaged in studying the literary tradition of the *Book of Martyrs*,
a Middle High German legendary which I had undertaken

1. [Added 1907.]   2. [Added 1910.]
3. [Added 1919.]   4. [Added 1912.]

to edit in the series of "German Mediaeval Texts" published by the Prussian Akademie der Wissenschaften. Very little was known about the work, which had never seen print. There was a single essay on it in existence, by Joseph Haupt (1872, 101 ff.). Haupt based his work not on an old manuscript but on a copy of the principal source, Manuscript C (Klosterneuburg). This copy had been made at a comparatively recent date (in the nineteenth century). It is preserved in the Hofbibliothek [Imperial Library]. At the end of the copy the following subscription[1] is to be found:

'"Anno Domini MDCCCL in vigilia exaltacionis sancte crucis ceptus est iste liber et in vigilia pasce anni subsequentis finitus cum adiutorio omnipotentis per me Hartmanum de Krasna tunc temporis ecclesie niwenburgensis custodem."[2]

'Now in his essay Haupt quotes this subscription in the belief that it comes from the writer of C himself, and supposes C to have been written in 1350 – a view involving a consistent misreading of the date 1850 in Roman numerals – in spite of his having copied the subscription perfectly correctly and in spite of its having been printed perfectly correctly (i.e. as MDCCCL) in the essay, in the passage referred to.

'Haupt's information proved the source of much embarrassment to me. In the first place, being an entire novice in the world of scholarship, I was completely dominated by Haupt's authority, and for a long time I read the date given in the subscription lying in front of me – which was perfectly clearly and correctly printed – as 1350 instead of 1850, just as Haupt had done. I did this even though no trace of any subscription could be found in the original Manuscript C, which I used, and though it further transpired that no monk by the name of

1. [I.e. signature or explanatory paragraph at the end of a document.]
2. ['This book was begun on the Eve of Holy Cross Day in the Year of Our Lord 1850, and was finished on Easter Saturday in the following year; it was made, with the aid of the Almighty, by me, Hartman of Krasna, at that time sacrist of Klosterneuburg.']

Hartman had lived at Klosterneuburg at any time in the fourteenth century. And when at last the veil fell from before my eyes I guessed what had happened; and further investigation confirmed my suspicion. The subscription so often referred to is in fact to be found *only* in the copy used by Haupt, and is the work of its copyist, P. Hartman Zeibig, who was born at Krasna in Moravia, was Master of the Augustinian choir at Klosterneuburg, and who as sacrist of the monastery made a copy of Manuscript C and appended his name in the ancient fashion at the end of his copy. The mediaeval phraseology and the old orthography of the subscription doubtless played their part in inducing Haupt always to read 1350 instead of 1850, alongside his *wish* to be able to tell his readers as much as possible about the work he was discussing, and therefore also *to date Manuscript C*. (This was the motive for the parapraxis.)'

(8)[1] In Lichtenberg's *Witzige und satirische Einfälle* ['Witty and Satirical Thoughts', 1853] a remark occurs which is no doubt derived from a piece of observation and which comprises virtually the whole theory of misreading: 'He had read so much Homer that he always read "*Agamemnon*" instead of "*angenommen* [supposed]".'[2]

For in a very large number of cases[3] it is the reader's preparedness that alters the text and reads into it something which he is expecting or with which he is occupied. The only contribution towards a misreading which the text itself need make is that of affording some sort of resemblance in the verbal image, which the reader can alter in the sense he requires. Merely glancing at the text, especially with uncorrected vision, undoubtedly increases the possibility of such an illusion, but it is certainly not a necessary precondition for it.

1. [Added 1910.]
2. [Lichtenberg was a favourite author of Freud's. The present epigram is quoted again by Freud in his book on jokes (1905*c*), *P.F.L.*, 6, 136, and in his *Introductory Lectures* (1916–17), *P.F.L.*, 1, 65.]
3. [This paragraph and Examples 9 and 10 were added in 1917.]

(9) I have an impression that no parapraxis was so greatly encouraged by war conditions – which brought us all such constant and protracted preoccupations – as this particular one of misreading. I have been able to observe a large number of instances of it, but unfortunately I have kept records of only a few of them. One day I picked up a mid-day or evening paper and saw in large print: '*Der Friede von Görz* [The Peace of Gorizia].' But no, all it said was: '*Die Feinde vor Görz* [The Enemy before Gorizia].' It is easy for someone who has two sons fighting at this very time in that theatre of operations to make such a mistake in reading. – Someone else found an 'old *Brotkarte* [bread card]' mentioned in a certain context; when he looked at this more attentively, he had to replace it by 'old *Brokate* [brocades]'. It is perhaps worth mentioning that at a particular house, where this man is often a welcome guest, it is his habit to make himself agreeable to the mistress by handing his bread cards over to her. – An engineer, whose equipment had never stood up for long to the dampness in a tunnel that was under construction, was astonished to read a laudatory advertisement of goods made of '*Schundleder* [shoddy leather]'. But tradesmen are not usually so candid; what was being recommended was '*Seehundleder* [sealskin]'.

The reader's profession or present situation, too, determines the outcome of his misreading. A philologist, whose most recent, and excellent, works had brought him into conflict with his professional colleagues, read '*Sprachstrategie* [language strategy]' in mistake for '*Schachstrategie* [chess strategy]'. – A man who was taking a walk in a strange town just when the action of his bowels was timed to occur by a course of medical treatment read the word 'Closet-House' on a large sign on the first storey of a tall shop-building. His satisfaction on seeing it was mixed with a certain surprise that the obliging establishment should be in such an unusual place. The next moment, however, his satisfaction vanished; a more correct reading of the word on the sign was 'Corset-House'.

(10) In a second group of cases the part which the text contributes to the misreading is a much larger one. It contains something which rouses the reader's defences – some information or imputation distressing to him – and which is therefore corrected by being misread so as to fit in with a repudiation or with the fulfilment of a wish. In such cases we are of course obliged to assume that the text was first correctly understood and judged by the reader before it underwent correction, although his consciousness learnt nothing of this first reading. Example (3) above [p. 157] is of this kind; and I include here a further, highly topical one given by Eitingon (1915), who was at the military hospital at Igló at the time.

'Lieutenant X., who is in our hospital suffering from a traumatic war neurosis, was one day reading me a poem by the poet Walter Heymann, who fell in battle at so early an age. With visible emotion he read the last lines of the final stanza as follows.

> Wo aber steht's geschrieben, frag' ich, dass von allen
> Ich übrig bleiben soll, ein andrer für mich fallen?
> Wer immer von euch fällt, der stirbt gewiss für mich;
> Und ich soll übrig bleiben? *warum denn nicht?*[1]

> [But where is it decreed, I ask, that out of all
> I should alone be left, my fellow for me fall?
> Whoever of you falls, for me that man doth die;
> And I – am I alone to live? *Why should not I?*]

'My surprise caught his attention, and in some confusion he read the line correctly:

> Und ich soll übrig bleiben? warum denn *ich*?
> [And I – am I alone to live then? Why should *I*?]

'I owe to Case X. some analytic insight into the psychical material of these "traumatic war neuroses", and in spite of the

1. From 'Den Ausziehenden' ['To Those who are Going Forth'] in *Kriegsgedichte und Feldpostbriefe* [War Poems and Letters from the Front] by Walter Heymann.

circumstances prevailing in a war hospital with a large number of patients and only a few doctors – circumstances so unfavourable to our way of working – it was then possible for me to see a little way beyond the shell explosions which were so highly esteemed as the "cause" of the illness.

'In this case, too, were to be seen the severe tremors which give pronounced cases of these neuroses a similarity that is so striking at the first glance, as well as apprehensiveness, tearfulness, and a proneness to fits of rage, accompanied by convulsive infantile motor manifestations, and to vomiting ("at the least excitement").

'The psychogenic nature of this last symptom in particular – above all in its contribution to the secondary gain from the illness – must have impressed everyone. The appearance in the ward of the hospital commandant who from time to time inspected the convalescent cases, or a remark made by an acquaintance in the street – "You look in really excellent form, you're certainly fit now"– is enough to produce an immediate attack of vomiting.

'"Fit . . . go back to service . . . why should I?"'

(11)[1] Dr Hanns Sachs (1917) has reported some other cases of 'war' misreading:

'A close acquaintance of mine had repeatedly declared to me that when his turn came to be called up he would not make any use of his specialist qualifications, which were attested by a diploma; he would waive any claim based on them for being found suitable employment behind the lines and he would enlist for service at the front. Shortly before the call-up date in fact arrived, he told me one day in the curtest way, and without giving any further reason, that he had submitted the evidence of his specialist training to the proper authorities and as a result would shortly be assigned to a post in industry. Next day we happened to meet in a post-office. I was standing up at a desk and writing; he came in, looked over my shoulder for a while and then said: "Oh! the word at the top there's '*Druckbogen*

1. [The remainder of this section (Examples 11–13) was added in 1919.]

[printer's proofs]' – I'd read it as '*Drückeberger* [shirker]'."'

(12) 'I was sitting in a tram and reflecting on the fact that many of the friends of my youth who had always been taken as frail and weakly were now able to endure the most severe hardships – ones which would quite certainly be too much for me. While in the middle of this disagreeable train of thought, I read, only half attentively, a word in large black letters on a shop-sign that we were passing: "Iron Constitution". A moment later it struck me that this word was an inappropriate one to be found on the board of a business-firm; I turned round hastily and catching another glimpse of the sign saw that it really read: "Iron Construction".' (Sachs, ibid.)

(13) 'The evening papers carried a Reuter message, which subsequently proved to be incorrect, to the effect that Hughes had been elected President of the United States. This was followed by a short account of the supposed President's career, in which I came across the information that Hughes had completed his studies at *Bonn* University. It struck me as strange that this fact had received no mention in the newspaper discussions during all the weeks before the day of the election. On taking a second look I found that all the text in fact contained was a reference to *Brown* University [at Providence, Rhode Island, U.S.A.]. The explanation of this gross case, in which the misreading had called for a fairly violent twist, depended – apart from my haste in reading the newspaper – chiefly upon my thinking it desirable that the new President's sympathy for the Central European Powers, as the basis for good relations in the future, should be based on personal motives as well as political ones.' (Sachs, ibid.)

(B) SLIPS OF THE PEN

(1)[1] On a sheet of paper containing short daily notes mainly of a business kind I was surprised to find, among some entries

1. [Example 1, apart from the penultimate and final sentences (added in 1907 and 1912 respectively), and Example 2 date back to 1901.]

correctly dated 'September', the wrongly written date 'Thursday, October 20'. It is not difficult to explain this anticipation – and to explain it as the expression of a wish. A few days before, I had returned fresh from my holiday travels, and I felt ready for plenty of professional work; but there were not yet many patients. On my arrival I had found a letter from a patient to say she was coming on October 20. When I made an entry for the same day of the month in September I may well have thought: 'X. should have been here already; what a waste of a whole month!', and with that thought in mind I brought the date forward a month. In this case the disturbing thought can scarcely be called an objectionable one; and for this reason I knew the solution of the slip of the pen as soon as I had noticed it. – In the autumn of the following year I made another slip of the pen which was precisely analogous and had a similar motive. – Ernest Jones (1911b) has made a study of slips like these in writing dates; in most cases they could be clearly recognized as having [psychological] reasons.

(2) I had received the proofs of my contribution to the *Jahresbericht für Neurologie und Psychiatrie*,[1] and I had naturally to revise the names of authors with particular care, since they are of various nationalities and therefore usually cause the compositor very great difficulty. I did in fact find some foreign-sounding names which were still in need of correction; but strangely enough there was one name which the compositor had corrected by *departing from* my manuscript. He was perfectly right to do so. What I had in fact written was 'Buckrhard', which the compositor guessed should be 'Burckhard'. I had actually praised the useful treatise which an obstetrician of that name had written on the influence of birth upon the origin of children's palsies, and I was not aware of having anything to hold against him; but he has the same name as a writer in

1. [*Annual Review of Neurology and Psychiatry*. Freud wrote the abstracts and reviews for the section 'Infantile Cerebral Palsy' in the first three volumes of this annual; the contribution here referred to appeared in the third (1899) volume (Freud, 1900b).]

Vienna who had annoyed me by an unintelligent review of my *Interpretation of Dreams*. It is just as if in writing the name Burckhard, meaning the obstetrician, I had had a hostile thought about the other Burckhard, the writer,[1] for distorting names is very often a form of insulting their owners, as I have mentioned above [p. 128] in discussing slips of the tongue.

(3)[2] This assertion is very neatly confirmed by a self-observation of Storfer's (1914), in which the author exposes with commendable frankness the motives that prompted him to recollect the name of a supposed rival wrongly and then to write it down in a distorted form:

'In December, 1910, I saw a book by Dr Eduard *Hitschmann* in the window of a bookshop in Zurich. Its subject was Freud's theory of the neuroses and it was new at the time. Just then I was at work on the manuscript of a lecture on the basic principles of Freud's psychology, which I was shortly to give before a University society. In the introductory part of the lecture which I had already written, I had referred to the historical development of Freud's psychology from his researches in an applied field, to certain consequent difficulties in giving a comprehensive account of its basic principles, and also to the fact that no general account of them had yet appeared. When I saw the book (whose author was till then unknown to me) in the shop window, I did not at first think of buying it. Some days later, however, I decided to do so. The book was no

---

1. Compare the scene in *Julius Caesar*, III, 3:

CINNA:	Truly, my name is Cinna.
A CITIZEN:	Tear him to pieces; he's a conspirator.
CINNA:	I am Cinna the poet ....
	·I am not Cinna the conspirator.
ANOTHER CITIZEN:	It is no matter, his name's Cinna; pluck but his name out of his heart, and turn him going.

[In the original this footnote is wrongly attached to the end of the sentence.]

2. [Added 1917.]

longer in the window. I asked the bookseller for it and gave the author's name as "Dr Eduard *Hartmann*". The bookseller corrected me: "I think you mean *Hitschmann*", and brought me the book.

'The unconscious motive for the parapraxis was obvious. I had so to speak given myself the credit for having written a comprehensive account of the basic principles of psycho-analytic theory, and obviously regarded Hitschmann's book with envy and annoyance since it took some of the credit away from me. I told myself, on the lines of *The Psychopathology of Everyday Life*, that the changing of the name was an act of unconscious hostility. At the time I was satisfied with this explanation.

'Some weeks later I noted down this parapraxis. On this occasion I raised the further question of why Eduard Hitsch-mann had been altered precisely to Eduard *Hart*mann. Could I have been brought to the name of the well-known philoso-pher[1] merely because it was similar to the other one? My first association was the memory of a pronouncement which I once heard from Professor Hugo von Meltzl, an enthusiastic admirer of Schopenhauer, and which ran roughly as follows: "Eduard von Hartmann is a botched Schopenhauer, a Schopenhauer turned inside out." The affective trend by which the substitutive formation for the forgotten name was determined was there-fore: "No, there will probably not be much in this Hitschmann and his comprehensive account; he probably stands to Freud as Hartmann does to Schopenhauer."

'I had, as I say, noted down this case of [psychologically] determined forgetting with the forgotten word replaced by a substitute.

'Six months later I came upon the sheet of paper on which I had made the note. I then observed that instead of Hitsch-mann I had throughout written *Hintsch*mann.'[2]

1. [Eduard von Hartmann (1842–1906), author of *Philosophie des Unbewussten* (*Philosophy of the Unconscious*).]

2. ['*Hintsch*' is a dialect word for 'asthma' or, more generally, 'pest'.]

(4)[1] Here is what seems to be a more serious slip of the pen; I might perhaps equally well have included it among 'bungled actions' [Chapter VIII]:

I intended to draw the sum of 300 kronen[2] from the Post Office Savings Bank, which I wanted to send to an absent relative for purposes of medical treatment. At the same time I noticed that my account stood at 4,380 kronen and decided to bring it down on this occasion to the round sum of 4,000 kronen which was not to be touched in the near future. After I had duly written out the cheque and cut off the figures corresponding to the sum,[3] I suddenly noticed that I had not asked for 380 kronen as I intended, but for exactly 438 kronen, and I took alarm at the unreliability of my conduct. I soon realized that my alarm was not called for; I was not now any poorer than I had been before. But it took me a good deal of reflection to discover what influence had disturbed my first intention, without making itself known to my consciousness. To begin with I started on the wrong line; I tried subtracting 380 from 438, but I had no idea afterwards what to do with the difference. Finally a thought suddenly struck me which showed me the true connection. Why, 438 was *ten per cent* of the total account, 4,380 kronen! Now a ten per cent discount is given by *booksellers*. I recalled that a few days earlier I had picked out a number of medical books in which I was no longer interested in order to offer them to a bookseller for precisely 300 kronen. He thought the price I was asking was too high, and promised to give me a definite answer within the next few days. If he accepted my offer he would replace the exact sum which I was to spend on the invalid. There is no doubt that I regretted this expenditure. My affect on perceiving my error can be under-

1. [This example dates back to 1901.]
2. [At that time equivalent to about £12 10s. or $62.]
3. [In Austria at that time, withdrawals from the Post Office Savings Bank involved cutting off portions of a sheet of paper printed with columns of digits: the point at which the cut was made indicated the number of kronen to be withdrawn.]

stood better as a fear of growing poor as a result of such expenditures. But both these feelings, my regret at the expenditure and my anxiety over becoming poor that was connected with it, were entirely foreign to my consciousness; I did not have a feeling of regret when I promised the sum of money, and would have found the reason for it laughable. I should probably not have believed myself in any way capable of such an impulse had I not become fairly familiar, through my psychoanalytic practice with patients, with the part played by the repressed in mental life, and had I not had a dream a few days before which called for the same solution.[1]

(5)[2] I quote the following case from Wilhelm Stekel, and can also vouch for its authenticity:

'A simply incredible example of a slip of the pen and misreading occurred in the editing of a widely-read weekly periodical. The proprietors in question had been publicly described as "venal"; and an article in defence and vindication was clearly called for. One was in fact prepared: it was written with great warmth and feeling. The editor-in-chief read the article, while the author naturally read it several times in manuscript and then once more in galley-proof; everyone was perfectly satisfied. Suddenly the printer's reader came forward and pointed out a small mistake which had escaped everyone's notice. There it was, plainly enough: "Our readers will bear witness to the fact that we have always acted in the most *self-seeking* manner for the good of the community." It is obvious that it should have read: "in the most *unself-seeking* manner". But the true thoughts broke through the emotional statement with elemental force.'

(6)[3] A reader of the *Pester Lloyd*,[4] Frau Kata Levy of Budapest, recently came across a similar unintended display of candour

1. This is the one which I took as the specimen dream in my short work *On Dreams* (1901a). [Another episode related to the same dream is mentioned below, on p. 186–7.]

2. [Added 1907.]   3. [Added 1919.]

4. [The well-known Budapest German-language daily.]

in a telegram from Vienna which appeared in the paper on October 11, 1918:

'In view of the complete mutual confidence which has prevailed between ourselves and our German allies throughout the war, it may be taken for certain that the two Powers would reach a unanimous decision in all circumstances. It is unnecessary to state specifically that active and *interrupted* co-operation between the allied diplomatists is taking place at the present stage as well.'

Only a few weeks later it was possible to express one's opinion more frankly about this 'mutual confidence', and there was no longer any need to take refuge in a slip of the pen (or misprint).

(7)[1] An American living in Europe who had left his wife on bad terms felt that he could now effect a reconciliation with her, and asked her to come across the Atlantic and join him on a certain date. 'It would be fine,' he wrote, 'if you could come on the *Mauretania* as I did.' He did not however dare to send the sheet of paper which had this sentence on it. He preferred to write it out again. For he did not want her to notice how he had had to correct the name of the ship. He had first written '*Lusitania*'.

This slip of the pen needs no explanation: its interpretation is perfectly plain. But a happy chance enables a further point to be added. Before the war his wife paid her first visit to Europe after the death of her only sister. If I am not mistaken, the *Mauretania* is the surviving sister-ship of the *Lusitania*, which was sunk in the war.

(8)[2] A doctor had examined a child and was making out a prescription for it, which included the word '*alcohol*'. While he was occupied in doing so the child's mother pestered him with stupid and unnecessary questions. He privately determined not to let this make him angry, and actually succeeded in keeping his temper, but made a slip of the pen in the course of the

1. [Added 1920.]   2. [Added 1910.]

interruptions. Instead of *alcohol* the word *achol*[1] could be read on the prescription.

(9)[2] The following example, which Ernest Jones [1911*b*, 501] reports about A. A. Brill, has a similar subject-matter, and I therefore insert it here. Although by custom a total abstainer, he allowed himself to be persuaded by a friend to drink a little wine. Next morning an acute headache gave him cause to regret having yielded in this way. He had occasion to write the name of a patient called *Ethel*; instead he wrote *Ethyl*.[3] It was no doubt of some relevance that the lady in question used to drink more than was good for her.

(10)[4] Since a slip of the pen on the part of a doctor who is writing a prescription possesses a significance which goes far beyond the practical importance of ordinary parapraxes [cf. p. 231 ff.], I take the opportunity of reporting in full the only analysis published up to now of such a slip made by a doctor:

From Dr Eduard Hitschmann (1913*b*): 'A colleague tells me that several times over a period of years he had made an error in prescribing a certain drug for women patients of an advanced age. On two occasions he prescribed ten times the correct dose; only later did he suddenly realize this and was obliged, in the greatest anxiety in case he had harmed his patient and put himself in a very unpleasant position, to take the most hurried steps to recall the prescription. This singular symptomatic act deserves to be clarified by a more precise description of the individual instances and by an analysis.

'For instance: In treating a poor woman bordering on extreme old age who was suffering from spastic constipation the doctor prescribed belladonna suppositories ten times too strong. He left the out-patients' department, and his error suddenly sprang to his mind about an hour later while he was at home reading the paper and having lunch; he was overcome by

1. Approximately [in classical Greek]: 'No choler [anger].'
2. [Added 1912.]
3. I.e. ethyl alcohol [the chemical name for ordinary alcohol].
4. [Added 1917.]

anxiety, rushed first to the out-patients' department to obtain the patient's address and hastened from there to her home, which was a long way off. He was delighted to find that the old woman had not yet had the prescription made up, and he returned home much relieved. The excuse that he gave himself on this occasion was the not unjustified one that the talkative head of the out-patients' department had looked over his shoulder while he was writing the prescription and had distracted him.

'Second instance: The doctor was obliged to tear himself away from a consultation with a flirtatious and provocatively attractive patient in order to pay a professional visit to an elderly spinster. He took a taxi, not having much time to spare for the visit; for he was due to keep a secret rendezvous with a girl he was in love with, at a certain time, near her house. Here, too, belladonna was indicated because of troubles analogous to those in the first instance. Once again he made the mistake of prescribing a quantity ten times too strong. The patient raised a question that was of some interest but irrelevant to the matter in hand; the doctor, however, showed impatience, though his words denied it, and left the patient, so that he appeared at the rendezvous in very good time. Some twelve hours later, at about seven o'clock in the morning, the doctor woke up; the thought of his slip of the pen and a feeling of anxiety came almost simultaneously to his consciousness, and he sent a hasty message to the patient in the hope that the medicine had not yet been collected from the chemist's, and asked for the prescription to be sent back in order to be revised. On receiving it however he found that the prescription had already been made up; with a somewhat stoical resignation and an optimism born of experience he went to the chemist, where the dispenser reassured him by explaining that he had naturally (or perhaps by mistake too?) made up the drug in a smaller dose.

'Third instance: The doctor wanted to prescribe a mixture of *Tinct. belladonnae* and *Tinct. opii* in a harmless dose for his old aunt, his mother's sister. The prescription was immediately taken to the chemist by the maid. A very short time later it occurred to the doctor that instead of "tincture" he had written "extract", and immediately afterwards the chemist telephoned to question him about the error. The doctor gave as an excuse the untruthful explanation that he had not completed the prescription – it had been carried off from his table with unexpected suddenness, so it was not his fault.

'These three errors in making out prescriptions have the following striking points of resemblance. Up to now it has only happened to the doctor with this one drug; each time it involved a woman patient of advanced years, and each time the dose was *too strong*. From the brief analysis it emerged that the doctor's relation to his mother must have been of decisive importance. For he recalled that on one occasion – one, moreover, which most probably occurred *before* these symptomatic acts – he had made out the same prescription for his mother, who was also an old woman; he had ordered a dose of 0.03, although he was more familiar with the usual dose of 0.02. This, as he told himself, was in order to give her radical help. His frail mother reacted to the drug with congestion in the head and an unpleasant dryness of the throat. She complained of this, alluding half-jokingly to the risks that could come from a consultation with a son. There were in fact other occasions when his mother, who was, incidentally, a doctor's daughter, raised similar critical and half jocular objections to drugs recommended at various times by her doctor son, and spoke of being poisoned.

'So far as the present writer can fathom this son's relations with his mother, there is no doubt that he is an instinctively affectionate child, but his mental estimate of his mother and his personal respect for her are by no means exaggerated. He shares a household with a brother a year younger than himself and with his mother, and has felt for years that this arrangement was inhibiting his erotic freedom. We have, of course, learnt from psychoanalytic experience that such reasons are readily misused as an excuse for an internal [incestuous] attach-ment. The doctor accepted the analysis, being fairly well satis-fied with the explanation, and laughingly suggested that the word '*belladonna*' (i.e., beautiful woman) could also have an erotic reference. He had also occasionally used the drug himself in the past.'

In my judgement serious parapraxes like the present ones are brought about in exactly the same way as the innocent ones that we normally investigate.

(11)[1] The next slip of the pen, reported by Sándor Ferenczi, will be thought quite especially innocent. It can be understood as being an act of condensation, resulting from impatience (com-pare the slip of the tongue, 'Der Apfe', above, p. 103); and this view might have been maintained if a penetrating analysis of the occurrence had not revealed a stronger disturbing factor:

'"I am reminded of the *Anektode*",[2] I once wrote in my note-book. Naturally I meant "*Anekdote* [anecdote]"; actually it was the one about a gipsy who had been sentenced to death [*Tode*], and who asked as a favour to be allowed himself to choose the tree from which he was to be hanged. (In spite of a keen search he failed to find any suitable tree.)'

(12) On the other hand there are times when the most in-significant slip in writing can serve to express a dangerous secret meaning. An anonymous correspondent reports:

'I ended a letter with the words: "Herzlichste Grüsse an Ihre Frau Gemahlin und *ihren* Sohn."[3] Just before I put the sheet in the envelope I noticed the error I had made in the first letter of "ihren" and corrected it. On the way home from my last visit to this married couple the lady who was with me had remarked that the son bore a striking resemblance to a family friend and was in fact undoubtedly his child.'

1. [This example and No. 12 were added in 1919.]
2. [A non-existent word; but the last part of it, '*Tode*', means 'death'.]
3. ['Warmest greetings to your wife and her son.' The German possessive adjective '*ihr*', as spelt with a small 'i', means 'her'; when spelt with a capital 'I', it means 'your'.]

(13)[1] A lady sent her sister a message of good wishes on the occasion of her taking up residence in a new and spacious house. A friend who was present noticed that the writer had put the wrong address on the letter. She had not even addressed it to the house that her sister had just left, but to her first house which she had moved into immediately after her marriage and had given up long before. This friend drew the lady's attention to the slip. 'You're right', she was forced to confess; 'but how did the idea come into my head? Why did I do it?' 'I think', said her friend, 'you probably grudge her the fine large home which will now be hers, while you feel yourself cramped for space; and therefore you put her back in her first home where she was no better off than you are.' 'I certainly grudge her her new home', the other frankly admitted, and added: 'What a pity one's always so petty in such things!'

(14)[2] Ernest Jones [1911b, 499] reports the following slip of the pen, which was supplied to him by A. A. Brill:

'A patient wrote to him [Dr Brill] on the subject of his sufferings, which he tried to attribute to worry about his financial affairs induced by a cotton crisis: "My trouble is all due to that d——d frigid wave; there isn't even any seed." (By "wave" he meant of course a trend in the money market.) What he really wrote, however, was not "wave" but "wife". In the bottom of his heart he cherished half-avowed reproaches against his wife on account of her sexual anaesthesia and childlessness, and he dimly realized, with right, that his life of enforced abstinence played a considerable part in the genesis of his symptoms.'

(15) Dr R. Wagner (1911) relates of himself:

'In reading through an old lecture note-book I found that I had made a small slip in the hurry of taking down the notes. Instead of "*Epithel* (epithelium]", I had written "*Edithel*". If we stress the first syllable we have the diminutive form of a girl's name.[3] The retrospective analysis is simple enough. At the

1. [Added 1910.]   2. [Examples 14–16 were added in 1912.]
3. [In Austria 'l' is the common diminutive termination.]

time I made the slip I was only very superficially acquainted
with the lady of this name; it was not till much later that our
relations became intimate. The slip of the pen is therefore a
neat indication of the break-through of the unconscious attraction I felt to her at a time when I myself actually had no inkling
of it, and my choice of the diminutive form at the same time
showed the nature of the accompanying feelings.'

(16) From Frau Dr von Hug-Hellmuth (1912):

'A doctor prescribed "*Leviticowasser* [Levitical water]" for a
woman patient instead of "*Levicowasser*".[1] This error, which
gave a chemist a welcome opportunity for passing adverse
comments, may very well be viewed in a milder light if one
looks out for the possible motivations arising from the unconscious and is prepared at any rate to concede them a certain
plausibility – even though they are merely the subjective conjectures of someone who is not closely acquainted with the
doctor. In spite of his habit of using somewhat harsh language
to scold his patients for their far-from-rational diet – to read
them a lecture ["*die Leviten lesen*"], so to speak – the doctor
enjoyed great popularity, so that his waiting-room was crowded
before and during his consulting hour; and this provided a
justification for his wish that the patients he had seen should
dress as quickly as possible – "*vite, vite*" [French for: "quickly,
quickly"]. If I remember correctly, his wife was French by
birth: this lends some support to my seemingly rather bold
assumption that he used *French* in his wish for greater speed
from his patients. It is in any case a habit of many people to draw
on foreign words to express such wishes: my own father hurried
us along as children on our walks by calling out "*avanti gioventù*"
[Italian for "forward, youth"] or "*marchez au pas*" [French for
"forward march"]; while a very elderly physician, with whom
I was in treatment for a throat complaint as a girl, used to try to
inhibit my movements, which seemed much too hasty to him,
by murmuring a soothing "*piano, piano*" [Italian for "gently,

1. [A mineral water from the arsenical and chalybeate springs of
Levico, a health-resort in South Tyrol.]

gently"]. Thus I can very easily imagine that the other doctor had the same habit too, and so made the slip of writing "*Leviticowasser*" instead of "*Levicowasser*".'

The same paper contains other examples recalled from its author's youth ('*frazösisch*' instead of '*französisch*', and a slip in writing the name 'Karl').

(17)[1] I have to thank Herr J. G., who also contributed an example mentioned above[2] for the following account of a slip of the pen. In content it is identical with a notorious bad joke, but in this case the intention of making a joke could be definitely ruled out:

'While I was a patient in a (lung-) sanatorium I learnt to my regret that the same illness which had forced me to seek treatment in an institution had been diagnosed in a close relative of mine. In a letter to my relative I recommended him to go to a specialist, a well-known professor, with whom I was myself in treatment, and of whose authority in medical matters I was fully satisfied, while having at the same time every reason to deplore his discourteousness: for, only a short time before, this same professor had refused to write me a testimonial which it was very important for me to have. In his reply to my letter my relative drew my attention to a slip of the pen which, since I immediately recognized the cause of it, gave me particular amusement. In my letter I had used the following phrase: "and so I advise you to *in*sult Professor X. without delay". I had of course, intended to write "*con*sult". I should perhaps point out that my knowledge of Latin and French rules out the possibility of explaining it as a mistake due to ignorance.'

(18)[3] Omissions in writing have naturally a claim to be considered in the same light as slips of the pen. Dattner (1911) has reported a curious instance of a 'historical parapraxis'. In one of the sections of the law dealing with the financial obligations of Austria and Hungary, settled in the 'Compromise' of 1867

1. [Added 1920.]
2. [This other example seems actually to appear *below*, on p. 284.]
3. [Added 1912.]

between the two countries, the word 'actual' was left out of the Hungarian translation; and Dattner makes it plausible to suppose that the unconscious desire of the Hungarian parliamentary draftsmen to grant Austria the least possible advantages played a part in causing the omission.[1]

We have every reason to suppose,[2] too, that the very frequent repetitions of the same word in writing and copying – 'perseverations' – are likewise not without significance. If the writer repeats a word he has already written, this is probably an indication that it was not so easy for him to get away from it: that he could have said more at that point but had omitted to do so, or something of the kind. Perseveration in copying seems to be a substitute for saying 'I too'. I have had lengthy medicolegal 'opinions' before me which show perseverations on the copyist's part at particularly important passages. The interpretation I should have liked to give them would be that, bored with his impersonal role, the copyist was introducing his own gloss: 'Just my case' or 'it's just the same with us.'

(19) Furthermore, there is nothing to prevent our treating misprints as 'writing mistakes' on the compositor's part, and our regarding them as being in a very great measure [psychologically] motivated. I have not set about making a systematic collection of such parapraxes, which could be very amusing and instructive. In the work which I have already referred to a number of times, Jones [1911b, 503–4] has devoted a special section to misprints.

The distortions[3] found in the text of telegrams can also at times be understood as writing mistakes on the telegraphist's part. In the summer holidays I received a telegram from my publishers, the text of which was unintelligible to me. It ran:

1. [Dattner's article gives a detailed account of the intricate way in which the omission of the word would have damaged Austria financially.]

2. [This paragraph and the next one were added in 1917.]

3. [This paragraph was added in 1920, and the reference to Silberer's paper in 1924.]

'Vorräte erhalten, Einladung X. dringend.' ['Provisions received, invitation X. urgent.'] The solution of the riddle starts from the name X. mentioned in it. X. was the author of a book to which I was to write an '*Einleitung* [introduction]'. This '*Einleitung*' was what had been turned into the '*Einladung* [invitation]'. I was then able to recall that some days earlier I had sent my publishers a '*Vorrede* [preface]' to another book; so this was the acknowledgement of its arrival. The true text had very probably run: 'Vorrede erhalten, Einleitung X. dringend.' ['Preface received, introduction X. urgent.'] We may assume that it had fallen victim to a revision by the telegraphist's hunger-complex, in the course of which, moreover, the two halves of the sentence became linked more closely than the sender had intended. It is, incidentally, a pretty instance of the 'secondary revision' that can be seen at work in most dreams.[1]

The possibility of 'tendentious misprints' has been discussed by Herbert Silberer (1922).

(20)[2] From time to time other writers have drawn attention to misprints the tendentiousness of which cannot easily be challenged. See, for example, Storfer's paper. 'The Political Demon of Misprints' (1914) and his short note (1915) which I reprint here:

'A political misprint is to be found in the issue of *März* for April 25 of this year. A dispatch from Argyrokastron reported some remarks made by Zographos, the leader of the insurgent Epirotes in Albania (or, if that is preferred, the President of the Independent Government of the Epirus). It included the following phrase: "Believe me: a self-governing Epirus would be in the most fundamental interest of Prince Wied. He could fall down ["*sich stürzen*", a misprint for "*sich stützen*", "support himself"] on it." Even without this fatal misprint the Prince of Albania is no doubt well aware that the acceptance

1. Cf. [Section I of] the chapter on the dream-work in my *Interpretation of Dreams* [1900a, P.F.L., 4, 628 ff.].

2. Examples 20 and 21 were added in 1917.]

of the support [" *Stütze* "] offered him by the Epirotes would mean his downfall [" *Sturz* "].'

(21) I myself recently read an article in one of our Vienna daily papers, the title of which – 'The Bukovina under *Rumanian* Rule' – would have at least to be called premature, since at the time Rumania had not yet disclosed herself as an enemy. From the content of the article it was quite clear that the word should have been 'Russian', not 'Rumanian'; yet the censor, too, seems to have found the phrase so little surprising that even he overlooked this misprint.

It is hard[1] to avoid suspecting a 'political' misprint on coming across the following 'literal' misprint in a circular from the celebrated (formerly the Imperial and Royal) printing firm of Karl Prochaska in Teschen:

'By a decree of the Entente Powers, fixing the frontier at the River Olsa, not only Silesia but Teschen as well have been divided into two parts, of which one *zuviel*[2] to Poland and the other to Czecho-Slovakia.'

Theodor Fontane was once obliged to take up arms in an amusing way against a misprint which was only too full of meaning. On March 29, 1860, he wrote to the publisher Julius Springer:

Dear Sir,

I seem to be fated not to see my modest wishes fulfilled. A glance at the proof sheets[3] which I enclose will tell you what I mean. What is more, I have been sent only *one* set of proofs, although I need two, for reasons which I have already given. And my request that the first set should be returned to me for further revision – *with special regard to the English words and phrases* – has not been carried out. I set great store by this. For instance, on page 27 of the present sheets a scene

---

1. [This example and the following one were added in 1924.]

2. ['Too much.' The word should have been the similarly pronounced '*zufiel*', 'fell to the share of'. The German-Austrian compositor objected to the distribution of what had been part of the Hapsburg Empire.]

3. The book in question was *Beyond the Tweed: Sketches and Letters from Scotland*, which Julius Springer published in 1860.

between John Knox and the Queen contains the words: 'worauf Maria aasrief.'[1] In the face of such a fulminating mistake, it would be a relief to know that it has really been removed. The unfortunate 'aas' for 'aus' is made all the worse by there being no doubt that she (the queen) must really have called him that to herself.

Yours faithfully,
Theodor Fontane.

Wundt (1900, 374) gives an explanation[2] which deserves notice for the fact (which can easily be confirmed) that we make slips of the pen more readily than slips of the tongue. 'In the course of normal speaking the inhibitory function of the will is continuously directed to bringing the course of ideas and the articulatory movements into harmony with each other. If the expressive movement which follows the ideas is retarded through mechanical causes, as is the case in writing . . . , such anticipations make their appearance with particular ease.'[3]

Observation of the conditions under which misreadings occur gives rise to a doubt which I should not like to leave unmentioned, because it can, I think, become the starting-point for a fruitful investigation. Everyone knows how frequently the reader finds that in *reading aloud* his attention wanders from the text and turns to his own thoughts. As a result of this digression on the part of his attention he is often unable, if interrupted and questioned, to give any account of what he has read. He has read, as it were, automatically, but almost always correctly. I do not think that under such conditions mistakes in reading show a noticeable increase. There is in fact a whole series of functions which we are accustomed to assume will be performed most exactly when done automatically – that is, with scarcely

1. ['On which Mary "*aasrief*"': i.e., cried '*Aas*' (literally, 'carrion'; colloquially, 'filthy blackguard'). The word should have been '*ausrief*', meaning simply 'cried out'.]

2. [This paragraph and the following one date back to 1901.]

3. [For an example (from Meringer and Mayer, 1895) of what Wundt means by an 'anticipation' see p. 95 above.]

any conscious attention.[1] From this it seems to follow that the factor of attention in mistakes in speaking, reading and writing must be determined in a different way from that described by Wundt (cessation or diminution of attention). The examples which we have subjected to analysis have not really justified us in assuming that there was a quantitative lessening of attention; we found something which is perhaps not quite the same thing: a *disturbance* of attention by an alien thought which claims consideration.

Between 'slips of the pen' and 'forgetting'[2] may be inserted the case of someone who forgets to append a signature. An unsigned cheque comes to the same thing as a forgotten cheque. For the significance of a forgetting of a similar kind I will cite a passage from a novel, which Dr Hanns Sachs came upon:

'A very instructive and transparent example of the sureness with which imaginative writers know how to employ the mechanism of parapraxes and symptomatic acts in the psycho-analytic sense is contained in John Galsworthy's novel *The Island Pharisees*. The story centres round the vacillations of a young man of the well-to-do middle-class between his strong social sympathy and the conventional attitudes of his class. Chapter XXVI portrays the way in which he reacts to a letter from a young ne'er-do-weel, to whom – prompted by his original attitude to life – he had supplied help on two or three occasions. The letter contains no direct request for money, but paints a picture of great distress which can have no other meaning. Its recipient at first rejects the idea of throwing the money away on a hopeless case instead of using it to support charitable causes. "To give a helping hand, a bit of himself, a nod of fellowship to any fellow-being irrespective of a claim, merely because he happened to be down, was sentimental

1. [In his book on jokes (1905c), Freud points out that attention can interfere with the automatic process involved in the appreciation of jokes. (See *P.F.L.*, 6, 204–7.) Cf. also p.337 f. below.]

2. [The remainder of the chapter was added in 1919.]

nonsense! The line must be drawn! But in the muttering of this conclusion he experienced a twinge of honesty. 'Humbug! You don't want to part with your money, that's all!'"

'Thereupon he wrote a friendly letter, ending with the words: "I enclose a cheque. Yours sincerely, Richard Shelton."

'"Before he had written out the cheque, a moth fluttering round the candle distracted his attention, and by the time he had caught and put it out he had forgotten that the cheque was not enclosed." The letter was posted in fact just as it was.

'There is however an even subtler motivation for the lapse of memory than the break-through of the selfish purpose, which had apparently been surmounted, of avoiding giving away the money.

'At the country seat of his future parents-in-law, surrounded by his fiancée, her family and their guests, Shelton felt isolated; his parapraxis indicates that he longed for his protégé who, as a result of his past and of his view of life, forms a complete contrast to the irreproachable company, uniformly moulded by one and the same set of conventions, that surround him. And in fact this person, who can no longer keep his place without being supported, does in fact arrive some days later to get an explanation of why the promised cheque was not there.'

CHAPTER VII

THE FORGETTING OF IMPRESSIONS AND INTENTIONS[1]

IF anyone should feel inclined to over-estimate the state of our present knowledge of mental life, a reminder of the function of memory is all that would be needed to force him to be more modest. No psychological theory has yet succeeded in giving a connected account of the fundamental phenomenon of remembering and forgetting; in fact, the complete analysis of what can actually be observed has so far scarcely been begun. To-day, forgetting has perhaps become more of a puzzle than remembering, ever since we have learnt from the study of dreams and pathological phenomena that even something we thought had been forgotten long ago may suddenly re-emerge in consciousness.[2]

There are, it is true, a few indications already in our possession which we expect to be accepted generally. We assume that forgetting is a spontaneous process which may be regarded as requiring a certain length of time. We lay stress on the fact that forgetting involves a certain selection taking place from among the impressions presented to us, and similarly from among the details of each impression or experience. We know some of the conditions enabling what would otherwise have been forgotten to be retained in the memory and to be re-

1. [The first part of this chapter, up to p. 190, dates back to 1901.]

2. [The following note is to be found at this point in Freud's interleaved copy of the 1904 edition (cf. Editor's Introduction, p. 35): 'Normal forgetting takes place by way of condensation. In this way it becomes the basis for the formation of concepts. What is isolated is perceived clearly. Repression makes use of the mechanism of condensation and produces a confusion with other similar cases. – In addition, trends from other quarters take possession of the indifferent material and cause it to be distorted and falsified.' Cf. a footnote added in 1907, p. 339 below, where these ideas are developed.]

awakened. Nevertheless, on countless occasions in daily life we can observe how imperfect and unsatisfactory our understanding of these conditions is. Thus we may listen to two people who were in receipt of the same external impressions – who took a journey together, for example [cf. p. 70 ff.] – exchanging recollections at some later date. What has remained firm in the memory of one of them has often been forgotten by the other, as if it had never happened; and this is true even where there is no justification for assuming that the impression was psychically of greater importance for the one than for the other. A whole quantity of factors determining the choice of what is to be remembered are obviously still beyond our ken.

With the aim of making a small contribution to our knowledge of the determinants of forgetting I make it my practice to submit to a psychological analysis those cases in which I myself forget something. I am as a rule only concerned with a certain group of these cases, namely those in which the forgetting surprises me because I should have expected to know the thing in question. I may add that I am not in general inclined to forget things (things I have experienced, that is, not things I have learned!), and that for a short period of my youth some unusual feats of memory were not beyond me. When I was a schoolboy I took it as a matter of course that I could repeat by heart the page I had been reading; and shortly before I entered the University I could write down almost verbatim popular lectures on scientific subjects directly after hearing them. In the period of tension before my final medical examination I must have made use once more of what remained of this faculty, for in some subjects I gave the examiners, as though it were automatically, answers which faithfully followed the words of the textbook that I had skimmed through only once in the greatest haste.

Since then the command that I have over my store of memories has steadily deteriorated; yet right up to the most recent times I have convinced myself over and over again that with the aid of a certain device I can remember far more than

I would otherwise have believed possible. When, for instance, a patient in my consulting hour claims that I have seen him before and I can recall neither the fact nor the time, I help myself by guessing: that is to say, I quickly think of a number of years, counting back from the present. In cases where records or more definite information from the patient enable me to check what has come to my mind, they show that I have rarely been more than half a year out in ten.[1] I have a similar experience when I meet a distant acquaintance and out of politeness enquire after his small children. If he describes their progress I try to think at random of the child's present age. I afterwards check my estimate by what the father tells me; and at the most I am wrong by a month, or with older children by three months, although I am unable to say on what my estimate was based. I have latterly grown so bold that I always produce my estimate spontaneously without running any risk of offending the father by exposing my ignorance about his offspring. In this way I extend my conscious memory by invoking my unconscious memory, which is in any case far more extensive.

I shall accordingly cite some *striking* examples of forgetting, most of which I observed in myself. I distinguish the forgetting of impressions and experiences – i.e., of knowledge – from the forgetting of intentions – i.e., from omission to do things. I can state in advance the invariable result of the entire series of observations: *in every case the forgetting turned out to be based on a motive of unpleasure.*

(A) The Forgetting of Impressions and Knowledge

(1) One summer holiday my wife made me greatly annoyed though the cause was innocent enough. We were sitting at table d'hôte opposite a gentleman from Vienna whom I knew and who no doubt remembered me too. However, I had reasons of

1. In the course of the subsequent consultation the details of the previous visit usually emerge into my consciousness.

my own for not renewing the acquaintance. My wife, who had heard no more than his distinguished name, revealed too plainly that she was listening to his conversation with his neighbours, for from time to time she turned to me with questions that took up the thread of their discussion. I became impatient and finally irritated.[1] Some weeks later I was complaining to a relative about this behaviour on my wife's part but was unable to recall a single word of the gentleman's conversation. As I am normally rather apt to harbour grievances and can forget no detail of an incident that has annoyed me, my amnesia in the present case was probably motivated by consideration for my wife. A short time ago I had a similar experience. I wished to have a good laugh with an intimate friend over a remark made by my wife only a few hours before, but was prevented from doing so by the singular fact that I had utterly forgotten what she had said. I had first to ask my wife to remind me what it was. It is easy to understand my forgetfulness here as being analogous to the typical disturbance of judgement to which we are subject where those nearest to us are concerned.

(2) I had undertaken to get a lady who was a stranger to Vienna a small strong-box for her documents and money. When I offered my services I had in my mind's eye an unusually vivid picture of a shop-window in the Inner Town[2] in which I was sure I had seen boxes of the kind. I could not, it was true, recall the name of the street, but I felt sure that I would find the shop if I walked through the town, since my memory told me I had passed it on countless occasions. To my chagrin I had no success in finding the shop-window with the strong-boxes, though I walked all over the Inner Town in every direction. I decided that the only course left was to look up the firms of safe-manufacturers in a trades directory, so as to be able to identify the shop on a second walk round the town. Such

1. [The episode appears also among the associations to a dream related in *On Dreams* (1901*a*). This dream is referred to above in connection with another episode. See footnote 1, p. 169.]
2. [The central part of Vienna.]

extreme measures, however, did not prove necessary; among the addresses given in the directory was one which I immediately recognized as the one I had forgotten. It was true that I had passed the shop-window innumerable times – every time, in fact, that I had visited the M. family, who have lived for many years in the same building. Our intimate friendship later gave place to a total estrangement; after that, I fell into the habit – the reasons for which I never considered – of also avoiding the neighbourhood and the house. On my walk through the town in search of the shop-window with the strong-boxes I had passed through every street in the district but this one, which I had avoided as if it were forbidden territory. The motive of unpleasure responsible in the present case for my failure to find my way is easy to recognize. The mechanism of forgetting, however, is not so simple here as in the preceding example. My aversion naturally applied not to the safe-manufacturer but to another person, whom I did not want to think about; and from this latter person it was then transferred to this occasion where it produced the forgetting. The case of 'Burckhard' [p. 165 f.] was very similar; my grudge against one person of this name induced me to make a slip in writing the same name when it referred to someone else. The part there played by identity of name in establishing a connection between two essentially different groups of thoughts was able to be replaced in the example of the shop-window by spatial contiguity, inseparable proximity. This latter case was, incidentally, more firmly knit; there was a second connection there, one involving its subject-matter, for money played a part among the reasons for my estrangement from the family living in the building.

(3) I was requested by the firm of B. and R. to pay a professional visit to one of their staff. On my way there I was possessed by the thought that I must repeatedly have been in the building where their firm had its premises. It was as if I had noticed their plate on a lower storey while I was paying a professional visit on a higher one. I could however recall neither what house it was nor whom I had visited there. Although the

whole matter was of no importance or consequence, I nevertheless turned my mind to it and finally discovered in my usual roundabout way, by collecting the thoughts that occurred to me in connection with it, that the premises of the firm of B. and R. were on the floor below the Pension Fischer, where I have frequently visited patients. At the same time I also recalled the building that housed the offices and the pension. It was still a puzzle to me what motive was at work in this forgetting. I found nothing offensive to my memory in the firm itself or in the Pension Fischer or the patients who lived there. Moreover, I suspected that nothing very distressing could be involved; otherwise I would hardly have succeeded in recovering in a roundabout way what I had forgotten, without resorting to external assistance as I had in the previous example. It finally occurred to me that while I was actually on my way to this new patient, a gentleman whom I had difficulty in recognizing had greeted me in the street. I had seen this man some months before in an apparently grave condition and had passed sentence on him with a diagnosis of progressive paralysis; but later I heard he had recovered, so that my judgement must have been wrong. Unless, that is, there had been a remission of the type that is also found in dementia paralytica – in which case my diagnosis would be justified after all! The influence that made me forget where the offices of B. and R. were came from my meeting with this person, and my interest in solving the problem of what I had forgotten was transferred to it from this case of disputed diagnosis. But the associative link (for there was only a slender internal connection – the man who recovered contrary to expectation was also an official in a large firm which used to recommend patients to me) was provided by an identity of names. The physician with whom I had seen the supposed case of paralysis was also called Fischer, like the pension which was in the building and which I had forgotten.

(4) Mislaying something is really the same as forgetting where it has been put. Like most people who are occupied with writing and books I know my way about on my writing-table

and can lay my hands straight away on what I want. What appears to other people as disorder is for me order with a history behind it. Why, then, did I recently mislay a book-catalogue, which had been sent to me, so that it was impossible to find it? I had in fact intended to order a book, *Über die Sprache* [On Language], which was advertised in it, since it was by an author whose witty and lively style I like and whose insight in psychology and knowledge of the history of civilization I have learnt to value. I believe that this is precisely why I mislaid the catalogue. For it is my habit to lend books by this author to my acquaintances for their enlightenment, and a few days previously one of them had remarked as he returned a copy: 'His style reminds me very much of your own, and his way of thinking, too, is the same as yours.' The speaker did not know what he was touching on by that remark. Years before, when I was younger and in greater need of outside contacts, an elder colleague to whom I had praised the writings of a well-known medical author had made almost the same comment: 'It's just your style and your manner.' Prompted by this remark I had written a letter to the author seeking closer relations with him, but had been put in my place by a chilly answer. Perhaps still earlier discouraging experiences as well lie concealed behind this one, for I never found the mislaid catalogue and was in fact deterred by this omen from ordering the advertised book, although the disappearance of the catalogue formed no real hindrance since I could remember the names of both book and author.[1]

(5)[2] Another case of mislaying merits our interest on account of the conditions under which the mislaid object was rediscovered. A youngish man told me the following story: 'Some years ago there were misunderstandings between me and my wife. I found her too cold, and although I willingly recognized

1. Accidental occurrences of various sorts which since Theodor Vischer [see footnote 1, p. 224 below] have been put down to 'the perverseness of things' might, I think, be similarly explained.

2. [Added 1907].

her excellent qualities we lived together without any tender feelings. One day, returning from a walk, she gave me a book which she had bought because she thought it would interest me. I thanked her for this mark of 'attention', promised to read the book and put it on one side. After that I could never find it again. Months passed by, in which time I occasionally remembered the lost book and made vain attempts to find it. About six months later my dear mother, who was not living with us, fell ill. My wife left home to nurse her mother-in-law. The patient's condition became serious and gave my wife an opportunity of showing the best side of herself. One evening I returned home full of enthusiasm and gratitude for what my wife had accomplished. I walked up to my desk, and without any definite intention but with a kind of somnambulistic certainty[1] opened one of the drawers. On the very top I found the long-lost book I had mislaid.'

(6)[2] A case of mislaying which shares the last characteristic of the above example – namely, the remarkable sureness shown in finding the object again once the motive for its being mislaid had expired – is reported by Stärcke (1916):

'A girl had spoilt a piece of material in cutting it out to make a collar; so the dressmaker had to come and do her best to put it right. When she had arrived and the girl wanted to fetch the badly-cut collar, she went to the drawer where she thought she had put it; but she could not find it. She turned the contents upside down without discovering it. Sitting down in exasperation she asked herself why it had suddenly disappeared and whether there was not some reason why she did not *want* to find it. She came to the conclusion that of course she felt ashamed in front of the dressmaker for having bungled something so simple as a collar. After this reflection she stood up, went to another cupboard and was able to lay her hands straight away on the badly-cut collar.'

(7)[3] The following example of 'mislaying' is of a type that

1. [See footnote, p. 221, below.]
2. [Added 1917.]   3. [Added 1910.]

has become familiar to every psychoanalyst. I may remark that the patient responsible for it found the solution himself:

'A patient, whose psychoanalytic treatment was interrupted by the summer holidays at a time when he was in a state of resistance and felt unwell, put his bunch of keys in its usual place – or so he thought – when he undressed for the night. Then he remembered that there were a few more things that he needed for his journey next day – the last day of treatment and the date on which his fee was due – and he went to get them out of the writing-desk, in which he had also put his money. But the keys had disappeared. He began to make a systematic but increasingly agitated search of his small flat – with no success. Since he recognized the "mislaying" of the keys as a symptomatic act – that is, as something he had done intentionally – he woke his servant in order to continue the search with the aid of an "unprejudiced" person. After another hour he gave it up and was afraid he had lost the keys. Next morning he ordered new keys from the makers of the desk, and they were hastily made for him. Two friends, who had come home with him in the same cab, thought they remembered hearing something fall with a clink on the ground as he stepped out of the cab. He was convinced that his keys had fallen from his pocket. That evening the servant triumphantly presented him with the keys. They had been found lying between a thick book and a thin pamphlet (a work by one of my pupils) which he wanted to take away to read on his holiday. They were so cleverly placed that no one would have suspected they were there. He found himself afterwards unable to replace them so that they were equally invisible. The unconscious dexterity with which an object is mislaid on account of hidden but powerful motives is very reminiscent of "somnambulistic certainty".[1] The motive, as one would expect, was ill-temper at the treatment being interrupted and secret rage at having to pay a high fee when he was feeling so unwell.'

1. [See footnote below, p. 221.]

(8)[1] 'A man', Brill [1912] relates, 'was urged by his wife to attend a social function in which he really took no interest . . . Yielding to his wife's entreaties, he began to take his dress-suit from the trunk when he suddenly thought of shaving. After accomplishing this he returned to the trunk and found it locked. Despite a long, earnest search the key could not be discovered. No locksmith was available on Sunday evening, so that the couple had to send their regrets. When he had the trunk opened the next morning the lost key was found within. The husband had absent-mindedly dropped the key into the trunk and sprung the lock. He assured me that this was wholly un-intentional and unconscious, but we know that he did not wish to go to this social affair. The mislaying of the key therefore lacked no motive.'

Ernest Jones [1911b, 506] observed in himself that he was in the habit of mislaying his pipe whenever he had smoked too much and felt unwell in consequence. The pipe then turned up in all sorts of places where it did not belong and where it was not normally put away.

(9)[2] An innocent case, in which the motivation was admitted, is reported by Dora Müller (1915):

'Fräulein Erna A. told me two days before Christmas: "Can you imagine? Yesterday evening I took a piece of my ginger-bread from the packet and ate it; at the same time I thought I would have to offer some to Fräulein S." (her mother's com-panion) "when she came to say goodnight to me. I didn't par-ticularly want to, but I made up my mind to do so all the same. Later on when she came I reached out to get the packet from my table; but it was not there. I had a look for it and found it inside my cupboard. I had put the packet away there without realizing." No analysis was necessary; the narrator herself understood the sequence of events. The impulse of wanting to keep the cake all to herself, which had just been repressed, had

---

1. [Added 1912. – This is quoted from Brill's original, of which Freud has made a very slightly modified translation.]

2. [This example and No. 10 were added in 1917.]

nevertheless achieved its end in the automatic act, though in this case it was cancelled out once more by the subsequent conscious act.'

(10) Sachs describes how, by a similar act of mislaying, he once avoided the duty of working: 'Last Sunday afternoon I hesitated for some time over whether I should work or take a walk and pay a visit at the end of it; but after a bit of a struggle I decided in favour of the former. After about an hour I noticed that my supply of paper was exhausted. I knew that somewhere in a drawer there was a stack of paper that I had had for years, but I looked in vain for it in my writing desk and in other places where I thought I might find it, although I went to a lot of trouble and rummaged round in every possible place – old books, pamphlets, letters and so on. Thus I finally found myself compelled to break off my work and go out after all. When I returned home in the evening, I sat down on the sofa, and, sunk in thought and half absent-mindedly, gazed at the bookcase in front of me. A box caught my eye and I remembered that I had not examined its contents for a long time. So I went over and opened it. At the very top was a leather portfolio containing unused paper. But it was only when I had taken it out and was on the point of putting it in the drawer of my desk that it occurred to me that this was the very same paper I had been unsuccessfully looking for in the afternoon. I must add here that although I am not ordinarily thrifty I am very careful with paper and keep any scraps that can be used. It was obviously this practice of mine, which is nourished by an instinct, that enabled my forgetfulness to be corrected as soon as the immediate motive for it had disappeared.'

If a survey is made of cases of mislaying,[1] it in fact becomes hard to believe that anything is ever mislaid except as a result of an unconscious intention.

(11)[2] One day in the summer of 1901 I remarked to a friend

1. [This paragraph was added in 1907.]
2. [Except where otherwise specified, the whole of what follows down to p. 201 dates back to 1901.]

with whom I used at that time to have a lively exchange of scientific ideas:[1] 'These problems of the neuroses are only to be solved if we base ourselves wholly and completely on the assumption of the original bisexuality of the individual.' To which he replied: 'That's what I told you two and a half years ago at Br. [Breslau] when we went for that evening walk. But you wouldn't hear of it then.' It is painful to be requested in this way to surrender one's originality. I could not recall any such conversation or this pronouncement of my friend's. One of us must have been mistaken and on the '*cui prodest*?' principle[2] it must have been myself. Indeed, in the course of the next week I remembered the whole incident, which was just as my friend had tried to recall it to me; I even recollected the answer I had given him at the time: 'I've not accepted that yet; I'm not inclined to go into the question.' But since then I have grown a little more tolerant when, in reading medical literature, I come across one of the few ideas with which my name can be associated, and find that my name has not been mentioned.

Finding fault with one's wife, a friendship which has turned into its opposite, a doctor's error in diagnosis, a rebuff by someone with similar interests, borrowing someone else's ideas – it can hardly be accidental that a collection of instances of forgetting, gathered at random, should require me to enter into such distressing subjects in explaining them. On the contrary, I suspect that everyone who is willing to enquire into the motives behind his lapses of memory will be able to record a similar sample list of objectionable subjects. The tendency to forget what is disagreeable seems to me to be a quite universal one; the capacity to do so is doubtless developed with different

1. [The friend was Wilhelm Fliess. The date of the conversation was not 1901 but 1900. This was in fact the last occasion on which the two men were together. A full account of the episode will be found in Jones, 1953, 344 ff.]

2. ['Who benefits?' – the traditional question the answer to which points to the person guilty of a crime.]

degrees of strength in different people. It is probable that many instances of *disowning* which we encounter in our medical work are to be traced to *forgetting*.[1] It is true that our view of such forgetting limits the distinction between the two forms of behaviour [disowning and forgetting] to purely psychological

---

1. [*Footnote added* 1907:] If we ask someone whether he suffered from a luetic infection ten or fifteen years ago, we are too apt to overlook the fact that, from a psychical point of view, he will have regarded this illness quite differently from, let us say, an acute attack of rheumatism. – In the anamneses which parents give about their daughters' neurotic illnesses, it is hardly possible to distinguish with certainty between what has been forgotten and what is being concealed, since everything standing in the way of a girl's future marriage is systematically set aside, i.e. repressed, by the parents. – [*Added* 1910:] A man who had recently lost his dearly-loved wife from an affection of the lungs reported the following instance to me in which misleading answers given to the doctor's enquiries could only be ascribed to forgetting of this kind. 'As my poor wife's pleuritis had still not improved after many weeks, Dr P. was called into consultation. In taking the anamnesis he asked the usual questions, including whether there were any cases of lung illness in my wife's family. My wife said there were none and I could not recall any either. As Dr P. was leaving, the conversation turned, as though accidentally, to the subject of excursions and my wife said: "Yes, it's a long journey, too, to Langersdorf, *where my poor brother's buried*." This brother died about fifteen years ago after suffering for years from tuberculosis. My wife was very fond of him and had often spoken to me about him. In fact it now occurred to me that at the time that her pleuritis was diagnosed she was very worried and remarked gloomily: "My brother died of a lung complaint too." But now, the memory was so strongly repressed that even after her remark about the excursion to Langersdorf she was not led to correct the information she had given about illnesses in her family. I myself became aware of the lapse of memory at the very moment she spoke of Langersdorf.' – [*Added* 1912:] A completely analogous experience is related by Jones in the work to which I have referred several times already [Jones, 1911*b*, 484]. A physician, whose wife suffered from an abdominal complaint the diagnosis of which was uncertain, remarked by way of comforting her: 'It is fortunate at any rate that there has been no tuberculosis in your family.' 'Have you forgotten', answered his wife in the greatest astonishment, 'that my mother died of tuberculosis and that my sister recovered from it only after having been given up by the doctors?'

factors and allows us to see in both modes of reaction the expression of the same motive. Of all the numerous examples of the disavowal of unpleasant memories which I have observed on the part of relatives of patients, one remains in my recollection as especially singular. A mother was giving me information about the childhood of her neurotic son, now in his puberty, in the course of which she said that, like his brothers and sisters, he had been a bed-wetter till late on – a fact which is certainly of some significance in the case history of a neurotic patient. A few weeks later, when she was wanting to find out about the progress of the treatment, I had occasion to draw her attention to the signs of a constitutional disposition to illness on the young man's part, and in doing so I referred to the bed-wetting which she had brought out in the anamnesis. To my astonishment she contested this fact in regard both to him and to the other children, and asked me how I could know it. Finally I told her that she herself had informed me a short time before. She must therefore have forgotten it.[1]

1. In the days while I was engaged in writing these pages the following almost incredible instance of forgetting happened to me. On the first of January I was going through my medical engagement book so that I could send out my accounts. Under the month of June I came across the name 'M—l' but could not recall who it belonged to. My bewilderment grew when I turned the pages and discovered that I treated the case in a sanatorium and made daily visits over a period of weeks. A patient treated under such conditions cannot be forgotten by a doctor after scarcely six months. Could it have been a man, I asked myself, a case of general paralysis, an uninteresting case? Finally the record of the fees I had received brought back to me all the facts that had striven to escape my memory. M—l was a fourteen-year-old girl, the most remarkable case I had had in recent years, one which taught me a lesson I am not likely ever to forget and whose outcome cost me moments of the greatest distress. The child fell ill of an unmistakable hysteria, which did in fact clear up quickly and radically under my care. After this improvement the child was taken away from me by her parents. She still complained of abdominal pains which had played the chief part in the clinical picture of her hysteria. Two months later she died of sarcoma of the abdominal glands. The hysteria, to which she was at the same time predisposed, used the tumour as a provoking

There are thus abundant signs to be found in healthy, non-neurotic people that the recollection of distressing impressions and the occurrence of distressing thoughts are opposed by a resistance.[1] But the full significance of this fact can be estimated only when the psychology of *neurotic* people is investigated. We are forced to regard as one of the main pillars of the mechanism supporting hysterical symptoms an *elementary endeavour* of this kind *to fend off* ideas that can arouse feelings of unpleasure – an endeavour which can only be compared with the flight-reflex in the presence of painful stimuli. The assumption that a defensive trend of this kind exists cannot be objected to on the ground that one often enough finds it impossible, on the contrary, to get rid of distressing memories that pursue one, and to banish distressing affective impulses like remorse and the pangs of conscience. For we are not asserting that this defensive trend is able to put itself into effect in every case, that in the interplay of psychical forces it may not come up against factors which, for other purposes, aim at the opposite effect and bring it about in spite of the defensive trend. It may be surmised that *the architectonic principle of the mental apparatus lies in a stratification – a building up of superimposed agencies*; and it is quite possible that this defensive endeavour belongs to a lower psychical agency

---

cause, and I, with my attention held by the noisy but harmless manifestations of the hysteria, had perhaps overlooked the first signs of the insidious and incurable disease.

1. [*Footnote added* 1910:] A. Pick (1905) has recently brought together a number of quotations from authors who appreciate the influence of affective factors on the memory and who – more or less clearly – recognize the contribution towards forgetting made by the endeavour to fend off unpleasure. But none of us has been able to portray the phenomenon and its psychological basis so exhaustively and at the same time so impressively as Nietzsche in one of his aphorisms (*Jenseits von Gut und Böse*, IV, 68): '"I did this", says my Memory. "I cannot have done this", says my Pride and remains inexorable. In the end – Memory yields.' [Freud had had his attention drawn to this saying by the 'Rat Man', whose case history was published very shortly before the date of this footnote (1909*d*), Section I (D), *P.F.L.*, 9, 64.]

and is inhibited by higher agencies. At all events, if we can trace back processes such as those found in our examples of forgetting to this defensive trend, that fact speaks in favour of its existence and power. As we have seen, a number of things are forgotten on their own account; where this is not possible, the defensive trend shifts its target and causes something else at least to be forgotten, something less important which has come into associative connection with the thing that is really objectionable.

The view developed here, that distressing memories succumb especially easily to motivated forgetting, deserves to find application in many spheres where no attention, or too little, has so far been paid to it. Thus it seems to me that it has still not yet been sufficiently strongly emphasized in assessing testimony in courts of law,[1] where the process of putting a witness on oath is clearly expected to have much too great a purifying influence on the play of his psychical forces. It is universally acknowledged that where the origin of a people's traditions and legendary history are concerned, a motive of this kind, whose aim is to wipe from memory whatever is distressing to national feeling, must be taken into consideration.[2] Closer investigation would perhaps reveal a complete analogy between the ways in which the traditions of a people and the childhood memories of the individual come to be formed. – The great Darwin[3] laid down a 'golden rule' for the scientific worker based on his insight into the part played by unpleasure as a motive for forgetting.[4]

1. Cf. Gross (1898). [See footnote 4, p. 316, below.]
2. [Cf. above, p. 88.]
3. [This sentence was added in 1912.]
4. [*Footnote added* 1912:] Ernest Jones [1911*b*, 480] has drawn attention to the following passage in Darwin's autobiography [1958, 123], which convincingly reflects his scientific honesty and his psychological acumen:

'I had, during many years, followed a golden rule, namely, that whenever a published fact, a new observation or thought came across me, which was opposed to my general results, to make a memorandum

In a very similar way to the forgetting of names [p. 37], the forgetting of impressions can be accompanied by faulty recollection; and this, where it finds credence, is described as paramnesia. Paramnesia in pathological cases – in paranoia it actually plays the part of a constituent factor in the formation of the delusion – has brought forth an extensive literature in which I have entirely failed to find any hint whatever as to its motivation. As this is also a subject which belongs to the psychology of the neuroses it is inappropriate to consider it in the present context. Instead, I shall describe a singular paramnesia of my own, in which the motivation provided by unconscious, repressed material and the manner and nature of the connection with this material can be recognized clearly enough.

While I was writing the later chapters of my book on dream-interpretation, I happened to be at a summer resort without access to libraries and works of reference, and I was forced to incorporate in my manuscript from memory all sorts of references and quotations, subject to later correction. In writing the passage on day-dreams[1] I thought of the excellent example of the poor book-keeper in Alphonse Daudet's Le Nabab, in whose person the writer was probably portraying his own reveries. I imagined I had a distinct memory of one of the phantasies which this man – I called him Monsieur Jocelyn – hatched out on his walks through the streets of Paris; and I began to reproduce it from memory. It was a phantasy of how Monsieur Jocelyn boldly threw himself at the head of a runaway horse in the street, and brought it to a stop; how the carriage door opened and a great personage stepped out, pressed Monsieur Jocelyn's hand and said: 'You are my saviour. I owe my life to you. What can I do for you?'

Any inaccuracies in my own account of this phantasy could,

---

of it without fail and at once; for I had found by experience that such facts and thoughts were far more apt to escape from the memory than favourable ones.'

1. [*The Interpretation of Dreams* (1900a), P.F.L., 4, 631 f. and 683.]

I assured myself, easily be corrected at home when I had the book in front of me. But when I finally looked through *Le Nabab* to check this passage in my manuscript, which was ready to go to press, I found, to my very great shame and consternation, no mention of any such reverie on the part of Monsieur Jocelyn; in fact the poor book-keeper did not have this name at all but was called Monsieur Joyeuse. This second error quickly gave me the key to the solution of the first one – the paramnesia. 'Joyeux', of which 'Joyeuse' is the feminine form, is the only possible way in which I could translate my own name, Freud, into French. Where then could the phantasy, which I had remembered wrongly and ascribed to Daudet, have come from? It could only be a product of my own, a day-dream which I had formed myself and which had not become conscious or which had once been conscious and had since been totally forgotten. Perhaps I invented it myself in Paris where I frequently walked about the streets, lonely and full of longings, greatly in need of a helper and protector, until the great Charcot took me into his circle. Later I more than once met the author of *Le Nabab* in Charcot's house.[1]

1. [In all the editions before 1924 this paragraph continued: 'But the irritating part of it is that there is scarcely any group of ideas to which I feel so antagonistic as that of being someone's protégé. What can be seen in our country of this relation is enough to rob one of all desire for it, and the role of the favourite child is one which is very little suited indeed to my character. I have always felt an unusually strong urge "to be the strong man myself". And yet *I* had to be reminded of daydreams like this – which, incidentally, were never fulfilled. Over and above this, the incident is a good illustration of the way in which the relation to one's own self, which is normally kept back, but which emerges victoriously in paranoia, disturbs and confuses us in our objective view of things.']

[*Footnote added* 1924:] Some time ago one of my readers sent me a small volume from Franz Hoffmann's *Jugendbibliothek* [Library for Young People] in which a rescue scene like the one in my phantasy in Paris is recounted in detail. The agreement between the two extends even to certain not quite ordinary expressions that occur in both. It is not easy to avoid suspecting that I had in fact read this children's book while I was myself a boy. The library at my secondary school contained

Another paramnesia,[1] which it was possible to explain satisfactorily, is reminiscent of *fausse reconnaissance*, a subject that will be discussed later [p. 328 ff. below]. I had told one of my patients, an ambitious and capable man, that a young student had recently gained admittance to the circle of my followers on the strength of an interesting work, '*Der Künstler, Versuch einer Sexualpsychologie*' [The Artist, an Attempt at a Sexual Psychology].[2] When this work appeared in print a year and a quarter later, my patient maintained that he could remember with certainty having read an announcement of this book somewhere (perhaps in a bookseller's prospectus) even before – a month or six months before – I had first mentioned it to him. This announcement, he said, had come into his mind at the time; and he further remarked that the author had changed the title: it no longer read '*Versuch*' but '*Ansätze zu einer Sexualpsychologie*' [Approach to a Sexual Psychology]. Careful enquiry of the author and a comparison of all the dates nevertheless showed that my patient was claiming to recall something impossible. No announcement of this work had appeared any-

---

Hoffmann's series and was always ready to offer these books to pupils in place of any other mental pabulum. The phantasy which, at the age of 43, I thought I remembered as having been produced by someone else, and which I was subsequently forced to recognize as a creation of my own at the age of 28, may therefore easily have been an exact reproduction of an impression which I had received somewhere between the ages of 11 and 13. After all, the rescue phantasy which I attributed to the unemployed book-keeper in *Le Nabab* was merely meant to prepare the way for the phantasy of my own rescue, to make my longing for a patron and protector tolerable to my pride. This being so, it will not surprise anyone with an understanding of the mind to hear that in my conscious life I myself was highly resistant to the idea of being dependent on a protector's favour, and that I found it hard to tolerate the few real situations in which something of that nature occurred. Abraham (1922*b*) has brought to light the deeper meaning of phantasies with such a content [rescue phantasies] and has provided an almost exhaustive explanation of their special features.

1. [The rest of this section was added in 1907.]
2. [This was the first work of Otto Rank (1907).]

where before publication, and certainly none a year and a quarter before it went to press. When I omitted to interpret this paramnesia, my patient produced a repetition of it of the same kind. He believed he had recently seen a work on agoraphobia in a bookshop window and was now looking through all the publishers' catalogues in order to get a copy. I was then able to explain to him why his efforts were bound to be fruitless. The work on agoraphobia existed only in his phantasy, as an unconscious intention: he meant to write it himself. His ambition to emulate the young man and become one of my followers on the strength of a similar scientific work was responsible for the first paramnesia and then for its repetition. Thereupon he recalled that the bookseller's announcement which had led him to make this false recognition dealt with a work entitled 'Genesis, das Gesetz der Zeugung' [Genesis, the Law of Generation]. However, it was I who was responsible for the change in the title mentioned by him, for I could remember having myself been guilty of that inaccuracy – 'Versuch' instead of 'Ansätze' – in repeating the title.

(B) THE FORGETTING OF INTENTIONS[1]

No group of phenomena is better qualified than the forgetting of intentions for demonstrating the thesis that, in itself, lack of attention does not suffice to explain parapraxes. An intention is an impulse to perform an action: an impulse which has already found approval but where execution is postponed to a suitable occasion. Now it can happen that during the interval thus created a change of such a kind occurs in the motives involved that the intention is not carried out; but in that case it is not forgotten: it is re-examined and cancelled. The *forgetting* of intentions, to which we are subject every day and in every possible situation, is *not* a thing that we are in the habit of explaining in terms of such a revision in the balance

1. [Except where otherwise specified, the whole of this section dates back to 1901.]

of motives. In general we leave it unexplained; or we try to find a psychological explanation by supposing that at the time when the intention was due to be carried out the attention necessary for the action was no longer at hand – attention which was, after all, an indispensable precondition for the coming into being of the intention and had therefore been available for the action at that time. Observation of our normal behaviour in regard to intentions leads us to reject this attempt at an explanation as being arbitrary. If I form an intention in the morning which is to be carried out in the evening, I may be reminded of it two or three times in the course of the day. It *need* not however become conscious at all throughout the day. When the time for its execution draws near, it suddenly springs to my mind and causes me to make the necessary preparations for the proposed action. If I am going for a walk and take a letter with me which has to be posted, it is certainly not necessary for me, as a normal individual, free from neurosis, to walk all the way with it in my hand and to be continually on the look-out for a letter-box in which to post it; on the contrary I am in the habit of putting it in my pocket, of walking along and letting my thoughts range freely, and I confidently expect that one of the first letter-boxes will catch my attention and cause me to put my hand in my pocket and take out the letter. Normal behaviour after an intention has been formed coincides fully with the experimentally-produced behaviour of people to whom what is described as a 'post-hypnotic suggestion at long range' has been given under hypnosis.[1] This phenomenon is usually described in the following way. The suggested intention slumbers on in the person concerned until the time for its execution approaches. Then it awakes and impels him to perform the action.

There are two situations in life in which even the layman is aware that forgetting – as far as intentions are concerned – cannot in any way claim to be considered as an elementary phenomenon not further reducible, but entitles him to conclude

1. Cf. Bernheim (1891, [130 ff.]) [which Freud translated (1892*a*)].

that there are such things as unavowed motives. What I have in mind are love-relationships and military discipline. A lover who has failed to keep a *rendezvous* will find it useless to make excuses for himself by telling the lady that unfortunately he completely forgot about it. She will not fail to reply: 'A year ago you wouldn't have forgotten. You evidently don't care for me any longer.' Even if he should seize on the psychological explanation mentioned above [p. 204] and try to excuse his forgetfulness by pleading pressure of business, the only outcome would be that the lady, who will have become as sharp-sighted as a doctor is in psychoanalysis, would reply: 'How curious that business distractions like these never turned up in the past!' The lady is not of course wanting to deny the possibility of forgetting; it is only that she believes, not without reason, that practically the same inference – of there being some reluctance present – can be drawn from unintentional forgetting as from conscious evasion.

Similarly, under conditions of military service, the difference between a failure to carry out orders which is due to forgetting and one which is deliberate is neglected on principle – and justifiably so. A soldier *must* not forget what military service orders him to do. If he *does* forget in spite of knowing the order, that is because the motives that drive him to carry out the military order are opposed by other, counter-motives. A one year volunteer[1] who at inspection tries to offer the excuse that he has *forgotten* to polish his buttons is sure to be punished. But this punishment is trifling in comparison to the one to which he would expose himself if he admitted to himself and his superiors that the motive for his failure to carry out orders was that 'I'm heartily sick of this wretched spit-and-polish'. For the sake of this saving of punishment – for reasons of economy, so to speak – he makes use of forgetting as an excuse, or it comes about as a compromise.

1. [Young men of higher social and educational standing in Austria who volunteered might have their term of military service reduced to one year.]

Both the service of women and military service demand that everything connected with them should be immune to forgetting. In this way they suggest the notion that, whereas in unimportant matters forgetting is permissible, in important matters it is a sign that one wishes to treat them as unimportant, i.e. to deny their importance.[1] This view, which takes psychical considerations into account, cannot in fact be rejected here. No one forgets to carry out actions that seem to himself important, without incurring suspicion of being mentally disordered. Our investigation can therefore only extend to the forgetting of intentions of a more or less minor character; we cannot consider any intention as being *wholly* indifferent, for otherwise it would certainly never have been formed.

As with the functional disturbances described on earlier pages, I have made a collection of the cases of omitting to do something as a result of forgetting which I have observed in myself, and I have endeavoured to explain them. I have invariably found that they could be traced to interference by unknown and unavowed motives – or, as one may say, to a *counter-will*. In a number of these cases I found myself in a position which was similar to being under conditions of service; I was under a constraint, against which I had not entirely given up struggling, so that I made a demonstration against it by forgetting. This accounts for the fact that I am especially prone to forget to send congratulations on occasions such as birthdays, anniversaries, wedding celebrations and promotions. I keep on making new resolutions on the subject and become more and more convinced that I shall not succeed. I am now on the point of giving the effort up and of yielding consciously to the motives that oppose it. While I was in a transitional stage, a friend asked

1. [*Footnote added* 1912:] In Bernard Shaw's play *Caesar and Cleopatra*, Caesar, as he is leaving Egypt, is worried for a time by the idea that there is something he has meant to do but has forgotten. Finally he remembers: he has forgotten to say goodbye to Cleopatra! This small detail is meant to illustrate – incidentally in complete contrast to the historical truth – how little Caesar cared for the young Egyptian princess. (From Jones, 1911*b*, 488*n*.)

me to send a congratulatory telegram on a certain day on his behalf along with my own, but I warned him that I should forget both; and it was not surprising that the prophecy came true. It is due to painful experiences in the course of my life that I am unable to manifest sympathy on occasions where the expression of sympathy must necessarily be exaggerated, as an expression corresponding to the slight amount of my feeling would not be allowable. Since I have come to recognize that I have often mistaken other people's ostensible sympathy for their real feelings, I have been in revolt against these conventional expressions of sympathy, though on the other hand I recognize their social usefulness. Condolences in the case of death are excepted from this divided treatment: once I have decided to send them I do not fail to do so. Where my emotional activity no longer has anything to do with social duty, its expression is never inhibited by forgetting.

Writing from a prisoner-of-war camp,[1] Lieutenant T. reports an instance of a forgetting of this kind, in which an intention that had in the first place been suppressed broke through in the form of 'counter-will' and led to an unpleasant situation:

'The most senior officer in a prisoner-of-war camp for officers was insulted by one of his fellow prisoners. To avoid further complications he wished to use the only authoritative measure at his disposal and have the officer removed and transferred to another camp. It was only on the advice of several friends that he decided – contrary to his secret wish – to abandon his plan and seek to satisfy his honour immediately, although this was bound to have a variety of disagreeable results. The same morning, as senior officer, he had to call the roll of the officers, under the supervision of the camp-guard. He had known his fellow officers for quite a long time and had never before made any mistakes over this. This time he passed over the name of the man who had insulted him, with the result that when all the others had been dismissed this man alone was obliged to

1. [This example was added in 1920.]

remain behind till the error was cleared up. The name that had been overlooked was perfectly plainly written in the middle of a sheet. The incident was regarded by one party as a deliberate insult, and by the other as an unfortunate accident that was likely to be misinterpreted. Later on, however, after making the acquaintance of Freud's *Psychopathology of Everyday Life*, the chief actor in the episode was able to form a correct picture of what had occurred.'

The conflict between a conventional duty and the unavowed view which we privately take of it similarly provides an explanation for those cases in which we forget to carry out actions that we promised to do as a favour to someone. Here the regular result is that it is only the would-be benefactor who believes that forgetting has the power to act as an excuse; the person who asked the favour gives what is unquestionably the right answer: 'He is not interested in the matter, otherwise he would not have forgotten.' There are some people who are known as being forgetful in general, and who are for that reason excused their lapses in the same kind of way as short-sighted people who fail to greet us in the street.[1] These people forget all their small promises, and they fail to carry out any of the commissions they receive. In this way they show themselves unreliable in little things, and they demand that we should not take these minor offences amiss – that is, that we should not attribute them to their character but refer them to an organic idiosyncrasy.[2] I am not one of these people myself, and have

1. Women, with their subtler understanding of unconscious mental processes, are as a rule more apt to take offence when someone does not recognize them in the street and therefore fails to greet them, than to think of the most obvious explanations – namely that the offender is short-sighted, or was so engrossed in his thoughts that he did not notice them. They conclude that he would have seen them if he had 'set any store by them'.

2. [*Footnote added* 1910:] Ferenczi reports that he himself was once an 'absent-minded person' [*ein 'Zerstreuter'*] and that he was noted by acquaintances for the frequency and strangeness of his parapraxes. But, he says, the signs of this absent-mindedness have almost completely

had no opportunity of analysing the actions of a person of this kind, so that, by examining the choice of occasions for forgetting, I might discover its motivation. I cannot however help suspecting on the basis of analogy that in these cases the motive is an unusually large amount of unavowed contempt for other people which exploits the constitutional factor for its own ends.[1]

In other cases the motives for forgetting are less easy to discover, and when found arouse greater surprise. Thus, for instance, in former years I noticed that, out of a fairly large number of visits to patients, I only forgot those to non-paying patients or to colleagues. My shame at this discovery led me to adopt the habit of making a note beforehand in the morning of the visits I intended to make during the day. I do not know if other doctors have arrived at the same practice by the same road. But in this way we get some idea of what causes the so-called neurasthenic patient to jot down, in his notorious 'notes', the various things he wants to tell the doctor. The ostensible reason is that he has no confidence in the reproductive capacity of his memory. That is perfectly correct, but the scene usually proceeds as follows. The patient has recounted his various complaints and enquiries in a very long-winded manner. After he

---

disappeared since he began treating patients by psychoanalysis and found himself obliged to turn his attention to the analysis of his own self as well. He thinks that one gives up these parapraxes in proportion as one learns to enlarge one's own responsibility. He therefore justly maintains that absent-mindedness is a condition which is dependent on unconscious complexes and which can be cured by psychoanalysis. One day, however, he was blaming himself for having committed a technical error in a patient's psychoanalysis. That day all his former absent-minded habits reappeared. He stumbled several times as he walked along the street (a representation of his *faux pas* [false step – blunder] in the treatment), left his pocket book at home, tried to pay a kreutzer too little for his tram-fare, found his clothes were not properly buttoned, and so on.

1. [*Footnote added* 1912:] In this connection Ernest Jones [1911b, 483] observes: 'Often the resistance is of a general order. Thus a busy man forgets to post letters entrusted to him – to his slight annoyance – by his wife, just as he may "forget" to carry out her shopping orders.'

has finished he pauses for a moment, then pulls out the jottings and adds apologetically: 'I've made some notes, as I can't remember things.' As a rule he finds that they contain nothing new. He repeats each point and answers it himself: 'Yes, I've asked about that already.' With the notes he is probably only demonstrating one of his symptoms: the frequency with which his intentions are disturbed through the interference of obscure motives.

I pass on to ailments that afflict the greater number of my healthy acquaintances as well as myself. I confess that – especially in former years – I was very apt to forget to return borrowed books, which I kept for long periods, and that it came about especially easily that I put off paying bills by forgetting them. One morning not long ago I left the tobacconist's where I had made my daily purchase of cigars without having paid for them. It was a most harmless omission, as I am well known there and could therefore expect to be reminded of my debt next day. But my trivial act of negligence, my attempt to contract a debt, was certainly not unconnected with budgetary thoughts which had occupied my mind during the preceding day. Among the majority even of what are called 'respectable' people traces of divided behaviour can easily be observed where money and property are concerned. It may perhaps be generally true that the primitive greed of the suckling, who wants to take possession of every object (in order to put it into his mouth), has only been incompletely overcome by civilization and upbringing.[1]

1. For the sake of preserving the unity of the subject [of money] I may perhaps interrupt the general arrangement I have adopted, and, in addition to what I have said above, point out that people's memories show a particular partiality in money matters. Paramnesias of having already paid for something can often be very obstinate, as I know from my own experience. When free play is given to avaricious aims apart from the serious interests of life – for fun, in fact –, as in card-playing, the most honourable men show an inclination to make errors and mistakes in memory and counting, and, without quite knowing how, they even find themselves involved in petty cheating. The psychically refresh-

I am afraid all the examples I have given up to now will seem merely commonplace. But after all it can only suit my aim if I come upon things that are familiar to everyone and that everyone understands in the same way, for my whole purpose is to collect everyday material and turn it to scientific use. I fail to see why the wisdom which is the precipitate of men's common experience of life should be refused inclusion among the acquisitions of science. The essential character of scientific work derives not from the special nature of its objects of study but from its stricter method of establishing the facts and its search for far-reaching correlations.

Where intentions of some importance are concerned, we have found in general that they are forgotten when obscure motives rise against them. In the case of rather less important intentions we can recognize a second mechanism of forgetting: a counter-will is transferred to the intention from some other topic, after an external association has been formed between the other topic and the content of the intention. Here is an example. I set store by high-quality blotting-paper ['*Löschpapier*'] and I

---

ing nature of these games is partly due to liberties of this kind. We must admit the truth of the saying that in play we can get to know a person's character – that is, if we are not thinking of his *manifest* character. – If waiters still make unintentional mistakes in the bill, the same explanation obviously applies to them. – In commercial circles a certain delay can frequently be observed in paying out sums of money (for settling accounts and so on) which in point of fact brings the owner no profit and can only be understood in psychological terms – as an expression of a counter-will against paying out money. – [*The next sentence was added in* 1912:] Brill [1912] puts the matter with epigrammatic brevity: 'We are more apt to mislay letters containing bills than cheques.' – The fact that women in particular evince a special amount of unpleasure at paying their doctor is connected with the most intimate impulses, which are very far from having been elucidated. Women patients have usually forgotten their purse and so cannot pay at the time of consultation; they then regularly forget to send the fee after they reach home, and thus arrange things so that one has treated them for nothing – 'for the sake of their *beaux yeux*'. They pay one, as it were, by the sight of their countenance.

decided one day to buy a fresh supply that afternoon in the course of my walk to the Inner Town.[1] But I forgot for four days running, till I asked myself what reason I had for the omission. It was easy to find after I had recalled that though I normally *write* '*Löschpapier*' I usually *say* '*Fliesspapier*' [another word for 'blotting-paper']. 'Fliess' is the name of a friend in Berlin who had on the days in question given me occasion for a worrying and anxious thought. I could not rid myself of this thought, but the defensive tendency (cf. above, p. 198 f.) manifested itself by transferring itself, by means of the verbal similarity, to the indifferent intention which on account of its indifference offered little resistance.

Direct counter-will and more remote motivation are found together in the following example of dilatoriness. I had written a short pamphlet *On Dreams* (1901*a*), summarizing the subject-matter of my *Interpretation of Dreams* [1900*a*], for the series *Grenzfragen des Nerven- und Seelenlebens* [Frontier Problems of Nervous and Mental Life]. Bergmann [the publisher] of Wiesbaden had sent me the proofs, and had asked for them back by return of post, as the book was to be issued before Christmas. I corrected the proofs the same night and placed them on my desk so as to take them with me next morning. In the morning I forgot about them, and only remembered them in the afternoon when I saw the wrapper on my desk. In the same way I forgot the proofs that afternoon, that evening and the following morning, till I pulled myself together and took them to a letter-box on the afternoon of the second day, wondering what could be the reason for my procrastination. It was obvious that I did not want to send them off, but I could not discover why. However, in the course of the same walk I called in at my publishers' in Vienna – the firm that had published my *Interpretation of Dreams*.[2] I placed an order for something and then said, as if impelled by a sudden thought: 'I suppose you know I've written the dream-book over again?' – 'Oh, you can't mean that!' he said. 'Don't be alarmed', I replied; 'it's only a

1. [See footnote 2, p. 187.]   2. [Franz Deuticke.]

short essay for the Löwenfeld-Kurella series.' But he was still not satisfied; he was worried that the essay would interfere with the sales of the book. I disagreed with him and finally asked: 'If I'd come to you before, would you have forbidden my publishing it?' – 'No, I certainly wouldn't.' Personally I believe I acted quite within my rights and did nothing contrary to common practice; nevertheless it seems certain that a misgiving similar to that expressed by the publisher was the motive for my delay in sending back the proofs. This misgiving goes back to an earlier occasion, on which a different publisher raised difficulties when it seemed unavoidable for me to introduce unaltered a few pages from an earlier work of mine on children's palsies published by another firm, into my monograph on the same subject in Nothnagel's *Handbuch*.[1] But in this case, as well, the reproach was not justified; this time, too, I had loyally informed my first publisher (the same one who published *The Interpretation of Dreams*) of my intention. However, if this chain of memories is followed back still further, it brings to light an even earlier occasion involving a translation from the French, in which I really did infringe the rights of property that apply to publications. I added notes to the text which I translated, without asking the author's permission, and some years later I had reason to suspect that the author was displeased with my arbitrary action.[2]

There is a proverb which reveals the popular knowledge that the forgetting of intentions is not accidental: 'If one forgets to do a thing once, one will forget to do it many times more.'

Indeed,[3] sometimes we cannot avoid an impression that everything that can be said about forgetting and about parapraxes is already familiar and self-evident to everyone. It is sufficiently surprising that it is nevertheless necessary to present

1. [Published by Hölder of Vienna (Freud, 1897a).]
2. [This relates to a volume of lectures by Charcot which Freud translated (Freud, 1892–94), and to which he added a large number of footnotes.]
3. [This paragraph was added in 1910, and the final one in 1907.]

to consciousness things that are so well-known. How often have I heard people say: 'Don't ask me to do that, I'm certain to forget it!' There is surely nothing mystical, then, if this prophecy is subsequently fulfilled. A person who talks in this way senses an intention not to carry out the request, and is merely refusing to admit it to himself.

Much light is thrown, moreover, on the forgetting of intentions by what may be called 'the forming of spurious intentions'. I once promised a young author that I would write a review of his short work; but because of internal resistances, which I knew about, I put off doing so, till one day I yielded to pressure from him and promised it would be done that same evening. I really had seriously meant to do it then, but I had forgotten that I had set the evening aside for preparing a specialist report that could not be deferred. After this had shown me that my intention had been spurious, I gave up the struggle against my resistances and refused the author's request.

CHAPTER VIII

BUNGLED ACTIONS[1]

I WILL quote another passage from the work of Meringer and Mayer (1895, 98) which I have already mentioned [p. 94]:

'Slips of the tongue are not without their parallels. They correspond to the slips which often occur in other human activities and which are known by the somewhat foolish name of "oversights".'

Thus I am by no means the first to surmise that there is sense and purpose behind the minor functional disturbances in the daily life of healthy people.[2]

If slips in speaking – which is clearly a motor function – can be thought of in this way, it is a short step to extend the same expectation to mistakes in our other motor activities. I have here formed two groups of cases. I use the term 'bungled actions' ['*Vergreifen*'] to describe all the cases in which a wrong result – i.e. a deviation from what was intended – seems to be the essential element. The others, in which it is rather the whole action which seems to be inappropriate, I call 'symptomatic and chance actions' ['*Symptom- und Zufallshandlungen*']. But no sharp line can be drawn between them, and we are indeed forced to conclude that all the divisions made in this study have no significance other than a descriptive one and run counter to the inner unity in this field of phenomena.

It is clear that the psychological understanding of 'bungled actions' will not be conspicuously helped if we class them under the heading of 'ataxia' or, in particular, of 'cortical ataxia'. Let us rather try to trace the individual examples back to their

1. [Except where otherwise indicated, the earlier part of this chapter (up to p. 222) dates back to 1901.]

2. [*Footnote added* 1910:] A second publication by Meringer [1908] has later shown me how great an injustice I did to that author when I credited him with any such understanding.

particular determinants. For this purpose I shall once more make use of self-observations, though in my case the occasions for these are not particularly frequent.

(a) In former years I visited patients in their homes more frequently than I do at present; and on numerous occasions when I was at the front door, instead of knocking or ringing the bell, I pulled my own latch key out of my pocket, only to thrust it back again in some confusion. When I consider the patients at whose houses this happened, I am forced to think that the parapraxis – taking out my key instead of ringing the bell – was in the nature of a tribute to the house where I made the mistake. It was equivalent to the thought 'Here I feel I am at home', for it only occurred at places where I had taken a liking to the patient. (Of course I never ring my own door bell.)

Thus the parapraxis was a symbolic representation of a thought which was not after all really intended to be accepted seriously and consciously; for a nerve specialist is in fact well aware that his patients remain attached to him only so long as they expect to be benefited by him, and that he in turn allows himself to feel an excessively warm interest in them only with a view to giving them psychical help.

Numerous self-observations made by other people[1] show that handling a key in this significantly incorrect way is certainly not a peculiarity of mine.

Maeder (1906) describes what is an almost identical repetition of my experiences: 'Il est arrivé à chacun de sortir son trousseau, en arrivant à la porte d'un ami particulièrement cher, de se surprendre pour ainsi dire, en train d'ouvrir avec sa clé comme chez soi. C'est un retard, puisqu'il faut sonner malgré tout, mais c'est une preuve qu'on se sent – ou qu'on voudrait se sentir – comme chez soi, auprès de cet ami.'[2]

---

1. [This and the next four paragraphs were added in 1912.]

2. ['Everyone has had the experience of taking out his bunch of keys on reaching the door of a particularly dear friend, of catching himself, as it were, in the act of opening it with his key just as if he was at home.

Jones (1911*b*, 509): 'The use of keys is a fertile source of occurrences of this kind, of which two examples may be given. If I am disturbed in the midst of some engrossing work at home by having to go to the hospital to carry out some routine work, I am very apt to find myself trying to open the door of my laboratory there with the key of my desk at home, although the two keys are quite unlike each other. The mistake unconsciously demonstrates where I would rather be at the moment.

'Some years ago I was acting in a subordinate position at a certain institution, the front door of which was kept locked, so that it was necessary to ring for admission. On several occasions I found myself making serious attempts to open the door with my house key. Each one of the permanent visiting staff, to which I aspired to be a member, was provided with a key, to avoid the trouble of having to wait at the door. My mistakes thus expressed my desire to be on a similar footing, and to be quite "at home" there.'

Dr Hanns Sachs reports a similar experience: 'I always have two keys on me, one for the door of my office and one for my flat. They are not at all easily confused with each other, for the office key is at least three times as big as the flat key. Moreover, I carry the former in my trouser pocket and the latter in my waistcoat pocket. Nevertheless it often happened that I noticed as I stood at the door that I had got out the wrong key on the stairs. I determined to make a statistical experiment. Since I stood in front of both the doors every day in more or less the same emotional state, the confusion between the two keys was bound to show a regular tendency, if, indeed, it was true that it had some psychical determinant. My observation of later instances then showed that I quite regularly took out my flat key at the door of the office, whereas the opposite happened only once. I came home tired, knowing that a guest would be

---

This causes a delay, as he has to ring the bell in the long run, but it is a sign that he feels – or would like to feel – at home with this friend.']

waiting for me there. When I reached the door I made an attempt to unlock it with the office key – which was of course much too large.'

(b) There is a house where twice every day for six years, at regular hours, I used to wait to be let in outside a door on the second floor.[1] During this long period it has happened to me on two occasions, with a short interval between them, that I have gone a floor too high – i.e. I have '*climbed too high*'.[2] On the first occasion I was enjoying an ambitious day-dream in which I was 'climbing ever higher and higher'. On this occasion I even failed to hear that the door in question had opened as I put my foot on the first step of the third flight. On the other occasion, I again went too far while I was deep in thought; when I realized it, I turned back and tried to catch hold of the phantasy in which I had been absorbed. I found that I was irritated by a (phantasied) criticism of my writings in which I was reproached with always 'going too far'. This I had now replaced by the not very respectful expression 'climbing too high'.

(c) For many years a reflex hammer and a tuning fork have been lying side by side on my writing table. One day I left in a hurry at the end of my consulting hour as I wanted to catch a particular suburban train; and in broad daylight I put the tuning fork in my coat pocket instead of the hammer. The weight of the object pulling down my pocket drew my attention to my mistake. Anyone who is not in the habit of giving consideration to such minor occurrences will doubtless explain and excuse the mistake by pointing to the haste of the moment. Nevertheless I preferred to ask myself the question why it actually was that I took the tuning fork instead of the hammer. My haste could just as well have been a motive for picking up

1. [Cf. below, p. 232.]

2. [The German '*versteigen*' would, on the analogy of '*verlesen*', '*verschreiben*', etc., mean 'to mis-climb'; but its normal meaning is 'to climb too high' or, figuratively, 'to over-reach oneself'.]

the right object so as not to have to waste time in correcting my mistake.

'Who was the last person to take hold of the tuning fork?' was the question that sprang to my mind at that point. It was an *imbecile* child, whom I had been testing some days before for his attention to sensory impressions; and he had been so fascinated by the tuning fork that I had had some difficulty in tearing it away from him. Could the meaning be, then, that I was an imbecile? It certainly seemed so, for my first association to 'hammer' was '*Chamer*' (Hebrew for 'ass').

But why this abusive language? At this point we must look into the situation. I was hurrying to a consultation at a place on the Western railway line, to visit a patient who, according to the anamnesis I had received by letter, had fallen from a balcony some months earlier and had since then been unable to walk. The doctor who called me in wrote that he was nevertheless uncertain whether it was a case of spinal injury or of a traumatic neurosis – hysteria. That was what I was now to decide. It would therefore be advisable for me to be particularly wary in the delicate task of making a differential diagnosis. As it is, my colleagues are of the opinion that I make a diagnosis of hysteria far too carelessly where graver things are in question. But so far this did not justify the abusive language. Why, of course! it now occurred to me that the little railway station was at the same place at which some years before I had seen a young man who had not been able to walk properly after an emotional experience. At the time I made a diagnosis of hysteria and I subsequently took the patient on for psychical treatment. It then turned out that though my diagnosis had not, it is true, been incorrect, it had not been correct either. A whole number of the patient's symptoms had been hysterical, and they rapidly disappeared in the course of treatment. But behind these a remnant now became visible which was inaccessible to my therapy; this remnant could only be accounted for by multiple sclerosis. It was easy for those who saw the patient after me to recognize the organic affection. I could

hardly have behaved otherwise or formed a different judgement, yet the impression left was that a grave error had been
made; the promise of a cure which I had given him could
naturally not be kept.

The error of picking up the tuning fork instead of the
hammer could thus be translated into words as follows: 'You
idiot! You ass! Pull yourself together this time, and see that
you don't diagnose hysteria again where there's an incurable
illness, as you did years ago with the poor man from that same
place!' And fortunately for this little analysis, if not fortunately
for my mood, the same man, suffering from severe spastic
paralysis, had visited me during my consulting hour a few days
before, and a day after the imbecile child.

It will be observed that this time it was the voice of self-
criticism which was making itself heard in the bungled action.
A bungled action is quite specially suitable for use in this way
as a self-reproach: the present mistake seeks to represent the
mistake that has been committed elsewhere.

(*d*) Bungled actions can, of course, also serve a whole number
of other obscure purposes. Here is a first example. It is very
rare for me to break anything. I am not particularly dexterous
but a result of the anatomical integrity of my nerve-muscle
apparatus is that there are clearly no grounds for my making
clumsy movements of this kind, with their unwelcome consequences. I cannot therefore recall any object in my house
that I have ever broken. Shortage of space in my study has
often forced me to handle a number of pottery and stone
antiquities (of which I have a small collection) in the most uncomfortable positions, so that onlookers have expressed anxiety
that I should knock something down and break it. That
however has never happened. Why then did I once dash the
marble cover of my plain inkpot to the ground so that it
broke?

My inkstand is made out of a flat piece of Untersberg marble
which is hollowed out to receive the glass inkpot; and the ink-

pot has a cover with a knob made of the same stone. Behind this inkstand there is a ring of bronze statuettes and terra cotta figures. I sat down at the desk to write, and then moved the hand that was holding the pen-holder forward in a remarkably clumsy way, sweeping on to the floor the inkpot cover which was lying on the desk at the time.

The explanation was not hard to find. Some hours before, my sister had been in the room to inspect some new acquisitions. She admired them very much, and then remarked: 'Your writing table looks really attractive now; only the inkstand doesn't match. You must get a nicer one.' I went out with my sister and did not return for some hours. But when I did I carried out, so it seems, the execution of the condemned ink-stand. Did I perhaps conclude from my sister's remark that she intended to make me a present of a nicer inkstand on the next festive occasion, and did I smash the unlovely old one so as to force her to carry out the intention she had hinted at? If that is so, my sweeping movement was only apparently clumsy; in reality it was exceedingly adroit and well-directed, and understood how to avoid damaging any of the more precious objects that stood around.

It is in fact my belief that we must accept this judgement for a whole series of seemingly accidental clumsy movements. It is true that they make a show of something violent and sweep-ing, like a spastic-atactic movement, but they prove to be governed by an intention and achieve their aim with a certainty which cannot in general be credited to our conscious voluntary movements. Moreover they have both features – their violence and their unerring aim – in common with the motor manifesta-tions of the hysterical neurosis, and partly, too, with the motor performances of somnambulism.[1] This fact indicates that both in these cases and in the movements under consideration the

---

1. [Freud returned to the notion of 'somnambulistic certainty' at the end of this book, p. 312, below. In later editions it reappeared in two examples quoted by him, pp. 191 and 192, above.]

same unknown modification of the innervatory process is present.

Another self-observation,[1] reported by Frau Lou Andreas-Salomé, may give a convincing demonstration of how obstinate persistence in an act of 'clumsiness' serves unavowed purposes in a far from clumsy way:

'Just at the time when milk had become scarce and expensive I found that I let it boil over time and time again, to my constant horror and vexation. My efforts to get the better of this were unsuccessful, though I cannot by any means say that on other occasions I have proved absent-minded or inattentive. I should have had more reason to be so after the death of my dear white terrier (who deserved his name of "Druzhok" – the Russian for "Friend" – as much as any human being ever did). But – lo and behold! – never since his death has even a drop of milk boiled over. My first thought about this ran: "That's lucky, for the milk spilt over on to the hearth or floor wouldn't even be of any use!" And in the same moment I saw my "Friend" before my eyes, sitting eagerly watching the cooking, his head cocked a little to one side, his tail wagging expectantly, waiting in trustful confidence for the splendid mishap that was about to occur. And now everything was clear to me, and I realized too that I had been even *more* fond of him than I myself was aware.'

In the last few years,[2] during which I have been collecting such observations, I have had a few more experiences of smashing or breaking objects of some value, but the investigation of these cases has convinced me that they were never the result of chance or of unintentional clumsiness on my part. One morning, for example, when I was passing through a room in my dressing-gown with straw slippers on my feet, I yielded to a sudden impulse and hurled one of my slippers from my foot at the wall, causing a beautiful little marble Venus to fall down

1. [This example was added in 1919.]
2. [This paragraph and the four following ones were added in 1907.]

from its bracket. As it broke into pieces, I quoted quite un-
moved these lines from Busch:

'Ach! die Venus ist perdü –
Klickeradoms! – von Medici!'[1]

This wild conduct and my calm acceptance of the damage
are to be explained in terms of the situation at the time. One
of my family was gravely ill,[2] and secretly I had already given
up hope of her recovery. That morning I had learned that there
had been a great improvement, and I know I had said to myself: 'So she's going to live after all!' My attack of destructive
fury served therefore to express a feeling of gratitude to fate
and allowed me to perform a '*sacrificial act*' – rather as if I had
made a vow to sacrifice something or other as a thank-offering
if she recovered her health! The choice of the Venus of Medici
for this sacrifice was clearly only a gallant act of homage
towards the convalescent; but even now it is a mystery to me
how I made up my mind so quickly, aimed so accurately and
avoided hitting anything else among the objects so close to it.

Another case of breaking something, for which I once again
made use of a pen-holder that slipped from my hand, likewise
had the significance of a sacrifice; but on this occasion it took
the form of a propitiatory sacrifice to avert evil. I had once seen
fit to reproach a loyal and deserving friend on no other grounds
than the interpretation I placed on certain indications coming
from his unconscious. He was offended and wrote me a letter
asking me not to treat my friends psychoanalytically. I had to
admit he was in the right, and wrote him a reply to pacify him.
While I was writing this letter I had in front of me my latest
acquisition, a handsome glazed Egyptian figure. I broke it in
the way I have described, and then immediately realized that

1. ['Oh! the Venus! Lost is she!
Klickeradoms! of Medici!'
From Wilhelm Busch's *Die fromme Helene*, Chapter VIII.]
2. [This refers to the illness of Freud's eldest daughter in 1905. (Jones,
1957, 409.) Cf. also p. 235 below.]

I had caused this mischief in order to avert a greater one. Luckily it was possible to cement both of them together – the friendship as well as the figure – so that the break would not be noticed.

A third breakage was connected with less serious matters; it was only the disguised 'execution' – to borrow an expression from Vischer's *Auch Einer*[1] – of an object which no longer enjoyed my favour. For some time I used to carry a stick with a silver handle. On one occasion the thin metal got damaged, through no fault of mine, and was badly repaired. Soon after the stick came back, I used the handle in a mischievous attempt to catch one of my children by the leg – with the natural result that it broke, and I was thus rid of it.

The equanimity with which we accept the resulting damage in all these cases can no doubt be taken as evidence that there is an unconscious purpose behind the performance of these particular actions.

In investigating the reasons for the occurrence of even so trivial a parapraxis as the breaking of an object,[2] one is liable to come across connections which, besides relating to a person's present situation, lead deep into his prehistory. The following analysis by Jekels (1913) may serve as an example:

'A doctor had in his possession an earthenware flower vase which, though not valuable, was of great beauty. It was among the many presents – including objects of value – which had been sent to him in the past by a (married) woman patient. When a psychosis became manifest in her, he restored all the presents to her relatives – except for this far less expensive vase, with which he could not bear to part, ostensibly because it was so beautiful. But this embezzlement cost a man of his scrupulousness a considerable internal struggle. He was fully aware of the

1. [Theodor Vischer (1807–87), the author of this novel (1878), was a Professor of Aesthetics, who is repeatedly quoted in Freud's book on jokes (1905c). See also above, p. 190, *n*. 1.]

2. [This paragraph and the example which follows were added in 1917.]

improbpriety of his action, and only managed to overcome his pangs of conscience by telling himself that the vase was not in fact of any real value, that it was too awkward to pack, etc. – Some months later he was on the point of getting a lawyer to claim and recover the arrears (which were in dispute) of the fees for the treatment of this same patient. Once again the self-reproaches made their appearance; and he suffered some momentary anxiety in case the relatives discovered what could be called his embezzlement and brought it against him during the legal proceedings. For a while indeed the first factor (his self-reproaches) was so strong that he actually thought of renouncing all claims on a sum of perhaps a hundred times the value of the vase – a compensation, as it were, for the object he had appropriated. However, he at once got the better of the notion and set it aside as absurd.

'While he was still in this mood he happened to be putting some fresh water in the vase; and despite the extreme in-frequency with which he broke anything and the good control that he had over his muscular apparatus, he made an extra-ordinarily "clumsy" movement – one that was not in the least organically related to the action he was carrying out – which knocked the vase off the table, so that it broke into some five or six largish pieces. What is more, this was after he had made up his mind on the previous evening, though not without consider-able hesitation, to put precisely this vase, filled with flowers, on the dining-room table before his guests. He had remembered it only just before it got broken, had noticed with anxiety that it was not in his living-room and had himself brought it in from the other room. After his first moments of dismay he picked up the pieces and by putting them together was just deciding that it would still be possible to make an almost complete repair of the vase, when the two or three larger fragments slipped from his hand; they broke into a thousand splinters, and with that vanished all hope for the vase.

'There is no doubt that this parapraxis had the current purpose of assisting the doctor in his law-suit, by getting rid of something which he had kept back and which to some extent prevented his claiming what had been kept back from him.

'But apart from this direct determinant, every psychoanalyst will see in the parapraxis a further and much deeper and more important *symbolic* determinant; for a vase is an unmistakable symbol of a woman.

'The hero of this little story had lost his young, beautiful and dearly-loved wife in a tragic manner. He fell ill of a neurosis whose main theme was that he was to blame for the misfortune ("he had broken a lovely vase"). Moreover, he had no further relations with women and took a dislike to marriage and lasting love-relationships, which unconsciously he thought of as being unfaithful to his dead wife but which he consciously rationalized in the idea that he brought misfortune to women, that a woman might kill herself on his account, etc. (Hence his natural reluctance to keep the vase permanently!)

'In view of the strength of his libido it is therefore not surprising that the most adequate relationships appeared to him to be those – transient from their very nature – with married women (hence his keeping back of another person's vase).

'This symbolism is neatly confirmed by the two following factors. Because of his neurosis he entered psychoanalytic treatment. In the course of the session in which he gave an account of breaking the "earthenware" vase, he happened much later to be talking once more about his relations with women and said he thought he was quite unreasonably hard to please; thus for example he required women to have "unearthly beauty". This is surely a very clear indication that he was still dependent on his (dead, i.e., unearthly) wife and wanted to have nothing to do with "earthly beauty"; hence the breaking of the earthenware ("earthly") vase.

'And at the exact time when in the transference he formed a phantasy of marrying his physician's daughter, he made him a present of a vase, as though to drop a hint of the sort of return-present he would like to have.

'Probably the symbolic meaning of the parapraxis admits of a number of further variations – for example, his not wanting to fill the vase, etc. What strikes me, however, as more interesting is the consideration that the presence of several, at the least of two, motives (which probably operated separately out of the preconscious and the unconscious) is reflected in the doubling of the parapraxis – his knocking over the vase and then letting it fall from his hands.'[1]

(e)[2] Dropping, knocking over and breaking objects are acts which seem to be used very often to express unconscious trains of thought, as analysis can occasionally demonstrate, but as may more frequently be guessed from the superstitious or facetious interpretations popularly connected with them. The interpretations attached to salt being spilt, a wine-glass being knocked over, a dropped knife sticking in the ground, etc., are well known. I shall not discuss till later [p. 317 ff.] the question of what claims such superstitious interpretations have to being taken seriously. Here I need only remark that individual clumsy actions do not by any means always have the same meaning, but serve as a method of representing one purpose or another according to circumstances.

Recently we passed through a period in my house during which an unusually large amount of glass and china crockery was broken; I myself was responsible for some of the damage. But the little psychical epidemic could easily be explained; these were the days before my eldest daughter's wedding. On such festive occasions it used to be the custom deliberately to break some utensil and at the same time utter a phrase to bring good luck. This custom may have the significance of a sacrifice and it may have another symbolic meaning as well.

When servants drop fragile articles and so destroy them, our first thought is certainly not of a psychological explanation, yet it is not unlikely that here, too, obscure motives play their part.

1. [Cf. p. 152 (b).]
2. [The first and third paragraphs in this section date back to 1901; the second was added in 1910.]

Nothing is more foreign to uneducated people than an appreciation of art and works of art. Our servants are dominated by a mute hostility towards the manifestations of art, especially when the objects (whose value they do not understand) become a source of work for them. On the other hand people of the same education and origin often show great dexterity and reliability in handling delicate objects in scientific institutions once they have begun to identify themselves with their chief and to consider themselves an essential part of the staff.

I insert here[1] a communication from a young technician which gives us some insight into the mechanism of a case of material damage:

'Some time ago I worked with several fellow-students in the laboratory of the technical college on a series of complicated experiments in elasticity, a piece of work which we had undertaken voluntarily but which was beginning to take up more time than we had expected. One day as I returned to the laboratory with my friend F., he remarked how annoying it was to him to lose so much time on that particular day as he had so much else to do at home. I could not help agreeing with him and added half jokingly, referring to an incident the week before: "Let us hope that the machine will go wrong again so that we can stop work and go home early." – In arranging the work it happened that F. was given the regulation of the valve of the press; that is to say, he was, by cautiously opening the valve, to let the fluid under pressure flow slowly out of the accumulator into the cylinder of the hydraulic press. The man conducting the experiment stood by the manometer and when the right pressure was reached called out a loud "stop!". At the word of command F. seized the valve and turned it with all his might – to the left! (All valves without exception are closed by being turned to the right.) This caused the full pressure of the accumulator to come suddenly on to the

1. [This example was added in 1912.]

press, a strain for which the connecting-pipes are not designed, so that one of them immediately burst – quite a harmless accident to the machine, but enough to oblige us to suspend work for the day and go home. – It is characteristic, by the way, that when we were discussing the affair some time later my friend F. had no recollection whatever of my remark, which I recalled with certainty.'

Similarly,[1] falling, stumbling and slipping need not always be interpreted as purely accidental miscarriages of motor action. The double meanings that language attaches to these expressions are enough to indicate the kind of phantasies involved, which can be represented by such losses of bodily equilibrium. I can recall a number of fairly mild nervous illnesses in women and girls which set in after a fall not accompanied by any injury, and which were taken to be traumatic hysterias resulting from the shock of the fall. Even at that time I had an impression that these events were differently connected and that the fall was already a product of the neurosis and expressed the same unconscious phantasies with a sexual content, which could be assumed to be the forces operating behind the symptoms. Is not the same thing meant by a proverb which runs: 'When a girl falls she falls on her back'?

We can also count[2] as bungled actions cases of giving a beggar a gold piece instead of a copper or small silver coin. The explanation of such mistakes is easy. They are sacrificial acts designed to appease fate, to avert harm, and so on. If a devoted mother or aunt, directly before going for a walk in the course of which she displays unwilling generosity of this kind, is heard to express concern over a child's health, we can have no more doubts about the meaning of the apparently disagreeable accident. In this way our parapraxes make it possible for us to practise all those pious and superstitious customs that must shun the light of consciousness owing to opposition from our reason, which has now grown sceptical.

1. [This paragraph dates back to 1901.]   2. [Added in 1907.]

(*f*) There is no sphere[1] in which the view that accidental actions are really intentional will command a more ready belief than that of sexual activity, where the border line between the two possibilities seems really to be a faint one. A good example from my own experience of a few years ago shows how an apparently clumsy movement can be most cunningly used for sexual purposes. In the house of some friends I met a young girl who was staying there as a guest and who aroused a feeling of pleasure in me which I had long thought was extinct. As a result I was in a jovial, talkative and obliging mood. At the time I also endeavoured to discover how this came about; a year before, the same girl had made no impression on me. As the girl's uncle, a very old gentleman, entered the room, we both jumped to our feet to bring him a chair that was standing in the corner. She was nimbler than I was and, I think, nearer to the object; so she took hold of the chair first and carried it in front of her with its back towards her, gripping the sides of the seat with both hands. As I got there later, but still stuck to my intention of carrying the chair, I suddenly found myself standing directly behind her, and throwing my arms round her from behind; and for a moment my hands met in front of her waist. I naturally got out of the situation as rapidly as it had arisen. Nor does it seem to have struck anyone how dexterously I had taken advantage of this clumsy movement.

Occasionally, too, I have had to tell myself that the irritating and clumsy process of dodging someone in the street, when for several seconds one steps first to one side and then to the other, but always to the same side as the other person, till finally one comes to a standstill face to face with him (or her) – this 'getting in someone's way', I have had to tell myself, is once more a repetition of an improper and provocative piece of behaviour from earlier times and, behind a mask of clumsiness, pursues sexual aims. I know from my psychoanalyses of neurotics that what is described as the *naïveté* of young people and children is frequently only a mask of this sort, employed so that they may

1. [This paragraph and the following one date back to 1901.]

be able to say or do something improper without feeling embarrassed.

Wilhelm Stekel has reported very similar self-observations.[1] 'I entered a house and offered my right hand to my hostess. In a most curious way I contrived in doing so to undo the bow that held her loose morning-gown together. I was conscious of no dishonourable intention; yet I carried out this clumsy movement with the dexterity of a conjurer.'

I have already[2] been able again and again [cf. pp. 142 and 182] to produce evidence that creative writers think of parapraxes as having a meaning and a motive, just as I am arguing here. We shall not be surprised, therefore, to see from a fresh example how a writer invests a clumsy movement with significance, too, and makes it foreshadow later events.

Here is a passage from Theodor Fontane's novel *L'Adultera* [*The Adulteress*, 1882]. '. . . Melanie jumped up and threw one of the large balls to her husband as though in greeting. But her aim was not straight, the ball flew to one side and Rubehn caught it.' On the return from the outing that led to this little episode a conversation between Melanie and Rubehn takes place which reveals the first signs of a budding affection. This affection blossoms into passion, so that Melanie finally leaves her husband and gives herself entirely to the man she loves. (Communicated by H. Sachs.)

(g)[3] The effects produced by the parapraxes of normal people are as a rule of the most harmless kind. Precisely for this reason it is an especially interesting question whether mistakes of considerable importance which may be followed by serious consequences – for example, mistakes made by a doctor or a chemist – are in any way open to the approach presented here. [Cf. also above, pp. 171–4.]

As I very rarely find myself undertaking medical treatment,

1. [Added in 1907.]
2. [This paragraph and the following one were added in 1917.]
3. [The first four paragraphs in this section date back to 1901.]

I can report only one example from my personal experience of
a bungled action of a medical kind. There is a very old lady
whom I have been visiting twice a day for some years.[1] On my
morning visit my medical services are limited to two actions.
I put a few drops of eye-lotion into her eye and give her a
morphine injection. Two bottles are always prepared for me:
a blue one with the collyrium and a white one with the
morphine solution. During the two operations my thoughts are
no doubt usually busy with something else; by now I have
performed them so often that my attention behaves as if it were
at liberty. One morning I noticed that the automaton had
worked wrong. I had put the dropper into the white bottle
instead of the blue one and had put morphine into the eye
instead of collyrium. I was greatly frightened and then reassured
myself by reflecting that a few drops of a two per cent solution
of morphine could not do any harm even in the conjunctival
sac. The feeling of fright must obviously have come from
another source.

In attempting to analyse this small mistake I first thought of
the phrase 'sich an der Alten vergreifen',[2] which provided a
short cut to the solution. I was under the influence of a dream
which had been told me by a young man the previous evening
and the content of which could only point to sexual intercourse
with his own mother.[3] The strange fact that the [Oedipus]
legend finds nothing objectionable in Queen Jocasta's age
seemed to me to fit in well with the conclusion that in being in
love with one's own mother one is never concerned with her

1. [This old lady, who is also alluded to on pp. 218 and 319, appears
as well in *The Interpretation of Dreams* (1900a), Chapters II and V,
P.F.L., 4, 195 and 336.]

2. ['To do violence to the old woman.' The German word '*vergreifen*'
means both 'to make a blunder' and 'to commit an assault'.]

3. The 'Oedipus dream', as I am in the habit of calling it, because it
contains the key to the understanding of the legend of King Oedipus.
In the text of Sophocles a reference to such a dream is put into Jocasta's
mouth [line 982 ff.]. Cf. *The Interpretation of Dreams* (1900a), *P.F.L.*, 4,
362–6.

as she is in the present but with her youthful mnemic image carried over from one's childhood. Such incongruities always appear when a phantasy that fluctuates between two periods is made conscious and so becomes definitely attached to one of the two periods. While absorbed in thoughts of this kind I came to my patient, who is over ninety, and I must have been on the way to grasping the universal human application of the Oedipus myth as correlated with the Fate which is revealed in the oracles; for at that point I did violence to or committed a blunder on 'the old woman'. Here again the bungled action was a harmless one; of the two possible errors, using the morphine solution for the eye or the eye lotion for the injection, I had chosen by far the more harmless one. This still leaves the question open of whether we may admit the possibility of an unconscious intention in mistakes that can cause serious harm, in the same way as in the cases which I have discussed.

Here then my material leaves me in the lurch, as might be expected, and I have to fall back on conjectures and inferences. It is well known that in the severer cases of psychoneurosis instances of self-injury are occasionally found as symptoms and that in such cases suicide can never be ruled out as a possible outcome of the psychical conflict. I have now learnt and can prove[1] from convincing examples that many apparently accidental injuries that happen to such patients are really instances of self-injury. What happens is that an impulse to self-punishment, which is constantly on the watch and which normally finds expression in self-reproach or contributes to the formation of a symptom, takes ingenious advantage of an external situation that chance happens to offer, or lends assistance to that situation until the desired injurious effect is brought about. Such occurrences are by no means uncommon in cases even of moderate severity, and they betray the part which the unconscious intention plays by a number of special

1. [In the editions before 1924 the sentence ran: 'and shall one day prove. . .']

features – e.g. by the striking composure that the patients retain in what is supposed to be an accident.[1]

Instead of a number of cases[2] I will give a detailed report of only a single example from my medical experience. A young married woman broke her leg below the knee in a carriage accident, so that she was bed-ridden for weeks; what was striking was the absence of any expressions of pain and the calmness with which she bore her misfortune. This accident introduced a long and severe neurotic illness of which she was finally cured by psychoanalysis. In treating her I learnt of the circumstances surrounding the accident and of certain events that had preceded it. The young woman was staying with her very jealous husband on the estate of a married sister, in company with her numerous other sisters and brothers with their husbands and wives. One evening in this intimate circle she showed off one of her accomplishments: she gave an accurate performance of the can-can, which was received with hearty applause by her relatives but with scanty satisfaction by her husband, who afterwards whispered to her: 'Carrying on like a tart again!' The remark struck home – we will not enquire whether it was only on account of the dancing display. She spent a restless night. Next morning she felt a desire to go for a drive. She selected the horses herself, refusing one pair and asking for another. Her youngest sister wanted her baby and its nurse to go in the carriage with her; my patient vigorously opposed this. During the drive she showed signs of nerves; she warned the coachman that the horses were growing skittish, and when the restless animals were really causing a moment's difficulty she jumped out in a fright and broke her leg, while the others who stayed in the carriage were unharmed. Although

1. In the present state of our civilization self-injury which does not have total self-destruction as its aim has no other choice whatever than to hide itself behind something accidental or to manifest itself by imitating the onset of a spontaneous illness. Formerly self-injury was a customary sign of mourning; at other periods it could express trends towards piety and renunciation of the world.

2. [This paragraph and the next two were added in 1907.]

after learning these details we can hardly remain in doubt that this accident was really contrived, we cannot fail to admire the skill which forced chance to mete out a punishment that fitted the crime so well. For it had now been made impossible for her to dance the can-can for quite a long time.

As regards self-injuries of my own, there is little that I can report in uneventful times; but in extraordinary circumstances I find that I am not incapable of them. When a member of my family complains to me of having bitten his tongue, pinched a finger, or the like, he does not get the sympathy he hopes for, but instead the question: 'Why did you do that?' I myself once gave my thumb a most painful pinch when a youthful patient told me during the hour of treatment of his intention (not of course to be taken seriously) of marrying my eldest daughter – I knew that at the time she was lying critically ill in a sanatorium.[1]

One of my boys, whose lively temperament used to make it difficult to nurse him when he was ill, had a fit of anger one day because he was ordered to spend the morning in bed, and threatened to kill himself, a possibility that was familiar to him from the newspapers. In the evening he showed me a swelling on one side of his chest which he had got by bumping against a door-handle. To my ironical question as to why he had done it and what he meant by it, the eleven-year-old child answered as though it had suddenly dawned on him: 'That was my attempt at suicide that I threatened this morning.' I do not think, by the way, that my views on self-injury were accessible to my children at the time.

Anyone who believes[2] in the occurrence of half-intentional self-*injury* – if I may use a clumsy expression – will be prepared also to assume that in addition to consciously intentional suicide there is such a thing as half-intentional self-*destruction* (self-destruction with an unconscious intention), capable of making skilful use of a threat to life and of disguising it as a

1. [See footnote 2, p. 223.]
2. [This paragraph and the next one date back to 1901.]

chance mishap. There is no need to think such self-destruction rare. For the trend to self-destruction is present to a certain degree in very many more human beings than those in whom it is carried out; self-injuries are as a rule a compromise between this instinct and the forces that are still working against it, and even where suicide actually results, the inclination to suicide will have been present for a long time before in lesser strength or in the form of an unconscious and suppressed trend.

Even a *conscious* intention of committing suicide chooses its time, means and opportunity; and it is quite in keeping with this that an *unconscious* intention should wait for a precipitating occasion which can take over a part of the causation and, by engaging the subject's defensive forces, can liberate the intention from their pressure.[1] The views I am putting forward here are far from being idle ones. I have learned of more than one apparently chance mishap (on horseback or in a carriage) the details of which justify a suspicion that suicide was unconsciously allowed to come about. For example, an officer, riding in a race with some fellow-officers, fell from his horse and was so severely injured that he died some days later. His behaviour on regaining consciousness was striking in some ways; and his

1. After all, the case is no different from that of a sexual assault upon a woman, where the man's attack cannot be repelled by her full muscular strength because a portion of her unconscious impulses meets the attack with encouragement. It is said, as we know, that a situation of this kind *paralyses* a woman's strength; all we need do is to add the reasons for this paralysis. To that extent the ingenious judgement delivered by Sancho Panza as governor of his island is psychologically unjust (*Don Quixote*, Part 2, Chapter 45). A woman dragged a man before the judge alleging he had robbed her of her honour by violence. In compensation Sancho gave her a full purse of money which he took from the accused; but after the woman's departure he gave him permission to pursue her and snatch his purse back again from her. The two returned struggling, the woman priding herself on the fact that the villain had not been able to take the purse from her. Thereupon Sancho declared: 'If you had defended your honour with half the determination with which you have defended this purse, the man could not have robbed you of it.'

previous behaviour had been even more remarkable. He had been deeply depressed by the death of his beloved mother, had had fits of sobbing in the company of his fellow officers, and to his trusted friends had spoken of being weary of life. He had wanted to leave the service to take part in a war in Africa which had not interested him previously;[1] formerly a dashing rider, he now avoided riding whenever possible. Finally, before the race, from which he could not withdraw, he expressed gloomy forebodings; with the view that we hold in these matters, it will not remain a surprise to us that these forebodings turned out to be justified. I shall be told that it is not to be wondered at if a person in such a state of nervous depression cannot manage a horse as well as on normal days. I quite agree; but the mechanism of the motor inhibition produced by this state of 'nerves' should, I think, be looked for in the intention of self-destruction that I am insisting on.

S. Ferenczi of Budapest has handed over to me for publication the analysis of an ostensibly accidental injury by shooting,[2] which he explains as an unconscious attempt at suicide. I can only declare my agreement with his view of the matter:

'J. Ad., twenty-two years old, a journeyman carpenter, consulted me on January 16, 1908. He wanted to find out from me whether the bullet that penetrated his left temple on March 20, 1907 could or should be removed by operation. Apart from occasional, not too severe, headaches he felt perfectly well, and the objective examination revealed nothing at all apart from the characteristic powder-blackened bullet scar on the left temple, so I advised against an operation. When asked about the circumstances of the case he explained that he had injured himself accidentally. He was playing with his brother's revolver,

1. It is evident that conditions on a field of battle are such as to come to the help of a conscious intention to commit suicide which nevertheless shuns the direct way. Compare the words of the Swedish captain concerning the death of Max Piccolomini in [Schiller's] *Wallensteins Tod* [Act IV, Scene 11]: 'They say he wanted to die.'

2. [This example was added in 1910.]

thought it was not loaded, pressed it with his left hand against his *left* temple (he is not left-handed), put his finger on the trigger and the shot went off. *There were three bullets in the six-shooter.* I asked him how the idea of taking up the revolver came to him. He replied that it was the time of his medical examination for military service; the evening before, he took the weapon with him to the inn because he was afraid of brawls. At the examination he was found unfit because of varicose veins; he was very ashamed of this. He went home and played with the revolver, but had no intention of hurting himself – and then the accident happened. When questioned further whether he was otherwise satisfied with life, he sighed in answer and told the story of his love for a girl who also loved him but left him all the same. She emigrated to America simply out of desire for money. He wanted to follow her, but his parents prevented him. His sweetheart left on January 20, 1907; two months, that is, before the accident. In spite of all these supicious factors the patient stuck to his point that the shooting was an "accident". I was however firmly convinced that his negligence in failing to make sure the weapon was not loaded before play-ing with it, as well as his self-inflicted injury, were psychically determined. He was still labouring under the depressing effects of his unhappy love affair and obviously wanted to "forget it all" in the army. When he was deprived of this hope as well, he took to playing with the revolver – i.e. to an unconscious attempt at suicide. His holding the revolver in his left and not his right hand is strong evidence that he was really only "playing" – that is, that he did not consciously wish to commit suicide.'

Another analysis[1] of an apparently accidental self-inflicted injury, which its observer (Van Emden, 1912) has passed on to me, recalls the proverb: 'He who digs a pit for others falls in it himself.'[2]

'Fràu X., who comes of a good middle-class family, is married

1. [Added in 1912.]
2. [Cf. *Ecclesiastes*, x, 8: 'He that diggeth a pit shall fall into it.']

with three children. She suffers from her nerves, it is true, but has never needed any energetic treatment as she is sufficiently able to cope with life. One day she incurred a facial disfigurement which was somewhat striking at the time though it was only temporary. It happened as follows. She stumbled on a heap of stones in a street under repair and struck her face against the wall of a house. The whole of her face was scratched; her eyelids became blue and oedematous and as she was afraid that something might happen to her eyes she had the doctor called in. After she had been reassured on that score, I asked her: 'But why did you in fact fall in that way?' She replied that, directly before this, she had warned her husband, who had been suffering for some months from a joint affection and therefore had difficulty in walking, to take great care in that street, and it had been a fairly frequent experience of hers to find in cases of the kind that in some remarkable way the very thing happened to her that she had warned someone else against.

'I was not satisfied that this was what had determined her accident and asked if perhaps she had something more to tell me. Yes, just before the accident she had seen an attractive picture in a shop on the other side of the street; she had quite suddenly desired it as an ornament for the nursery and therefore wanted to buy it immediately. She walked straight towards the shop, without looking at the ground, stumbled over the heap of stones and in falling struck her face against the wall of the house without making even the slightest attempt to shield herself with her hands. The intention of buying the picture was immediately forgotten and she returned home as fast as possible. – "But why didn't you keep a better look-out?" I asked. "Well," she answered, "perhaps it was a *punishment* – on account of that episode I told you about in confidence." – "Has it gone on worrying you so much then?" – "Yes – I regretted it very much afterwards; I considered myself wicked, criminal and immoral, but at the time I was almost crazy with my nerves."

'The reference was to an abortion which she had had carried

out with her husband's consent, as, owing to their financial circumstances, the couple did not wish to be blessed with any further children. This abortion had been started by a woman quack but had had to be completed by a specialist.

"'I often reproach myself by thinking 'You really had your child killed' and I was afraid such a thing couldn't go unpunished. Now that you've assured me there's nothing wrong with my eyes, my mind's quite at rest: I've been *sufficiently punished* now in any case."

'This accident was therefore a self-punishment, firstly to atone for her crime, but secondly also to escape from an unknown punishment of perhaps much greater severity of which she had been in continual dread for months. In the moment that she dashed towards the shop to buy the picture, the memory of the whole episode with all its fears, which had already been fairly strongly active in her unconscious when she had warned her husband, became overwhelming and might perhaps have been expressed in some words like these: "Why do *you* need an ornament for the nursery? – you had your child destroyed! You're a murderess. The great punishment's just coming down on you for certain!"

'This thought did not become conscious; but instead of it she used the situation, at what I might call this psychological moment, for punishing herself unobtrusively with the help of the heap of stones which seemed suitable for the purpose. This is the reason why she did not even put out her hands as she fell and also why she was not seriously frightened. The second and probably less important determinant of her accident was no doubt self-punishment for her *unconscious* wish to be rid of her husband, who, incidentally, had been an accomplice in the crime. This wish was betrayed by her entirely superfluous warning to him to keep an eye open for the heap of stones in the street, since her husband walked with great care precisely because he was bad on his legs.'[1]

1. [*Footnote added* 1920:] A correspondent writes to me as follows on the subject of 'self-punishment by means of parapraxes': 'If one studies

When the details of the case are considered[1] one will also be likely to feel that Stärcke (1916) is right in regarding an apparently accidental self-injury by burning as a 'sacrificial act':

'A lady whose son-in-law had to leave for Germany for military service scalded her foot in the following circumstances. Her daughter was expecting her confinement soon and reflections on the perils of war naturally did not put the family into a very cheerful mood. The day before his departure she had asked her son-in-law and daughter in for a meal. She herself prepared the meal in the kitchen after having first – strangely enough – changed her high, laced boots with arch supports, which were comfortable for walking and which she usually wore indoors as well, for a pair of her husband's slippers that were too large and were open at the top. While taking a large pan of boiling soup off the fire she dropped it and in this way scalded one foot fairly badly – especially the instep, which was not protected by the open slipper. – Everyone naturally put this accident down to her understandable "nerves". For the first few days after this burnt offering she was particularly careful with anything hot, but this did not prevent her some days later from scalding her wrist with hot gravy.'[2]

---

the way people behave in the street one has a chance of seeing how often men who turn round to look back at passing women – not an unusual habit – meet with a minor accident. Sometimes they will sprain an ankle – on a level pavement; sometimes they will bump into a lamp-post or hurt themselves in some other way.'

1. [Added in 1917.]

2. [*Footnote added* 1924:] In a very large number of cases like these of injury or death in accidents the explanation remains a matter of doubt. The outsider will find no occasion to see in the accident anything other than a chance occurrence, while someone who is closely connected with the victim and is familiar with intimate details has reason to suspect the unconscious intention behind the chance occurrence. The following account by a young man whose fiancée was run over in the street gives a good example of the kind of intimate knowledge that I mean and of the type of accessory details in question:

'Last September I made the acquaintance of a Fräulein Z., aged 34.

She was in well-to-do circumstances, and had been engaged before the war, but her fiancé had fallen in action in 1916 while serving as an officer. We came to know and become fond of each other, not at first with any thought of marrying, as the circumstances on both sides, in particular the difference in our ages (I myself was 27), seemed to rule that out. As we lived opposite each other in the same street and met every day, our relationship took an intimate turn in course of time. Thus the idea of marriage came more into view and I finally agreed to it myself. The betrothal was planned for this Easter; Fräulein Z., however, intended first to make a journey to her relatives at M., but this was suddenly prevented by a railway strike that had been called as a result of the Kapp Putsch [an attempted counter-revolutionary *coup d'état* in Berlin in March, 1920]. The gloomy prospects that the workers'

victory and its consequences appeared to hold out for the future had their effect for a brief time on our mood, too, but especially on Fräulein Z., always a person of very changeable moods, since she thought she saw new obstacles in the way of our future. On Saturday, March 20, however, she was in an exceptionally cheerful frame of mind – a state of affairs that took me quite by surprise and carried me along with her, so that we seemed to see everything in the rosiest colours. A few days before, we had talked of going to church together some time, without however having fixed a definite date. At 9.15 the next morning, Sunday, March 21, she telephoned to ask me to fetch her to church straight away; but I refused, as I could not have got ready in time, and had, besides, work I wanted to finish. Fräulein Z. was noticeably disappointed; she then set out alone, met an acquaintance on the stairs at her house and walked with him for the short distance along the Tauentzienstrasse to the Rankestrasse, in the best of humour and without referring at all to our conversation. The gentleman bade her good-bye with a joking remark. [In order to reach the church] Fräulein Z. had only to cross the Kurfürstendamm [the main street in West Berlin] where it widened out and one could have a clear view along it; but, close to the pavement, she was run over by a horse-drawn cab. (Contusion of the liver, which led to her death a few hours later.) – We had crossed at that point hundreds of times before; Fräulein Z. was exceedingly careful, and very often prevented me from being rash; on this morning there was almost no traffic whatever, the trams, omnibuses, etc. were on strike. Just about that time there was almost *absolute quiet*; even if she did not see the cab she must at all events have heard it! Everybody supposed it was an "accident". My first thought was: "That's impossible – but on the other hand there can be no question of its having been intentional." I tried to find a psychological explanation. After some considerable time I thought I had found it in your *Psychopathology of*

If a furious raging[1] against one's own integrity and one's own life can be hidden in this way behind apparently accidental clumsiness and motor inefficiency, it is not a very large step to find it possible to transfer the same view to mistakes that seriously endanger the lives and health of other people. What evidence I have to show that this view is a valid one is drawn from my experience with neurotics, and thus does not wholly meet the demands of the situation. I will give an account of a case in which something that was not strictly a faulty action but that rather deserves the name of a symptomatic or chance action gave me the clue which subsequently made it possible to resolve the patient's conflict. I once undertook the task of bringing an improvement to the marriage of a very intelligent man, whose disagreements with his fondly attached young wife could undoubtedly be shown to have a real basis, but could not, as he himself admitted, be completely accounted for in that way. He was continually occupied with the thought of a divorce, which he then dismissed once more because of his warm love for his two small children. In spite of this he constantly returned to his intention and made no attempt to find a way of making the situation tolerable to himself. Such inability

---

Everyday Life. In particular, Fräulein Z. showed at various times a certain leaning in the direction of suicide and even tried to induce me to think the same way – thoughts from which I have often enough dissuaded her; for example, only two days before, after returning from a walk, she began, without any external reason at all, to talk about her death and the provisions for dealing with her estate. (She had not, by the way, done anything about this! – an indication that these remarks definitely did not have any intention behind them.) If I may venture on an opinion, I should regard this calamity not as an accident, nor as an effect of a clouding of consciousness, but as an intentional self-destruction performed with an unconscious purpose, and disguised as a chance mishap. This view of mine is confirmed by remarks which Fräulein Z. made to her relatives, both earlier, before she knew me, and also more recently, as well as by remarks to me up to within the last few days; so that I am tempted to regard the whole thing as an effect of the loss of her former fiancé, whom in her eyes nothing could replace.'

1. [This paragraph dates back to 1901.]

to deal with a conflict is taken by me as proof that unconscious and repressed motives have lent a hand in strengthening the conscious ones which are struggling against each other, and I undertake in such cases to end the conflict by psychical analysis. One day the man told me of a small incident which had frightened him extremely. He was romping ['*hetzen*'] with his elder child, who was by far his favourite; he was swinging him high in the air and down again, and once he swung him so high while he was standing at a particular spot that the top of the child's head almost struck the heavy gas chandelier that was hanging there. *Almost*, but not quite – or perhaps just! No harm came to the child, but it was made giddy with fright. The father stood horrified with the child in his arms, and the mother had a hysterical attack. The peculiar adroitness of this imprudent movement and the violence of the parents' reaction prompted me to look for a symptomatic act in this accident – one which aimed at expressing an evil intention directed against the beloved child. I was able to remove the contradiction between this and the father's contemporary affection for his child by shifting the impulse to injure it back to the time when this child had been the only one and had been so small that its father had not yet had any reason to take an affectionate interest in it. It was then easy for me to suppose that, as he was getting little satisfaction from his wife, he may at that time have had a thought or formed a decision of this kind: 'If this little creature that means nothing at all to me dies, I shall be free and able to get a divorce.' A wish for the death of the creature that he now loved so dearly must therefore have persisted unconsciously. From this point it was easy to find the path by which this wish had become unconsciously fixated. A powerful determinant was in fact provided by a memory from the patient's childhood: namely that the death of a small brother, for which his mother blamed his father's negligence, had led to violent quarrels between the parents and threats of a divorce. The subsequent course of my patient's marriage, as well as my therapeutic success, confirmed my conjecture.

Stärcke (1916)[1] has given an example of the way in which creative writers do not hesitate to put a bungled action in the place of an intentional action and to make it in this way the source of the gravest consequences:

'In one of Heijermans' (1914) sketches there occurs an example of a bungled action, or, more precisely, of a faulty action which the author uses as a dramatic *motif*.

'The sketch is called "Tom and Teddie". They are a pair of divers who appear in a variety theatre; their act is given in an iron tank with glass walls, in which they stay under water for a considerable time and perform tricks. Recently the wife has started an affair with another man, an animal-trainer. Her diver-husband has caught them together in the dressing-room just before the performance. Dead silence, menacing looks, with the diver saying: "Afterwards!" – The act begins. The diver is about to perform his hardest trick: he will remain "two and a half minutes under water in a hermetically sealed trunk". – This is a trick they had performed often enough; the trunk was locked and "Teddie used to show the key to the audience, who checked the time by their watches". She also used purposely to drop the key once or twice into the tank and then dive hurriedly after it, so as not to be too late when the time came for the trunk to be opened.

'"This particular evening, January 31st, saw Tom locked up as usual by the neat fingers of his brisk and nimble wife. He smiled behind the peep-hole – she played with the key and waited for his warning sign. The trainer stood in the wings, in his impeccable evening dress, with his white tie and his horse-whip. Here was the 'other man'. To catch her attention he gave a very short whistle. She looked at him, laughed, and with the clumsy gesture of someone whose attention is distracted she threw the key so wildly in the air that at exactly two minutes and twenty seconds, by an accurate reckoning, it fell by the side of the tank in the middle of the bunting covering the pedestal. No one had seen it. No one could see it. Viewed from the house

1. [This final example was added in 1917.]

the optical illusion was such that everyone saw the key fall into the water – and none of the stage hands heard it since the bunting muffled the sound.

"'Laughing, Teddie clambered without delay, over the edge of the tank. Laughing – Tom was holding out well – she came down the ladder. Laughing, she disappeared under the pedestal to look there, and, when she did not find the key at once, she bowed in front of the bunting with a priceless gesture, and an expression on her face as if to say 'Gracious me! what a nuisance this is!'.

"'Meanwhile Tom was grimacing in his droll way behind the peep-hole, as if he too was becoming agitated. The audience saw the white of his false teeth, the champing of his lips under the flaxen moustache, the comical bubble-blowing that they had seen earlier, when he was eating the apple. They saw his pale knuckles as he grappled and clawed, and they laughed as they had laughed so often already that evening.

"'Two minutes and fifty-eight seconds . . .

"'Three minutes and seven seconds . . . twelve seconds . . .

"'Bravo! Bravo! Bravo!

"'Then consternation broke out in the house and there was a shuffling of feet, when the stage hands and the trainer began to search too and the curtain came down before the lid had been raised.

"'Six English dancing-girls came on – then the man with the ponies, dogs and monkeys. And so on.

"'It was not till the next morning that the public knew there had been an accident, that Teddie had been left a widow . . ."

'It is clear from this quotation what an excellent understanding the author must himself have had of the nature of a symptomatic act, seeing that he demonstrates to us so strikingly the deeper cause of the fatal clumsiness.'

CHAPTER IX

SYMPTOMATIC AND CHANCE
ACTIONS[1]

THE actions described so far [Chapter VIII], in which we recognized the carrying out of an unconscious intention, made their appearance in the form of disturbances of other intended actions and concealed themselves behind the pretext of clumsiness. The 'chance' actions which are now to be discussed differ from 'bungled' actions merely in the fact that they scorn the support of a conscious intention and are therefore in no need of a pretext. They appear on their own account, and are permitted because they are not suspected of having any aim or intention. We perform them 'without thinking there is anything in them', 'quite accidentally', 'just to have something to do'; and such information, it is expected, will put an end to any enquiry into the significance of the action. In order to be able to enjoy this privileged position, these actions, which no longer put forward the excuse of clumsiness, have to fulfil certain conditions: they must be *unobtrusive* and their effects must be slight.

I have collected a large number of such chance actions from myself and from others, and after closely examining the different examples I have come to the conclusion that the name of *symptomatic acts* is a better one for them. They give expression to something which the agent himself does not suspect in them, and which he does not as a rule intend to impart to other people but to keep to himself. Thus, exactly like all the other phenomena which we have so far considered, they play the part of symptoms.

The richest supply of such chance or symptomatic acts is in fact to be obtained during the psychoanalytic treatment of

1. [The earlier portion of this chapter, up to p. 251, dates back to 1901.]

neurotics. I cannot resist quoting two examples from this source which show how extensively and in what detail these insignificant occurrences are determined by unconscious thoughts. The borderline between symptomatic acts and bungled actions is so ill-defined that I might equally well have included these examples in the last chapter.

(1) During a session a young married woman mentioned by way of association that she had been cutting her nails the day before and 'had cut into the flesh while she was trying to remove the soft cuticle at the bottom of the nail'. This is of so little interest that we ask ourselves in surprise why it was recalled and mentioned at all, and we begin to suspect that what we are dealing with is a symptomatic act. And in fact it turned out that the finger which was the victim of her small act of clumsiness was the ring-finger, the one on which a wedding ring is worn. What is more, it was her wedding anniversary; and in the light of this the injury to the soft cuticle takes on a very definite meaning, which can easily be guessed. At the same time, too, she related a dream which alluded to her husband's clumsiness and her anaethesia as a wife. But why was it the ring-finger on her *left* hand which she injured, whereas a wedding ring is worn [in her country] on the *right* hand? Her husband is a lawyer, a 'doctor of law' ['*Doktor der Rechte*', literally 'doctor of right(s)'], and as a girl her affections belonged in secret to a physician (jokingly called '*Doktor der Linke*' ['doctor of the left']). A 'left-handed marriage', too, has a definite meaning.

(2) A young unmarried lady said to me: 'Yesterday I quite unintentionally tore a hundred florin[1] note in two and gave half to a lady who was visiting me. Am I to take this as a symptomatic act as well?' Closer investigation disclosed the following particulars. The hundred florin note: – She devoted part of her time and means to charitable work. Together with another lady she was providing for the bringing up of an orphan. The hundred florins were the contribution sent to her

1. [Worth at the time approximately £8 or $40.]

by the other lady. She had put them in an envelope and placed it on her writing table for the time being.

The visitor was a lady of good standing whom she was assisting in another charitable cause. This lady wished to make a note of the names of a number of people whose support could be enlisted. There was no paper at hand, so my patient reached for the envelope on her desk, and without thinking of what it contained tore it in two: one piece she kept herself, so as to have a duplicate set of names, and the other she handed to her visitor. It should be observed that her act, though certainly inappropriate, was perfectly harmless. If a hundred florin note is torn up, it does not, as is well known, lose any of its value so long as it can be put together again completely from the fragments. The importance of the names on the piece of paper was a guarantee that the lady would not throw it away, and it was equally certain that she would restore the valuable contents as soon as she noticed them.

But what was the unconscious thought to which this chance action, made possible by forgetfulness, was meant to give expression? The visitor stood in a very definite relation to my patient's treatment. It was this lady who had formerly recommended me to her as a doctor, and, if I am not mistaken, my patient felt herself under an obligation to her for this advice. Was the half of the hundred florin note perhaps meant to represent a fee for her services as an intermediary? That would still be very strange.

Further material was however forthcoming. A little time before, a woman who was an intermediary of a very different kind had enquired of a relative of the patient's whether the young lady would perhaps like to make a certain gentleman's acquaintance; and that morning, a few hours before the lady's visit, the suitor's letter of proposal had arrived and had caused much amusement. So when the lady opened the conversation by enquiring after my patient's health, the latter might well have thought: 'You certainly found me the right doctor, but if you could help me to get the right husband' (with the further thought: 'and to get a child') 'I should be *more* grateful.' This thought, which was kept repressed, formed the starting-point from which the two intermediaries became fused into one, and she handed her visitor the fee which her phantasy was ready to give the other woman. This solution becomes entirely convincing when I add that I had been telling the patient about such chance or symptomatic acts only the evening before. She thereupon took the first opportunity of producing something analogous.

These extremely frequent chance and symptomatic acts might be arranged in three groups, according to whether they occur habitually, regularly under certain conditions, or sporadically.[1] Actions of the first group (such as playing with one's watch-chain, fingering one's beard and so on), which can almost be taken as characteristics of the person concerned, trench upon the multifarious movements known as *tics* and no doubt deserve to be dealt with in connection with them. In the second group I include playing with a stick or scribbling with a pencil that one happens to be holding, jingling coins in one's pocket, kneading bread-crumbs and other plastic materials, fiddling with one's clothing in all kinds of ways and so forth. During psychical treatment idle play of this sort regularly conceals a sense and meaning which are denied any other form of expression. Generally the person concerned is quite unaware that he is doing anything of the kind or that he has modified his usual play in certain ways; and he fails to see and hear the effects of these actions. He does not, for example, hear the noise made by the jingling of coins, and, if his attention is drawn to it, he behaves as though he were astonished and incredulous. All the things that a person does with his clothing, often without realizing it, are no less important and deserve

1. [The first two of these three groups are dealt with in the present paragraph. The third is not explicitly reached until p. 268, most of the intervening material having been added in the later editions of the book – though many of the interpolated examples seem in fact to belong already to the third 'sporadic' category.]

the doctor's attention. Every change in the clothing usually worn, every small sign of carelessness – such as an unfastened button – every trace of exposure, is intended to express something which the wearer of the clothes does not want to say straight out and which for the most part he is unaware of. The interpretations of these small chance actions, and the evidence for these interpretations, emerge each time with sufficient certainty from the material which accompanies them during the session, from the topic that is under discussion and from the associations that occur when attention is drawn to the apparently chance action. Because of this I shall not proceed to support my assertions with examples accompanied by analyses; but I mention these actions because I believe that they have the same meaning in the case of normal people as they have in my patients.

I cannot refrain from showing by at least one example[1] how close the connection can be between a symbolic action performed through force of habit and the most intimate and important aspects of a healthy person's life:[2]

'As Professor Freud has taught us, symbolism plays a greater role in the childhood of normal people than earlier psychoanalytical experiences had led one to expect. In this connection the following short analysis may be of some interest, especially in view of its medical subject-matter.

'A doctor on rearranging his furniture in a new house came across an old-fashioned, straight wooden stethoscope, and, after pausing to decide where he should put it, was impelled to place it on the side of his writing-desk in such a position that it stood exactly between his chair and the one reserved for his patients. The act in itself was somewhat odd, for two reasons. In the first

---

1. [Added in 1912.]

2. Ernest Jones (1910a). [The German text is considerably longer than the published English version, and differs slightly from it. The present version follows the German, though keeping to the English wherever possible.]

place he does not use a stethoscope at all often (he is in fact a neurologist) and if he needs one he uses a binaural one. In the second place all his medical apparatus and instruments were kept in drawers, with the sole exception of this one. However, he gave no further thought to the matter until one day a patient, who had never seen a straight stethoscope, asked him what it was. On being told, she asked why he kept it just there; he answered in an off-hand way that that place was as good as any other. This started him thinking, however, and he wondered whether there had been any unconscious motive in his action, and being familiar with the psychoanalytical method he decided to investigate the matter.

'The first memory that occurred to him was the fact that when a medical student he had been struck by the habit his hospital interne had of always carrying in his hand a straight stethoscope on his ward visits, although he never used it. He greatly admired this interne, and was much attached to him. Later on, when he himself became an interne, he contracted the same habit, and would feel very uncomfortable if by mistake he left his room without having the instrument to swing in his hand. The aimlessness of the habit was however shown, not only by the fact that the only stethoscope he ever used was a binaural one, which he carried in his pocket, but also in that it was continued when he was a surgical interne and never needed any stethoscope at all. The significance of these observations immediately becomes clear if we refer to the phallic nature of this symbolic action.

'He next recalled the fact that in his early childhood he had been struck by the family doctor's habit of carrying a straight stethoscope inside his hat; he found it interesting that the doctor should always have his chief instrument handy when he went to see patients and only had to take off his hat (i.e. a part of his clothing) and "pull it out". As a small child he had been strongly attached to this doctor; and a brief self-analysis enabled him to discover that at the age of three and a half he had had a double phantasy concerning the birth of a younger sister –

namely that she was the child, firstly, of himself and his mother, and secondly, of the doctor and himself. Thus in this phantasy he played both a masculine and a feminine part. He further recalled having been examined by the same doctor when he was six, and distinctly recollected the voluptuous sensation of feeling the doctor's head near him pressing the stethoscope into his chest, and the rhythmic to-and-fro respiratory movement. At the age of three he had had a chronic chest affection which necessitated repeated examination, although he could not in fact still remember it.

'At the age of eight he was impressed by being told by an older boy that it was the doctor's custom to get into bed with his women patients. There certainly was some real basis for this rumour; at all events the women of the neighbourhood, including the subject's own mother, were very attached to the young and handsome doctor. The subject had himself on several occasions experienced sexual temptations in regard to his women patients; he had twice fallen in love with one and finally had married one. It can hardly be doubted that his unconscious identification with the doctor was the chief motive for his adoption of the medical profession. Other analyses lead us to suppose that this is undoubtedly the commonest motive (though it is hard to determine just how common). In the present case it was doubly determined; firstly by the superiority of the doctor on several occasions over the father, of whom the son was very jealous, and secondly by the doctor's knowledge of forbidden topics and his opportunities for sexual satisfaction.

'Then came a dream which I have already published elsewhere (Jones 1910b); it was plainly of a homosexual-masochistic nature. In this dream a man who was a substitutive figure for the doctor attacked the subject with a "sword". The sword reminded him of a passage in the Völsung Nibelungen Saga, where Sigurd places a naked sword between himself and the sleeping Brünhilde. The same episode occurs in the Arthurian legend which our subject also knows well.

'The meaning of the symptomatic act now becomes clear.

Our doctor placed his straight stethoscope between himself and his women patients exactly as Sigurd placed his sword between himself and the woman he was not to touch. The act was a compromise-formation: it satisfied two impulses. It served to satisfy in his imagination the suppressed wish to enter into sexual relations with any attractive woman patient, but at the same time it served to remind him that this wish could not become a reality. It was, so to speak, a charm against yielding to temptation.

'I might add that the following lines from Lord Lytton's *Richelieu* made a great impresson on the boy:

> Beneath the rule of men entirely great
> The pen is mightier than the sword . . .[1]

and that he has become a prolific writer and uses an exceptionally large fountain pen. When I asked him why he needed it he gave the characteristic response: "I have so much to express."

'This analysis again reminds us what profound insight is afforded into mental life by "innocent" and "meaningless" acts, and how early in life the tendency to symbolization develops.'

I can quote a further instance from[2] my psychotherapeutic experience in which eloquent testimony was borne by a hand playing with a lump of bread-crumb. My patient was a boy of not yet thirteen: for almost two years he had been severely hysterical and I finally took him for psychoanalytic treatment after a lengthy stay in a hydropathic institution had brought no success. I was going on the assumption that he must have had sexual experiences and be tormented by sexual questions, which was likely enough at his age; but I refrained from helping him with explanations as I wished to put my hypotheses

1. 'Compare Oldham's: "I wear my pen, as others do their sword."'
[From 'Satire upon a Printer' by John Oldham (1653–83).]
2. [This example dates back to 1901.]

once again to the test. I was therefore naturally curious as to the way in which he would bring out what I was looking for. One day it struck me that he was rolling something between the fingers of his right hand; he would thrust it in his pocket and continue playing with it there, and then take it out again and so on. I did not ask what he had in his hand; but he suddenly opened his hand and showed me. It was bread-crumb kneaded into a lump. At the next session he again brought along a similar lump and this time, while we were talking, he modelled figures out of it which excited my interest; he did this with incredible rapidity, with his eyes closed. They were undoubtedly little men, with a head, two arms and two legs, like the crudest prehistoric idols, and with an appendage between the legs which he drew out into a long point. He had hardly completed this when he kneaded the figure together again; later he allowed it to remain, but drew out a similar appendage from the surface of the back and other parts of the body in order to disguise the meaning of the first one. I wanted to show him I had understood him, but at the same time I wanted to prevent him from pretending that he had not thought of anything while he was engaged in making these figures. With this in mind I suddenly asked him if he remembered the story of the Roman king who gave his son's envoy an answer in dumb-show in his garden. The boy failed to recall it, although he must have learnt it so much more recently than I. He asked whether it was the story of the slave and the answer that was written on his shaven head.[1] No, I answered, that is from Greek history, and I told him the story. King Tarquinius Superbus[2] had made

1. [The story is to be found in Herodotus, Book V, Chapter 35.]

2. [In the editions of 1901 and 1904: 'Tarquinius Priscus'. In his interleaved copy of the 1904 edition (cf. Editor's Introduction, p. 35) Freud has made an imperfectly legible comment on this slip. The gist of his comment is that in substituting the name of the father for that of the son he was anticipating the remarks which he makes later on in this book (p. 279) on a similar substitution of Zeus for Kronos in *The Interpretation of Dreams*. The topic of castration provided the link between the two examples.]

his son Sextus find his way secretly into a hostile Latin city. The son, who had meanwhile collected a following in the city, sent a messenger to the king asking what steps he should take next. The king did not answer, but went into his garden, had the question repeated to him there, and then silently struck off the heads of the tallest and finest poppies. All that the messenger could do was to report this to Sextus, who understood his father and arranged for the most distinguished citizens in the city to be removed by assassination.

While I was speaking, the boy stopped kneading and, as I was on the point of describing what the king did in his garden and had reached the words 'silently struck', he made a lightning movement and tore the head off his little man. He had therefore understood me and had seen that he had been understood by me. I could now question him directly, I gave him the information he needed, and in a short time we had brought the neurosis to an end.

The symptomatic acts[1] that can be observed in almost inexhaustible abundance in healthy people no less than in sick ones have more than one claim to our interest. To the doctor they often serve as valuable clues which enable him to get his bearings in new or unfamiliar situations; to the observer of human nature they often betray everything – and at times even more than he cares to know. A person who is familiar with their significance may at times feel like King Solomon who, according to oriental legend, understood the language of animals. One day I was to examine a young man, whom I did not know, at his mother's house. As he came towards me I was struck by a large stain on his trousers – made by albumen, as I could tell from its peculiar stiff edges. After a moment's embarrassment the young man apologized and said that he had felt hoarse and so had swallowed a raw egg; some of the slippery white of egg had probably fallen on his clothes. He was able to confirm this by pointing to the egg-shell, which was still visible in the room on a small plate. In this way the suspicious stain was given an

1. [This paragraph was added in 1907.]

innocent explanation; but when his mother had left us alone I thanked him for making my diagnosis so very much easier, and without more ado took as the basis of our discussion his confession that he was suffering from the troubles arising from masturbation. Another time I was paying a visit to a lady who was as rich as she was miserly and foolish, and who was in the habit of giving the doctor the task of working through a host of complaints before the simple cause of her condition could be reached. When I entered she was sitting at a small table and was busy arranging silver florins in little piles. On rising she knocked some of the coins on to the floor. I helped her to pick them up, and soon cut short her account of her sufferings by asking: 'Has your noble son-in-law robbed you of so much money then?' She denied this angrily, only to go on very soon afterwards to tell the sad story of the agitation which her son-in-law's extravagance had caused her. She has not however sent for me since. I cannot claim that one always makes friends of those to whom one shows the meaning of their symptomatic acts.

Dr J. E. G. van Emden (The Hague) reports another case of 'confession through a parapraxis'.[1] 'In making out my bill, the waiter in a small restaurant in Berlin announced that the price of a particular dish had been increased by ten pfennigs, owing to the war. When I asked why this was not shown on the menu he replied that that must just be an oversight – the price had certainly gone up. He pocketed the money clumsily and dropped a ten pfennig coin on the table right in front of me.

'"Now I know for certain that you've charged me too much. Would you like me to enquire at the cash desk?"

'"Excuse me . . . one moment, please," and he had gone.

'Needless to say, I allowed him his retreat, and, after he had apologized a couple of minutes later for having for some unknown reason confused my dish with another one, I let him keep the ten pfennigs as a reward for his contribution to the psychopathology of everyday life.'

1. [Added in 1919.]

Anyone[1] who cares to observe his fellow men while they are at table will be able to observe the neatest and most instructive symptomatic acts.

Thus Dr Hanns Sachs relates: 'I happened to be present when an elderly couple, relatives of mine, took their evening meal. The lady suffered from a gastric complaint and had to observe a very strict diet. A piece of roast meat had just been set before the husband, and he asked his wife, who was not allowed to join in this course, to pass him the mustard. His wife opened the cupboard, reached inside, and put her little bottle of stomach drops on the table in front of her husband. There was of course no resemblance between the barrel-shaped mustard pot and the little bottle of drops which might have accounted for her picking up the wrong one; yet the wife did not notice her confusion of the two until her husband laughingly called her attention to it. The meaning of the symptomatic act needs no explanation.'

I owe to Dr B. Dattner, of Vienna, an excellent example of this kind which the observer made very skilful use of:

'I was lunching in a restaurant with my colleague H., a doctor of philosophy. He spoke of the hardships of probationary students, and mentioned incidentally that before he had finished his studies he was given the post of secretary to the ambassador, or, more precisely, the minister plenipotentiary and extraordinary, of Chile. "But then the minister was transferred and I did not present myself to his successor." While he was uttering the last sentence he raised a piece of cake to his mouth, but let it drop from the knife in apparent clumsiness. I immediately grasped the hidden meaning of this symptomatic act, and, as it were casually, interjected to my colleague, who was unfamiliar with psychoanalysis: "You certainly allowed a tasty morsel to slip from you there." He did not, however, notice that my words could apply equally well to his symptomatic act, and repeated my exact words with a peculiarly

1. [This paragraph and the four examples which follow were added in 1912.]

charming and surprising liveliness just as if my remark had taken the words out of his mouth: "Yes, that was certainly a tasty morsel that I allowed to slip from me", and went on to unburden himself by means of a detailed description of the clumsiness which had lost him this well-paid position.

'The meaning of the symbolic symptomatic act becomes clearer if it is realized that my colleague had scruples about telling a fairly remote acquaintance like myself of his precarious material situation, and that the obstrusive thought thereupon disguised itself as a symptomatic act which expressed symbolically what was meant to be hidden and in this way afforded the speaker relief which arose from unconscious sources.'

The following examples will show how much meaning may turn out to lie in an apparently unintentional act of carrying something off or taking something away with one.

Dr B. Dattner relates: 'A colleague paid a visit to a friend, a lady he had much admired in the days of his youth; it was the first visit after her marriage. He told me of this visit and expressed his surprise at the fact that he had not succeeded in keeping his resolution to stay only a very short time with her. He then went on to recount a singular parapraxis which had happened to him there. His friend's husband, who had joined in the conversation, had looked for a box of matches which had quite definitely been on the top of the table when he arrived. My colleague, too, had looked through his pockets to see whether he had not accidentally "snapped it up",[1] but without avail. Some time later he had in fact found "it" in his pocket, and was struck by the fact that there was only a single match in the box. – A dream a few days later which prominently displayed the match-box symbolism and was concerned with this same friend of his youth confirmed my explanation that my colleague's symptomatic act was intended to announce that he had prior rights and to demonstrate his claim to exclusive possession (only one match in the box).'

1. [In German the word for 'box' ('*Schachtel*') is feminine; so that this might equally mean 'snapped *her* up'.]

Dr Hanns Sachs relates: 'Our maid is particularly fond of a certain kind of cake. There is no possible doubt of this, as it is the only thing that she always makes well. One Sunday she brought in this particular cake, put it down on the sideboard, removed the plates and cutlery of the previous course and stacked them on the tray on which she had brought in the cake; she then put the cake back on the top of this pile instead of on the table, and disappeared with it into the kitchen. Our first idea was that she had noticed something that ought to be put right about the cake, but when she failed to appear again my wife rang and asked: "Betty, what has happened to the cake?" "How do you mean?" replied the maid, not understanding. We had first to point out to her that she had taken the cake away with her again. She had put it on the pile of dishes, carried it out and put it away "without noticing". – Next day, as we were about to eat what remained of this cake, my wife noticed that there was just as much as we had left the day before – in other words, that the maid had rejected her own share of her favourite dish. When asked why she had not eaten any of the cake she replied in some embarrassment that she had not wanted any. – The infantile attitude is very clear on both occasions: first the childish insatiability which did not want to share the object of her wishes with anyone, followed by the equally childish defiant reaction: "If you grudge it me, keep it for yourselves; I don't want anything at all now."'

Chance actions and symptomatic acts[1] occurring in matrimonial matters often have the most serious significance and might induce people who disregard the psychology of the unconscious to believe in omens. [Cf. p. 320 f., footnote.] It is not a happy beginning when a young bride loses her wedding-ring on the honeymoon; but after all it is usually only mislaid and is soon found again. – I know a lady, now divorced from her husband, who in managing her money affairs frequently signed documents in her maiden name, many years before she in fact resumed it. – I was once the guest of a young married

1. [This paragraph was added in 1907.]

couple and heard the young woman laughingly describe her
latest experience. The day after her return from the honeymoon
she had called for her unmarried sister to go shopping with her
as she used to do, while her husband went to his business.
Suddenly she noticed a gentleman on the other side of the street,
and nudging her sister had cried: 'Look, there goes Herr L.'
She had forgotten that this gentleman had been her husband
for some weeks. I felt a cold chill as I heard the story, but I did
not dare to draw the inference. The little incident only occurred
to my mind some years later when the marriage had come to
a most unhappy end.

The following observation[1] is quoted from one of Alphonse
Maeder's valuable studies, published in French (Maeder, 1906).
It might equally well have been included among the examples
of forgetting:

'Une dame nous racontait récemment qu'elle avait oublié
d'essayer sa robe de noce et s'en souvint la veille du mariage
à huit heures du soir; la couturière désespérait de voir sa cliente.
Ce détail suffit à montrer que la fiancée ne se sentait pas
très heureuse de porter une robe d'épouse, elle cherchait à
oublier cette représentation pénible. Elle est aujourd'hui . . .
divorcée.'[2]

A friend who has learnt to read signs[3] has told me that the
great actress Eleonora Duse introduces into one of her parts a
symptomatic act which clearly shows the depths from which
she draws her artistry. It is a drama of adultery; she has just
had an altercation with her husband and now stands apart
deep in thought, before the seducer approaches. During the
short interval she plays with her wedding ring, takes it off her

1. [Added in 1910.]
2. ['A lady was telling us recently how she had forgotten to try on her
wedding dress and remembered it at eight o'clock on the eve of her
wedding. The dressmaker had given up hope of seeing her customer.
This detail was enough to show that the bride did not feel very happy
about wearing a wedding-dress; she was trying to forget the painful
performance. To-day . . . she is divorced.']
3. [This paragraph was added in 1907.]

finger, puts it on again, and then once more takes it off. She is now ready for the other man.

I add here an account by Theodor Reik (1915)[1] of some other symptomatic acts involving rings.

'We are familiar with the symptomatic acts of married people which consist in their taking off and replacing their wedding rings. My colleague M. produced a series of similar symptomatic acts. He had received a ring as a present from a girl he was in love with, with a note saying that he must not lose it or she would know that he did not love her any more. Subsequently he grew increasingly worried that he might lose the ring. If he had temporarily taken it off (for example while he was washing) it would regularly be mislaid, so that often it could only be found again after a long search. When he was posting a letter he could not suppress a slight fear that the ring might be pulled off by the edges of the letter-box. On one occasion he managed things so clumsily that the ring *did* fall into the box. The letter he was sending off on that occasion was a parting note to an earlier lady-love of his, and he felt guilty towards her. Simultaneously he was filled with a longing for this other lady which conflicted with his feelings towards his present love-object.'

The theme of the ring[2] leaves one once again with the impression of how hard it is for a psychoanalyst to discover anything new that has not been known before by some creative writer. In Fontane's novel *Vor dem Sturm*, Justizrat Turgany declares during a game of forfeits: 'You may be sure, ladies, that the deepest secrets of nature are revealed in the pledging of forfeits.' Among the examples he uses to support his claim there is one that deserves our special interest: 'I recall a professor's wife – she had reached the age of *embonpoint* – who again and again pulled off her wedding ring to offer it as a forfeit. Do not ask me to describe the happiness of her marriage.' He then went on: 'In the same company there was a gentleman who

1. [Added in 1917.]
2. [This paragraph and the next two were added in 1919.]

never tired of depositing his English pocket-knife, with its ten blades, corkscrew and flint and steel, in the ladies' laps, until the bladed monster, after tearing several silk dresses, finally disappeared amid general cries of indignation.'

We shall not be surprised if an object of such rich symbolic meaning as a ring should be made to play a part in some significant parapraxes, even where it does not, in the form of a wedding ring or an engagement ring, mark an erotic tie. The following example of an occurrence of this sort has been put at my disposal by Dr M. Kardos:

'Several years ago a man who is much my junior attached himself to me; he shares my intellectual endeavours and stands to me somewhat in the relation of a pupil to his teacher. On one particular occasion I presented him with a ring; and this ring has several times given rise to symptomatic acts or parapraxes, whenever anything in our relationship has met with his disapproval. A short time ago he was able to report the following case, which is particularly neat and transparent. We used to meet once a week, when he regularly came to see me and talk with me; but on one occasion he made an excuse to stay away, as a *rendezvous* with a young lady seemed more attractive to him. The following morning he noticed – not, however, until long after he had left the house – that the ring was not on his finger. He did not worry any more about it, since he assumed he had left it behind on his bedside table, where he put it every evening, and would find it there when he got home. As soon as he reached home he looked for it, without success, and then began a systematic search of the room, which was equally fruitless. At last it crossed his mind that the ring had been lying on the bedside table – just as had been the case, in fact, for more than a year – beside a small pocket-knife that he normally carried in his waistcoat pocket; the suspicion thus occurred to him that he might have "absent-mindedly" pocketed the ring with the knife. So he felt in his pocket and found that the missing ring was in fact there. "His wedding-ring in his waistcoat pocket" is a proverbial way of referring to

the place where the ring is kept by a husband who intends to
betray the wife who gave it to him. My friend's feeling of guilt
had therefore caused him first to punish himself ("you no
longer deserve to wear this ring") and secondly to confess his
unfaithfulness, though only in the form of an unwitnessed
parapraxis. It was only in a roundabout way, while he was
describing this parapraxis – an eventuality which could,
incidentally, have been foreseen – that he came to confess
his little "unfaithfulness".'

I also know of an elderly man[1] who married a very young
girl and who decided to spend the wedding night in a hotel in
town instead of on the honeymoon journey. Hardly had they
reached the hotel when he noticed in alarm that he was without his wallet, which contained all the money for the honeymoon; he had either mislaid it or lost it. He was still able to
reach his servant by telephone; the latter found the missing
wallet in the discarded wedding suit and brought it to the hotel
to the waiting bridegroom who had accordingly entered upon
his marriage without means [ohne Vermögen]. He was thus able
to start his journey with his young bride next morning. In the
night, however, he had, as he had apprehensively foreseen,
proved 'incapable [unvermögend]'.[2]

It is consoling to reflect that there is an unsuspected extension
of the human habit of 'losing things' – namely, symptomatic
acts, and that this habit is consequently welcome, at least to a
secret intention of the loser's. It is often only an expression of
the low estimation in which the lost object is held, or of a
secret antipathy towards it or towards the person that it came
from; or else the inclination to lose the object has been transferred to it from other more important objects by a symbolic
association of thoughts. Losing objects of value serves to express
a variety of impulses; it may either be acting as a symbolic
representation of a repressed thought – that is, it may be repeat-

1. [This paragraph and the following one were added in 1907.]
2. ['Unvermögend', 'without means', 'without power', and so 'im-
potent'.]

ing a warning that one would be glad enough to ignore –, or (most commonly of all) it may be offering a sacrifice to the obscure powers of destiny to whom homage is still paid among us to-day.[1]

Here are a few examples to illustrate these remarks about losing things.[2]

Dr B. Dattner: 'A colleague told me he had unexpectedly lost his "Penkala"[3] pencil which he had had for over two years and which he valued highly because of its superior quality. Analysis revealed the following facts. The day before, my colleague had received a thoroughly disagreeable letter from his brother-in-law, which concluded with the sentence: "I have neither the inclination nor the time at present to encourage you in your frivolity and laziness." The affect connected with this letter was so powerful that next day my colleague promptly sacrificed the pencil, *which was a present from this brother-in-law*, so as not to feel under too great an obligation to him.'

A lady of my acquaintance understandably refrained from visiting the theatre while in mourning for her old mother. There were only a few days still to elapse before the end of her year of mourning, and she allowed herself to be persuaded by her friends to buy a ticket for a particularly interesting performance. On reaching the theatre she made the discovery that she had lost the ticket. She thought afterwards that she had thrown it away with her tram ticket on leaving the tram. This lady used to pride herself on never losing anything through carelessness.

1. [A footnote inserted in the 1907 edition at this point, and extended in subsequent editions, contained a number of shorter examples of symptomatic acts. These were transferred to the text in the 1924 edition and will be found on pp. 272–5 below.]

2. [This last sentence, the example from Dattner which follows, and the sentence on p. 266 below referring to Rank's article, were added in 1912. The two intervening paragraphs on this page and the next were added in 1917 and 1920.]

3. [The trade name of a special form of pencil.]

It is therefore fair to assume that another experience she had of losing something was not without a good reason either. On her arrival at a health resort she decided to pay a visit to a pension where she had stayed on an earlier occasion. She was welcomed there as an old friend and entertained, and when she wanted to pay she was told she was to look on herself as a guest; but this she did not feel was quite proper. It was agreed that she might leave something for the maid who had waited on her, so she opened her purse to put a one mark note on the table. In the evening the pension's manservant brought her a five mark note which had been found under the table and which the proprietress thought must belong to the lady. She must therefore have dropped it from her purse in getting out the tip for the maid. She had probably wanted to pay her bill in spite of everything.

An article of some length by Otto Rank (1911 [450]) makes use of dream-analysis to expose the sacrificial mood that forms the basis of this act [of losing something], and to reveal its deeper motives.[1] It is of interest when he writes later that often not only losing objects but also *finding* them appears to be [psychologically] determined. In what sense this is to be understood may be gathered from his story, which I include here (Rank, 1915a). It is obvious that in cases of losing, the object is already provided; in cases of finding, it has first to be looked for.

'A girl who was materially dependent on her parents wished to buy a piece of cheap jewellery. She enquired in the shop about the price of the article she fancied, but was disappointed to find that it cost more than the sum she had saved. All the same, it was only a matter of two kronen that stood between her and this small pleasure. In a depressed mood she began to stroll home through the streets, which were thronged with the evening crowds. Though she describes herself as having been

1. [*Footnote added* 1917:] Other articles on the same topic will be found in the *Zentralblatt für Psychoanalyse*, **2** [1912], and in the *Internationale Zeitschrift für Psychoanalyse*, **1** (1913). – [The rest of the paragraph in the text, and the example which follows, were also added in 1917.]

deep in thought, she suddenly noticed lying on the ground, in one of the busiest squares, a small piece of paper which she had just passed by without attending to it. She turned round, picked it up and was astonished to find it was a folded two kronen note. She thought: "This has been sent me by fate so that I can buy the jewellery", and started happily back with the idea of taking the hint. But at the same moment she told herself that she ought not to do so, since money that one finds is lucky money and should not be spent.

'The bit of analysis which would make this "chance action" intelligible may probably be inferred from the situation described, even in the absence of personal information from the girl herself. Among the reflections that occupied her mind as she was walking home, the thought of her poverty and her restricted material position must no doubt have bulked large; moreover we may guess that that thought took the form of a wishful removal of her straitened circumstances. The idea of how the required sum could most easily be obtained will surely have arisen from her interest in satisfying her modest wish; and it will have suggested the simplest solution – namely, that of finding the money. In this way her unconscious (or preconscious) was predisposed towards "finding", even though – owing to claims on her attention from other quarters ("deep in thought") – the actual thought did not become fully conscious to her. We may go further and, on the strength of similar cases which have been analysed, actually assert that *unconscious* "readiness to look for something" is much more likely to lead to success than consciously directed attention. Otherwise it would be almost impossible to explain how it was that precisely this one person out of the many hundreds of passers-by – and with all the difficulties caused by the poor street-lighting and the dense crowds – was able to make the find that came as a surprise to her herself. Some indication of the actual strength of this unconscious or preconscious readiness may be obtained from the remarkable fact that *after* making this find – that is, at a time when the attitude had become superfluous and had certainly been removed from conscious attention – the girl found a handkerchief at a later point on her way home, in a dark and lonely part of a suburban street.'

It must be said[1] that it is precisely such symptomatic acts that often offer the best approach to an understanding of people's intimate mental life.

Turning now to the chance actions that occur sporadically,[2] I will report an example which suggested a comparatively deep interpretation even without analysis. It gives a clear illustration of the conditions under which such symptoms can be produced entirely unobtrusively, and it enables me to subjoin a remark of practical importance. In the course of a summer holiday it happened that I had to wait a few days at a particular place for the arrival of my travelling companion. In the meantime I made the acquaintance of a young man who also seemed to be lonely and was willing enough to join me. As we were staying at the same hotel it was natural for us to take all our meals and walks together. On the afternoon of the third day he suddenly told me that he was expecting his wife to arrive by train that evening. My psychological interest was now aroused, for I had already been struck that morning by my companion's rejecting my proposal for a longish expedition and objecting during our short walk to taking a certain path which he said was too steep and dangerous. On our afternoon walk he suddenly remarked that I must no doubt be hungry; I must certainly not delay my evening meal on his account – he was going to wait for his wife to arrive and have supper with her. I took the hint and sat down to dinner while he went to the station. Next morning we met in the hall of the hotel. He introduced me to his wife and then said: 'You'll have breakfast with us, won't you?' I had first to go on a small errand in the next street, but promised to be back soon. When I entered the breakfast room, I saw that the couple were both sitting on the same

1. [This paragraph was added in 1912.]
2. [See footnote, p. 250. – This paragraph and the following one date back to 1901.]

side of a small table by the window. On the opposite side there was only one chair; the husband's big, heavy waterproof cape had been hung over the back of it, covering the seat. I understood very well the meaning of the coat's being arranged in that way; it had certainly not been done deliberately and was therefore all the more expressive. It meant: 'There's no room for you here, you're superfluous now.' The husband failed to notice that I was standing in front of the table without sitting down; but his wife did, and quickly nudged her husband and whispered: 'Look, you've taken up the gentleman's seat.'

This and other similar experiences have led me to conclude that actions carried out unintentionally must inevitably become the source of misunderstandings in human relations. The agent, who knows nothing of there being an intention connected with these actions, does not feel that they are chargeable to him and does not hold himself responsible for them. The second party, on the other hand, since he regularly bases his conclusions as to the agent's intentions and sentiments on such actions among others, knows more of the other's psychical processes than that person himself is ready to admit or believes he has communicated. The agent, indeed, grows indignant if these conclusions drawn from his symptomatic acts are brought up against him; he declares them to be baseless, since he is not conscious of having had the intention at the time they were carried out, and complains of being misunderstood by the second party. Strictly considered, misunderstandings of this kind are based on too intimate and too extensive understanding. The more two people suffer from 'nerves', the more readily will they give each other cause for disputes the responsibility for which each disclaims just as decidely in regard to himself as he considers it certain in regard to the other person. And this is no doubt the punishment for people's internal dishonesty in only giving expression under the pretext of forgetting, bungling and doing things unintentionally to impulses that would better be admitted to themselves and to others if they can no longer be controlled. It can in fact be said quite generally that everyone is continually practising psychical analysis on his neighbours and consequently learns to know them better than they know themselves. The road whose goal it is to observe the precept γνῶθι σεαυτόν[1] runs *viâ* the study of one's own apparently accidental actions and omissions.

Of all the writers[2] who have from time to time passed comment on our minor symptomatic acts and parapraxes, or who have made use of them, none has understood their secret nature so clearly or exhibited them in so uncannily lifelike a manner as Strindberg – a man whose genius in recognizing such things was, it is true, assisted by grave mental abnormality.[3] Dr Karl Weiss of Vienna (1913) has drawn attention to the following passage in one of his works:

'After a while the Count did in fact come, and he approached Esther quietly, as though he had a *rendezvous* with her.

'"Have you been waiting long?" he asked in his low voice.

'"Six months, as you know," answered Esther; "but did you see me to-day?"

'"Yes, just now, in the tram: and I looked into your eyes feeling that I was talking to you."

'"A great deal has 'happened' since the last time."

'"Yes, and I believed it was all over between us."

'"How so?"

'"All the little gifts that I had from you broke in pieces – in an occult way, what is more. But that is something that has been noticed long, long ago."

'"Dear me! Now I remember a whole set of events that I took to be accidents. Once I was given a pair of pince-nez by my grandmother, at a time we were good friends. They were made of polished rock-crystal and were excellent for making

1. ['Know thyself' – the celebrated inscription in the Temple of Apollo at Delphi.]

2. [This paragraph and the passage from Strindberg were added in 1917.]

3. [The facility with which paranoics can correctly interpret symptomatic acts in other people is discussed below, pp. 317–18.]

post-mortems[1] – a real miracle of which I took the greatest care. One day I broke with the old lady and she was angry with me. And during the next post-mortem the lenses happened to fall out for no reason. I thought they were simply broken and sent them to be repaired. But no, they went on refusing to help me; they were put in a drawer and got lost."

"'Dear me! Strange that things that concern the eyes should be the most sensitive. I was once given some opera glasses by a friend; they suited my eyes so well that it was a pleasure to use them. This friend and I fell out. You know how it happens without visible cause; it seems as though one were not allowed to be in harmony. The next time I wanted to use the opera glasses I could not see clearly. The cross-piece was too short and I saw two images. I don't need to tell you that the cross-piece had not grown shorter and my eyes had not grown further apart! It was a miracle that happens every day – one that bad observers do not notice. How can we explain it? *The psychical power of hatred must be greater than we suppose.* – What is more, the ring that I had from you has lost its stone and will not let itself be repaired; no, it will not. Do you want to part from me, then? . . .'" (*The Gothic Rooms*, German trans., p. 258f.)

In the field of symptomatic acts, too,[2] psychoanalytic observation must concede priority to imaginative writers. It can only repeat what they have said long ago. Wilhelm Stross has drawn my attention to the following passage in Laurence Sterne's celebrated humorous novel, *Tristram Shandy* (Volume VI, Chapter V):

'. . . And I am not at all surprized that *Gregory of Nazianzum*, upon observing the hasty and untoward gestures of *Julian*, should foretel he would one day become an apostate; – or that St *Ambrose* should turn his *Amanuensis* out of doors, because of an indecent motion of his head, which went backwards and forwards like a flail; – or that *Democritus* should conceive *Prota-*

1. [Esther Borg, in Strindberg's novel, was a doctor.]
2. [This paragraph and the quotation from Sterne were added in 1920.]

goras to be a scholar, from seeing him bind up a faggot, and thrusting, as he did it, the small twigs inwards. – There are a thousand unnoticed openings, continued my father, which let a penetrating eye at once into a man's soul; and I maintain it, added he, that a man of sense does not lay down his hat in coming into a room, – or take it up in going out of it, but something escapes, which discovers him.'

I add here a brief and varied collection of symptomatic acts found in healthy and neurotic people:[1]

An elderly colleague who was not a good loser at cards had one evening paid up a largish sum of money that he had lost. He did this without complaining but in a peculiarly restrained mood. After his departure it was discovered that he had left behind at his seat more or less everything he had on him: spectacles, cigar-case and handkerchief. This no doubt calls for the translation: 'You robbers! You have well and truly plundered me!'

A man suffering from occasional sexual impotence, which originated from the intimacy of his relations with his mother in childhood, related that he was in the habit of decorating pamphlets and notes with the letter S, his mother's initial. He cannot bear letters from home coming in contact with other profane correspondence on his desk, and is therefore forced to put the former away separately.

A young lady suddenly flung open the door of the consulting room though the woman who preceded her had not yet left it. In apologizing she blamed her 'thoughtlessness'; it soon turned out that she had been demonstrating the curiosity that in the past had caused her to make her way into her parents' bedroom.

Girls who are proud of having beautiful hair are able to

1. [What follows from this point to the end of the chapter first appeared as a footnote in the 1907 edition (see p. 265 above), and was added to in later editions. It was transferred to the text and to its present position in 1924. – Except where otherwise stated the examples date from 1907.]

manage their combs and hairpins in such a way that their hair comes down in the middle of a conversation.

Some men scatter small change out of their trouser pockets while they are lying down during treatment and in that way pay whatever fee they think appropriate for the session.

People who forget to take away articles they have brought to the physician's house, such as pince-nez, gloves and purses, are showing by this that they cannot tear themselves away and would like to come back soon. Ernest Jones [1911b, 508] says: 'One can almost measure the success with which a physician is practising psychotherapy, for instance, by the size of the collection of umbrellas, handkerchiefs, purses, and so on, that he could make in a month.'[1]

The slightest actions of a habitual nature which are performed with a minimum of attention, such as winding up one's watch before going to sleep, switching off the light before leaving a room, etc., are subject from time to time to disturbances that unmistakably demonstrate the influence of unconscious complexes upon what would seem to be the most fixed habits. Maeder, writing in the periodical *Coenobium* [1909], tells of a house-physician who decided to go into town one evening for an important engagement, although he was on duty and was not supposed to leave the hospital. When he returned he was surprised to find the light on in his room. He had forgotten to turn it off when he went out, which was something that he had never failed to do before. But he soon grasped the motive for his forgetfulness. The chief resident medical officer in the hospital would naturally have concluded from the light in the house-physician's room that he was at home.

A man overburdened with worries and subject to occasional depressions assured me that he regularly found in the morning that his watch had run down whenever the evening before life had seemed to be altogether too harsh and unfriendly. By omit-

1. [This last sentence was added in 1912, and the following two paragraphs in 1910.]

ting to wind up his watch he was giving symbolic expression to his indifference about living till the next day.

Another man,[1] whom I do not know personally, writes: 'After fate had dealt me a hard blow, life seemed so harsh and unfriendly that I imagined I had not sufficient strength to live through the next day. I then noticed that almost every day I forgot to wind up my watch. Previously I have never failed to do so; it was something I did regularly before going to bed, as an almost mechanical and unconscious act. But now I only very rarely remembered to do it, and that was when I had something important or specially interesting ahead of me. Should this too be considered a symptomatic act? I could not explain it to myself at all.'

If anyone takes the trouble, as Jung (1907) and Maeder (1909)[2] have done, to note the tunes that he finds himself humming, unintentionally and often without noticing he is doing so, he will pretty regularly be able to discover the connection between the words of the song and a subject that is occupying his mind.

The subtler determinants, too,[3] of the expression of one's thoughts in speaking or writing deserve careful attention. We believe that in general we are free to choose what words we shall use for clothing our thoughts or what images for disguising them. Closer observation shows that other considerations determine this choice, and that behind the form in which the thought is expressed a glimpse may be had of a deeper meaning – often one that is not intended. The images and turns of phrase to which a person is particularly given are rarely without significance when one is forming a judgement of him; and others often turn out to be allusions to a theme which is being kept in the background at the time, but which has powerfully affected the speaker. In the course of some theoretical discussions I heard someone at a particular time repeatedly

1. [This paragraph was added in 1912.]
2. [The latter reference was added in 1910.]
3. [This final paragraph was added in 1917.]

using the expression: 'If something suddenly shoots through one's head'.[1] I happened to know that he had recently received news that a Russian bullet had passed right through the cap that his son was wearing on his head.

1. [I.e., 'if an idea suddenly springs to one's mind'.]

CHAPTER X

ERRORS[1]

ERRORS of memory are distinguished from forgetting accompanied by paramnesia by the single feature that in the former the error (the paramnesia) is not recognized as such but finds credence. The use of the term 'error', however, seems to depend on yet another condition. We speak of 'being in error' rather than of 'remembering wrongly' where we wish to emphasize the characteristic of objective reality in the psychical material which we are trying to reproduce – that is to say, where what we are trying to remember is something different from a fact of our own psychical life: something, rather, that is open to confirmation or refutation by the memory of other people. The antithesis to an error of memory in this sense is ignorance.

In my *Interpretation of Dreams* (1900a) I was responsible for a number of falsifications which I was astonished to discover after the book was published. They concerned historical points and, in general, points of fact. After closer examination I found that they did not owe their origin to my ignorance, but are traceable to errors of memory which analysis is able to explain.

(1) On page 266 (of the first edition) [Chapter VI (G)] I refer to the town of *Marburg* [in Hesse] – a name also found in Styria – as Schiller's birthplace. The error occurs in the analysis of a dream which I had during a journey by night and from which I was woken by the guard calling out the name of Marburg station. In the content of the dream someone asked a question about a book by Schiller. In fact Schiller was not born at the university town of Marburg [in Hesse] but at *Marbach* in Swabia. Moreover I can assert that I have always known this.

(2) On page 135 [Chapter V (B)] Hannibal's father is called

1. [The earlier portion of this chapter, up to p. 280, dates back to 1901.]

Hasdrubal. This error annoyed me especially, but it furnished me with the strongest corroboration of my view of such errors. There must be few readers of my book who are better acquainted with the history of the house of Barca than its author, who penned this error and who overlooked it in three sets of proofs. The name of Hannibal's *father* was *Hamilcar Barca* – *Hasdrubal* was the name of Hannibal's *brother*, as well as of his brother-in-law and predecessor in command.

(3) On pages 177 and 370 [Chapters V (D) and VII (F)] I state that Zeus emasculated his father Kronos and dethroned him. I was, however, erroneously carrying this atrocity a generation forward; according to Greek mythology it was Kronos who committed it on his father Uranus.[1]

How is it to be explained that my memory provided me at these points with what was incorrect, while otherwise – as the reader of the book can see for himself – it put at my disposal the most out-of-the-way and unusual material? And how, too, did I pass over these errors while I carefully went through three sets of proofs – as if I had been struck blind?

Goethe said of Lichtenberg.[2] 'Where he makes a jest a problem lies concealed.' Similarly it can be said of the passages in my book that I have quoted here: where an error makes its appearance a repression lies behind it – or more correctly, an insincerity, a distortion, which is ultimately rooted in repressed material. In analysing the dreams reported there I was compelled, by the very nature of the themes to which the dream-thoughts related, on the one hand to break off the analysis at some point before it had been rounded off, and on the other hand to take the edge off some indiscreet detail by mild distortion. I could not do otherwise, and I had in fact no other choice

1. This was not a complete error. The Orphic version of the myth makes Zeus repeat the process of emasculation on his father Kronos. (*See* Roscher's *Lexicon of Mythology*.) [Cf. footnote 2, p. 255.]

2. [Goethe's remark is also quoted by Freud in his book on jokes (1905c), a work in which many of Lichtenberg's epigrams are discussed, as well as at the end of Lecture 2 in his *Introductory Lectures* (1916–17). (Cf. *P.F.L.*, 6, 136 and 1, 65.) See also p. 160 and *n.* 2 above.]

if I wished to bring forward examples and evidence at all. My awkward position was a necessary result of the peculiar character of dreams, which consists in giving expression to repressed material – in other words, to material that is inadmissible to consciousness. (In spite of this it would seem that enough was still left to give offence to some sensitive souls.) I did not succeed, however, in carrying through the distortion or concealment of the thoughts, whose continuation was known to me, without leaving some trace of them behind. What I wanted to suppress often succeeded against my will in gaining access to what I had chosen to relate, and appeared in it in the form of an error that I failed to notice. Moreover, the same theme is at the bottom of all the three examples I have given: the errors are derivatives of repressed thoughts connected with my dead father.[1]

(1) Anyone who reads through the dream analysed on p. 266 [Chap. VI (G), VIII] will in part find undisguisedly, and will in part be able to guess from hints, that I have broken off at thoughts which would have contained an unfriendly criticism of my father. In the continuation of this train of thoughts and memories there in fact lies an annoying story in which books play a part, and a business friend of my father's who bears the name of *Marburg* – the same name that woke me when it was called out at Marburg station on the *Südbahn*. In the analysis I tried to suppress this Herr Marburg from myself and from my readers; he took his revenge by intruding where he did not belong and changing the name of Schiller's birthplace from *Marbach* to *Marburg*.

(2) The error of putting *Hasdrubal* instead of *Hamilcar*, the brother's name instead of the father's, occurred precisely in a context that concerned the Hannibal-phantasies of my school-years and my dissatisfaction with my father's behaviour towards

1. [In his preface to the second edition of *The Interpretation of Dreams*, written in 1908, Freud remarked that after he had completed the book he found that it was 'a portion of my own self-analysis, my reaction to my father's death'. (*P.F.L.*, **4**, 47.)]

the 'enemies of our people'.[1] I could have gone on to tell how my relationship with my father was changed by a visit to England, which resulted in my getting to know my half-brother, the child of my father's first marriage, who lived there. My brother's eldest son is the same age as I am. Thus the relations between our ages were no hindrance to my phantasies of how different things would have been if I had been born the son not of my father but of my brother. These suppressed phantasies falsified the text of my book at the place where I broke off the analysis, by forcing me to put the brother's name for the father's.

(3) It is to the influence of the memory of this same brother that I attribute my error in advancing by a generation the mythological atrocities of the Greek pantheon. One of my brother's admonitions lingered long in my memory. 'One thing,' he had said to me, 'that you must not forget is that as far as the conduct of your life is concerned you really belong not to the second but to the third generation in relation to your father.' Our father had married again in later life and was therefore much older than his children by his second marriage. I made the error already described at the exact point in the book at which I was discussing filial piety.

It has also occasionally happened that friends and patients, whose dreams I have reported, or have alluded to in the course of my dream-analyses, have drawn my attention to the fact that the details of the events experienced by us together have been inaccurately related by me. These again could be classified as historical errors. After being put right I have examined the various cases and here too I have convinced myself that my memory of the facts was incorrect only where I had purposely distorted or concealed something in the analysis. Here once again we find *an unobserved error taking the place of an intentional concealment or repression.*[2]

---

1. [See *The Interpretation of Dreams*, P.F.L. 4, 284 ff.]

2. [An instance of the same mechanism appears in 'A Seventeenth-Century Demonological Neurosis' (1923*d*), P.F.L., 14, 414 *n*.]

These errors that derive from repression are to be sharply distinguished from others which are based on genuine ignorance. Thus, for example, it was ignorance which made me think during an excursion to the Wachau that I had come to the home of Fischhof, the revolutionary leader. The two places merely have the same name: Fischhof's Emmersdorf is in Carinthia. I, however, knew no better. [1900a, Chap. V (B).]

(4)[1] Here is another instructive error that put me to shame, an example of what might be called temporary ignorance. One day a patient reminded me to give him the two books on Venice that I had promised him, as he needed them in preparing for a journey at Easter. 'I have them ready,' I replied, and went to the library to fetch them. The truth, however, was that I had forgotten to look them out, for I did not entirely approve of my patient's journey, which I saw as an unnecessary interruption of the treatment and a material loss to the physician. I therefore took a hasty look round the library for two books I had had my eye on. One was 'Venice, City of Art'; but besides this I thought I must own a historical work in a similar series. Quite right, there it was: 'The Medici'. I took it and brought it to my waiting patient, only ashamedly to acknowledge the error. In reality I of course knew that the Medici have nothing to do with Venice, but for a short time it did not strike me as in any way incorrect. I now had to be fair; as I had so frequently confronted my patient with his own symptomatic acts I could only vindicate my authority in his eyes by being honest and showing him the motives (which I had kept secret) for my disapproval of his journey.

It may, in general, seem astonishing that the urge to tell the truth is so much stronger than is usually supposed. Perhaps, however, my being scarcely able to tell lies any more is a consequence of my occupation with psychoanalysis. As often as I try to distort something I succumb to an error or some other parapraxis that betrays my insincerity, as can be seen in this last example and in the previous ones.

1. [What follows from here to the end of Example 5 was added in 1907.]

Of all parapraxes errors seem to have the least rigid mechanism. That is to say, the occurrence of an error is a quite general indication that the mental activity in question has had to struggle with a disturbing influence of some sort or other; but the particular form that the error takes is not determined by the quality of the concealed disturbing idea. We may add here retrospectively that the same thing can be assumed to be true of many simple cases of slips of the tongue and pen. Every time we make a slip in talking or writing we may infer that there has been a disturbance due to mental processes lying outside our intention; but it must be admitted that slips of the tongue and of the pen often obey the laws of resemblance, of indolence or of the tendency to haste, without the disturbing element succeeding in imposing any part of its own character on the resulting mistake in speech or writing. It is the compliance of the linguistic material[1] which alone makes the determining of the mistakes possible, and at the same time sets the limits up to which the determining can go.

To avoid confining myself entirely to my own errors, I shall report a few examples that might indeed have been included just as well among slips of the tongue and bungled actions; this is, however, a matter of indifference, since all these forms of parapraxis are equivalent to one another.

(5) I forbade a patient to telephone to the girl he was in love with – but with whom he himself wanted to break off relations – since each conversation served only to renew the struggle about giving her up. He was to write his final decision to her, though there were difficulties about delivering letters to her. He called on me at one o'clock to tell me he had found a way of getting round these difficulties, and amongst other things

---

1. [See also below, p. 338. Freud comments on this characteristic of language in several places. For example, in *The Interpretation of Dreams* (1900a), speaking of condensation: 'Words. . . may be regarded as predestined to ambiguity.' (*P.F.L.*, **4**, 456.) In '*Gradiva*' (1907a), too, Freud writes at the end of Chapter III of the ambiguity made possible 'by the malleable nature of the material of speech'.]

asked if he might quote my authority as a physician. At two o'clock he was occupied in composing the letter that was to end the relationship, when he suddenly broke off and said to his mother who was with him: 'Oh! I've forgotten to ask the professor if I may mention his name in the letter.' He rushed to the telephone, put through his call and said into the instrument: 'May I speak to the professor, please, if he's finished dinner?' In answer he got an astonished: 'Adolf, have you gone mad?' It was the same voice which by my orders he should not have heard again. He had simply 'made an error' and instead of the physician's number he had given the girl's.

(6)[1] A young lady was to pay a visit to the *Habsburgergasse* ['Hapsburg Street'] to a friend, a lady who had recently been married. She spoke about it while the family were at table, but said in error that she had to go to the *Babenbergergasse* ['Babenberg Street']. Some of those at the table laughingly drew her attention to her error – or slip of the tongue (according to choice) – which she had not noticed. In fact two days before this the republic had been proclaimed in Vienna; the black and yellow had vanished and been replaced by the colours of the old Ostmark – red, white and red – and the Hapsburgs had been deposed. Our speaker introduced the change of dynasty into her friend's address. In Vienna there is indeed a very well known Babenberger*strasse*, but no Viennese would speak of it as a '*Gasse*'.[2]

1. [Added in 1919.]
2. [In Vienna two terms are used for 'street'; '*Strasse*' for the more important streets and '*Gasse*' for the minor ones. – Charlemagne gave the name of '*Ostmark*' (Eastern Province) to the region which ultimately became Austria. It first attained importance under the Babenberg dynasty. This came to an end in the thirteenth century and was succeeded by the Hapsburgs (or Habsburgs) who ruled until the end of the first World War. The red, white and red colours adopted by the new Republic (in place of the Imperial black and yellow) were those of the Babenbergs.]

(7)[1] The local school-teacher at a summer resort, a quite poor but handsome young man, persisted in his courtship of the daughter of the proprietor of a villa, who came from the capital, until the girl fell passionately in love with him and even persuaded her family to give their approval to the marriage in spite of the differences in their social position and race. One day the teacher wrote a letter to his brother in which he said: 'The girl is certainly no beauty; but she is very sweet, and it would be all right as far as that goes. But whether I shall be able to make up my mind to marry a Jewess I cannot yet tell you.' This letter was received by his fiancée and it put an end to the engagement, while at the same time his brother was wondering at the protestations of love addressed to him. My informant assured me that this *was* an error and not a cunning device. I know of another case in which a lady who was dissatisfied with her old doctor but unwilling openly to get rid of him achieved her purpose by mixing up two letters. Here at least I can guarantee that it was error and not conscious cunning that made use of this *motif*, which is such a familiar one in comedy.

(8)[2] Brill [1912, 191] tells of a lady who asked him for news of a common acquaintance and in doing so called her in error by her maiden name. When her attention was drawn to the mistake she was forced to admit that she disliked the lady's husband and had been very unhappy about her marriage.

(9)[3] Here is an error which can also be described as a slip of the tongue. A young father presented himself before the registrar of births to give notice of the birth of his second daughter. When asked what the child's name was to be he answered: 'Hanna', and had to be told by the official that he already had a child of that name. We may conclude that the second daughter was not quite so welcome as the first had been.

(10)[4] I will add some other observations of confusion

1. [Added in 1907.]   2. [Added in 1912.]   3. [Added in 1907.]
4. [Examples 10 and 11 were added in 1920.]

between names; they might of course have been equally well included in other chapters of this book.

A lady is the mother of three daughters two of whom have long been married; the youngest is still awaiting her destiny. At both weddings a lady who is a friend of the family gave the same present, an expensive silver tea-service. Every time the conversation turns to this tea-service the mother makes the error of saying that the third daughter owns it. It is clear that this error expresses the mother's wish to see her last daughter married too – on the assumption that she would be given the same wedding present.

The frequent cases in which a mother confuses the names of her daughters, sons or sons-in-law are just as easy to interpret.

(11) Here is a good example of an obstinate interchange of names; I borrow it from a Herr J. G. who made the observation on himself during a stay in a sanatorium:

'At dinner one day (at the sanatorium) I was having a conversation, which did not interest me much and was entirely conventional in tone, with the lady who was next to me at table, when in the course of it I used a phrase of special affability. That somewhat elderly spinster could not help commenting that it was not usually my habit to behave to her with such affability and gallantry – a rejoinder which contained not only a certain regret but also an obvious dig at a young lady we both knew to whom I was in the way of being somewhat attentive. Naturally I understo d at once. In the course of our further conversation I had to have it repeatedly pointed out to me by my neighbour, to my great embarrassment, that I had addressed her by the name of the young lady whom she regarded with some justice as her more fortunate rival.'

(12)[1] I will also report as an 'error' an incident with a serious background, which was told me by a witness who was closely involved. A lady spent an evening out of doors with her husband and two strangers. One of these two 'strangers' was an intimate friend of hers; but the others knew nothing of this and were

1. [Added in 1917.]

meant to know nothing. The friends accompanied the married couple to the door of their house and while they were waiting for the door to be opened they took their leave of one another. The lady bowed to the stranger, gave him her hand and said a few polite words. Then she took the arm of her secret lover, turned to her husband and began to bid him good-bye in the same way. Her husband entered into the situation, raised his hat and said with exaggerated politeness: 'Good-bye, dear lady!' The horrified wife dropped her lover's arm and before the concierge appeared had time to exclaim: 'Goodness! What a stupid thing to happen!' The husband was one of those married men who want to put an act of infidelity on their wife's part beyond the bounds of possibility. He had repeatedly sworn that in such a case more than one life would be in jeopardy. He therefore had inner impediments of the strongest kind to prevent his noticing the challenge contained in this error.

(13)[1] Here is an error of one of my patients: the fact that it was repeated in order to express a contrary meaning makes it particularly instructive. After protracted internal struggles this over-cautious young man brought himself to the point of pro-posing marriage to the girl who had long been in love with him, as he was with her. He escorted his *fiancée* home, said good-bye to her, and, in a mood of the greatest happiness, got on to a tram and asked the conductress for *two* tickets. About six months later he had got married but could not yet adjust himself to his conjugal bliss. He wondered whether he had done the right thing in marrying, missed his former relations with his friends, and had every sort of fault to find with his parents-in-law. One evening he fetched his young wife from her parents' house, got on to a tram with her and contented himself with asking for one ticket only.

(14)[2] How a wish that has been reluctantly suppressed can be satisfied by means of an 'error' is described in a good example of Maeder's (1908). A colleague who had a day free from duties

1. [Added in 1919.]   2. [Added in 1910.]

wanted to enjoy it without any interruptions; but he was due to pay a visit to Lucerne to which he did not look forward. After long deliberation he decided to go there all the same. He passed the time on the journey from Zurich to Arth-Goldau in reading the daily papers. At the latter station he changed trains and continued reading. He travelled on till the ticket-inspector informed him that he was in the wrong train – the one travelling back from Goldau to Zurich, though he had a ticket for Lucerne.

(15)[1] An analogous, though not entirely successful, attempt to help a suppressed wish to find expression by means of the same mechanism of an error is described by Dr V. Tausk (1917) under the title of 'Travelling in the Wrong Direction':

'I had come to Vienna on leave from the front. An old patient had heard I was in town and invited me to visit him as he was ill in bed. I complied with his request and spent two hours with him. When I was leaving, the sick man asked how much he owed me. "I am here on leave and am not practising now," I replied. "Please regard my visit as a friendly turn." The patient hesitated, as he no doubt felt he had no right to claim my professional services in the form of an unremunerated act of friendship. But he finally accepted my answer by expressing the respectful opinion, which was dictated by his pleasure at saving money, that as a psychoanalyst I would no doubt do the right thing. A few moments later I myself had misgivings about the sincerity of my generosity, and with my mind full of doubts – which could hardly be explained in more than one way – I got on a tram of route X. After a short journey I had to change on to route Y. While waiting at the point where I was to change I forgot the business of the fee and was occupied with the symptoms of my patient's illness. Meanwhile the tram I was waiting for came and I got on it. But at the next stop I had to get off again. I had in fact inadvertently and without noticing got on to an X tram instead of a Y tram, and had travelled back again in the direction I had just come from – in the

1. [Added in 1919.]

direction of my patient from whom I did not wish to accept any fee. *But my unconscious wanted to collect it.*'

(16)[1] A trick very similar to the one in Example 14 was once brought off by me myself. I had promised my strict eldest brother that that summer I would make my long due visit to him at an English seaside resort, and had undertaken, as time was limited, to travel by the shortest route, without breaking my journey anywhere. I asked if I might stop for a day in Holland, but he thought I might postpone that till my journey back. So I travelled from Munich *via* Cologne to Rotterdam and the Hook of Holland from where the boat starts at midnight for Harwich. I had to change at Cologne; I left my train to change into the Rotterdam express, but it was nowhere to be found. I asked various railway officials, was sent from one platform to another, fell into a mood of exaggerated despair and soon realized that during this fruitless search I must have missed my connection. After this was confirmed I considered whether I should spend the night in Cologne. Among other considerations in favour of that plan was one of filial piety, since according to an old family tradition my ancestors had once fled from that city during a persecution of the Jews. However I decided against it, travelled by a later train to Rotterdam, which I reached late in the night, and was then obliged to spend a day in Holland. That day brought me the fulfilment of a long-cherished wish; I was able to see Rembrandt's magnificent paintings at the Hague and in the Rijksmuseum at Amsterdam. It was only the next morning, when I was travelling in the train across England and could collect my impressions, that a clear memory emerged of my having seen a large notice in the station at Cologne – a few steps from the place where I had got off the train and on the same platform – which read 'Rotterdam –Hook of Holland'. There, waiting for me, had been the train in which I ought to have continued my journey. My action in hurrying away in spite of this clear direction, and my search for the train in another place, would have to be described as an

1. [Added in 1910.]

incomprehensible 'blindness' unless one is prepared to assume that – contrary to my brother's instructions – I had really resolved to admire the Rembrandts on the journey out. Everything else – my well-acted perplexity, the emergence of the 'pious' intention to spend the night in Cologne – was merely a contrivance to keep my resolution hidden from myself till it had been completely carried out.

(17)[1] From his own personal experience J. Stärcke (1916) tells of a similar device produced by 'forgetfulness' for the purpose of fulfilling an ostensibly renounced wish.

'I once had to give a lecture with lantern slides at a village; but the lecture was postponed for a week. I had answered the letter about the postponement and had entered the new date in my notebook. I should have been glad to go to this village in the afternoon, for then I should have had time to pay a visit to a writer I knew who lived there. To my regret, however, I had at the time no afternoon that I could keep free. Somewhat reluctantly, I gave up the idea of the visit.

'When the evening of the lecture arrived I set out for the station in the greatest hurry with a case of lantern slides. I had to take a taxi to catch the train. (It happens frequently with me that I put things off so long that I have to take a taxi if I am to catch my train). When I reached my destination I was a little surprised that there was no one at the station to meet me (as is the usual practice with lectures in smallish places). It suddenly occurred to me that the lecture had been postponed for a week and that I had made a fruitless journey on the date that had originally been fixed. After I had roundly cursed my forgetfulness, I debated whether I should return home by the next train. However, upon closer consideration I reflected that I now had a fine opportunity of paying the visit I had wanted to, and I thereupon did so. It was only when I was on my way that it struck me that my unfulfilled wish to have sufficient time for this visit had neatly hatched the plot. Being weighed down by the heavy case of lantern slides and hurrying to catch the train

1. [Added in 1917.]

could serve excellently to hide the unconscious intention all the more effectively.'

It may perhaps be thought[1] that the class of errors whose explanation I have given here is not very numerous or particularly significant. But I leave it open for question whether there is not some ground for extending the same line of approach to our assessment of the far more important *errors of judgement* made by human beings in their lives and in scientific work. Only for the rarest and best adjusted mind does it seem possible to preserve the picture of external reality, as it is perceived, against the distortion to which it is normally subjected in its passage through the psychical individuality of the percipient.

1. [This paragraph dates back to 1901.]

CHAPTER XI

COMBINED PARAPRAXES[1]

TWO of the last-mentioned examples – my own error which transferred the Medici to Venice [p. 280], and that of the young man who succeeded in getting a conversation with his *fiancée* on the telephone in defiance of my prohibition [p. 281 f.] – have not in fact been described entirely accurately. Careful consideration reveals that they are a combination of an act of forgetting and an error. I can illustrate this combination still more clearly from some other examples.[2]

(1) A friend tells me of the following experience. 'Some years ago I allowed myself to be elected to the committee of a certain literary society, as I thought that the organization might one day be able to help me to have my play produced; and I took a regular part, though without being much interested, in the meetings, which were held every Friday. Then, a few months ago, I was given the promise of a production at the theatre at F.; and since then I have regularly *forgotten* the meetings of the society. When I read your book on the subject I felt ashamed of my forgetfulness. I reproached myself with the thought that it was shabby behaviour on my part to stay away now that I no longer needed these people, and resolved on no account to forget the next Friday. I kept on reminding myself of this resolution until I carried it into effect and stood at the door of the room where the meetings were held. To my astonishment it was locked; the meeting was over. I had in fact made a mistake over the day; it was now Saturday!'

---

1. [This chapter was first included in the 1907 edition. It then consisted of the first four and the last paragraphs only. Further examples were added in the later editions of the book.]

2. [The next three examples are among the large number repeated in Part I of the *Introductory Lectures* (1916–17). Example 2 is there attributed to R. Reitler (*P.F.L.*, **1**, 84).]

(2) The next example combines a symptomatic act with a case of mislaying. It reached me in a somewhat roundabout way, but comes from a reliable source.

A lady travelled to Rome with her brother-in-law, who is a famous artist. The visitor was received with great honour by the German community in Rome, and among other presents he was given an antique gold medal. The lady was vexed that her brother-in-law did not appreciate the lovely object sufficiently. When she returned home (her place in Rome having been taken by her sister) she discovered while unpacking that she had brought the medal with her – how, she did not know. She at once sent a letter with the news to her brother-in-law, and announced that she would send the article she had walked off with back to Rome next day. But next day the medal had been so cleverly mislaid that it could not be found and sent off; and it was at this point that the meaning of her 'absent-mindedness' dawned on the lady: she wanted to keep the object for herself.

(3)[1] There are some cases in which the parapraxis obstinately repeats itself, at the same time changing the method that it employs:

For reasons unknown to him, Ernest Jones (1911b, 483) once left a letter lying on his desk for several days without posting it. At last he decided to send it off, but he had it returned to him from the 'Dead Letter Office' since he had forgotten to address it. After he had addressed it he again took it to the post, but this time it had no stamp. He was then no longer able to overlook his reluctance to sending the letter off at all.

(4) The vain attempts to carry out an action in opposition to an internal resistance are most impressively depicted in a short communication by Dr Karl Weiss (1912) of Vienna:

'The following episode will show how persistently the unconscious can make itself felt if it has a motive for preventing an intention from being carried out, and how hard it is to guard against that persistence. An acquaintance asked me to lend him

1. [Examples 3–5 were added in 1912.]

a book and to bring it to him the next day. I immediately promised I would, but was aware of a lively feeling of unpleasure which I could not at first explain. Later on it became clear to me: the person in question had for years owed me a sum of money which he apparently had no idea of repaying. I thought no more of the matter, but I remembered it the next morning with the same feeling of unpleasure and at once said to myself: "Your unconscious will arrange for you to forget the book; but you don't want to be disobliging, so you will take all possible steps not to forget it." I came home, wrapped up the book and put it beside me on the desk where I write my letters. After some time I went out; I took a few steps and remembered I had left the letters I wanted to post on my desk. (One of them, by the way, was a letter in which I was obliged to write something disagreeable to someone from whom I was hoping to get support over a certain matter.) I turned back, took the letters and again set off. In the tram it occurred to me that I had promised my wife to buy something for her, and I was very pleased with the thought that it would only make a small parcel. At that point the association "parcel" – "book" suddenly occurred to me, and I now noticed that I was not carrying the book. So I had not only forgotten it the first time I went out, but had also persisted in overlooking it when I took the letters that it lay beside.'

(5) The same situation is found in an instance which Otto Rank (1912) analysed exhaustively:

'A scrupulously orderly and pedantically precise man reported the following experience, which was quite unusual for him. One afternoon he was in the street and wanted to know the time; and he found he had left his watch at home – a thing he did not remember ever having done before. As he had an evening engagement for which he had to be punctual, and as he had not enough time to fetch his own watch before it, he took advantage of a visit to a lady, a friend of his, to borrow her watch for the evening. This was all the more feasible since he already had an engagement to visit the lady next morning, and he promised to return the watch on that occasion. Next day, however, when he wanted to hand over the watch he had borrowed to its owner, he found to his astonishment that now he had left *it* at home. This time he had his own watch on him. He then firmly resolved to return the lady's watch the same afternoon and actually carried out this resolution. But when he wanted to see the time upon leaving her, he found to his immense annoyance and astonishment that he had again forgotten his own watch.

'The repetition of this parapraxis seemed so pathological to a man with his love of orderliness that he would have been glad to learn of its psychological motivation; and this was promptly revealed by the psychoanalytic enquiry as to whether anything disagreeable had happened to him on the crucial day when he was forgetful for the first time, and in what connection it had occurred. He immediately related how after lunch – shortly before he went out forgetting his watch – he had had a conversation with his mother, who told him that an irresponsible relative, who had already caused him much worry and expense, had pawned his [the relative's] watch, but, as it was needed in the house, was asking him [the narrator] to provide the money to redeem it. He was very much upset by what was a more or less forced loan, and it recalled to his mind all the annoyances that the relative had caused him over many years. His symptomatic act therefore proves to have had more than one determinant. In the first place it gave expression to a train of thought that ran somewhat as follows: "I won't allow money to be extorted from me in this way, and if a watch is needed I shall leave my own at home." But since he needed it in the evening for keeping an appointment, this intention could only come into effect by an unconscious path, in the form of a symptomatic act. In the second place, what the act of forgetting signified came to this: "The perpetual sacrifice of money on this good-for-nothing will be the utter ruin of me, so that I shall have to give up everything." Although, according to him, his indignation at this piece of news was only momentary, the repetition of the same symptomatic act nevertheless shows that it continued to operate intensively in the unconscious, somewhat as though his consciousness were saying: "I can't get this story out of my head."[1] In view of this attitude of the unconscious, it will come as no surprise to us that the same thing should have happened to the borrowed lady's watch. But perhaps there were also special motives that favoured this transference on to the "innocent" lady's watch. Probably the most obvious motive is that he would no doubt have liked to keep it to take the place of the watch of his own which he had sacrificed, and that he therefore forgot to return it the next day. He would also perhaps have been glad to have the watch as a souvenir of the lady. Furthermore, forgetting the lady's watch gave him the opportunity of paying the lady he admired a second visit. He was in any case obliged to call on her in the morning in connection with another matter, and by forgetting the watch he seems, as it were, to indicate that it was a shame to use this visit, which had been arranged some time before, for the incidental purpose of returning the watch. Moreover, having twice forgotten his own watch, and in that way being able to return the other watch, goes to show that unconsciously he was trying to avoid carrying both watches at once. He was obviously seeking to avoid giving this appearance of superfluity, which would have been in striking contrast to his relative's want. But on the other hand he contrived by these means to counter his apparent intentions of marrying the lady, by warning himself that he had indissoluble obligations to his family (his mother). Finally, another reason for forgetting a lady's watch may be sought in the fact that the evening before he had, as a bachelor, felt embarrassment in front of his friends about looking at the lady's watch, and only did so surreptitiously; and to avoid a repetition of this awkward situation he did not like to carry it any longer. But as he had on the other

1. 'The continued operation of an idea in the unconscious manifests itself sometimes in the form of a dream following the parapraxis, and sometimes in a repetition of the parapraxis or in a failure to correct it.'

hand to return it, the result here too was an unconsciously performed symptomatic act, which proved to be a compromise-formation between conflicting emotional impulses, and a dearly-bought victory by the unconscious agency.'

Here are three cases observed by J. Stärcke (1916, 108–9):[1]

(6) *Mislaying, breaking and forgetting as an expression of a counter-will that has been pushed back.* 'I had got together a number of illustrations for a scientific work, when one day my brother asked me to lend him some which he wanted to use as lantern slides in a lecture. Though I was momentarily aware of thinking I would prefer it if the reproductions I had collected at much pains were not exhibited or published in any way before I could do so myself, I promised him I would look out the negatives of the pictures he wanted and make lantern slides from them. These negatives however I was unable to find. I looked through the whole pile of boxes full of the relevant negatives, and a good two hundred negatives passed through my hands, one after the other; but the negatives I was looking for were not there. I had a suspicion that in fact I seemed not to want my brother to have the pictures. After I had made this unfriendly thought conscious and had combated it, I noticed I had put the top box of the pile on one side, and had not looked through it; and this box contained the negatives I was looking for. On the lid of this box there was a brief note of the contents, and it is likely that I had given it a hasty glance before I put the box aside. The unfriendly thought, however, seemed not yet to have been totally subdued, for there were a variety of further happenings before the slides were dispatched. I pressed too hard on one of the slides and broke it, while I was holding it in my hand and was wiping the glass clean. (In the ordinary way I never break a lantern slide like that.) When I had made a new copy of this slide it fell from my hand, and was only saved from being smashed by my stretching out my foot and breaking its fall. When I mounted the lantern slides the whole pile fell to the ground once more, fortunately with-

1. [Examples 6–8 were added in 1917.]

out any being broken. And finally, several days passed before I actually packed them and sent them off; for though I intended to do so afresh every day, each time I forgot my intention once again.'

(7) *Repeated forgetfulness – eventual performance bungled.* 'One day I had to send a postcard to an acquaintance; but I kept on postponing doing so for several days. I strongly suspected that this was due to the following causes: he had informed me by letter that a certain person would come to see me in the course of the week from whom I was not particularly anxious to have a visit. When the week had passed and the prospect of the unwanted visit had become very slender I finally wrote the postcard, in which I informed him when I should be free. When writing the postcard I thought at first of adding that I had been prevented from writing earlier by *druk werk* ([Dutch for] "laborious, exacting or burdensome work"); but in the end I did not do so as no reasonable human being believes this stock excuse any longer. Whether this little untruth was nevertheless bound to make its appearance I do not know; but when I pushed the postcard into the letter box I accidentally put it into the lower opening: *Drukwerk* ([Dutch for] "printed matter").'

(8) *Forgetting and error.* 'One morning, in very fine weather, a girl went to the Rijksmuseum to draw some plaster-casts there. Though she would have preferred to go for a walk, as the weather was so fine, she nevertheless made up her mind to be industrious for once and to do some drawing. First she had to buy some drawing paper. She went to the shop (about ten minutes' walk from the museum), and bought some pencils and other materials for sketching, but quite forgot to buy the drawing paper. Then she went to the museum, and as she was sitting on her stool ready to begin, she found she had no paper and had to go back to the shop. After fetching some paper she began to draw in earnest, made good progress and, after some time, heard the clock in the museum tower strike a large number of times. "That will be twelve o'clock", she thought,

and continued working until the clock in the tower struck the quarter ("that", she thought, "will be a quarter past twelve"), packed up her drawing materials and decided to walk through the Vondelpark[1] to her sister's house and have coffee there (which, in Holland, is equivalent to luncheon). At the Suasso Museum she saw to her astonishment that it was only twelve o'clock, not half past! The temptingly fine weather had got the better of her industriousness, and in consequence she had not recalled, when the clock struck twelve times at half past eleven, that belfry clocks strike the hour at the half hour as well.'

(9)[2] As some of the above instances have already shown, the unconsciously disturbing purpose can also achieve its aim by obstinately repeating the same kind of parapraxis. I borrow an amusing example of this from a small volume, *Frank Wedekind und das Theater*, which has been published in Munich by the Drei Masken Verlag; but I must leave the responsibility for the anecdote, which is told in Mark Twain's manner, to the author of the book.

'In Wedekind's one act play *Die Zensur* [The Censorship] there occurs at its most solemn moment the pronouncement: "The fear of death is an intellectual error ['*Denkfehler*']." The author, who set much store by the passage, asked the performer at rehearsal to make a slight pause before the word "*Denkfehler*". On the night, the actor entered wholeheartedly into his part, and was careful to observe the pause; but he involuntarily said in the most solemn tones: "The fear of death is a *Druckfehler* [a misprint]." In reply to the actor's enquiries at the end of the performance, the author assured him that he had not the smallest criticism to make; only the passage in question did not say that the fear of death is a misprint but that it is an intellectual error. – When *Die Zensur* was repeated on the following night, the actor, on reaching the same passage, declared, and once again in the most solemn tones: "The fear of death is a

1. [The 'Bois de Boulogne' of Amsterdam. The Suasso Museum is a portion of the Municipal Museum.]
2. [Added in 1919.]

Denkzettel [a memorandum]." Wedekind once more showered unstinted praise on the actor, only remarking incidentally that what the text said was not that the fear of death was a memorandum but that it was an intellectual error. – Next night *Die Zensur* was given again, and the actor, with whom the author had meanwhile struck up a friendship and had exchanged views on artistic questions, declared when he came to the passage, with the most solemn face in the world: "The fear of death is a *Druckzettel* [a printed label]." The actor received the author's unqualified appreciation, and the play was given many more performances; but the author had made up his mind that the notion of an "intellectual error" was a lost cause for good and all.'

Rank (1912 and 1915b[1]) has also given attention to the very interesting relations between 'Parapraxes and Dreams', but they cannot be followed without a thorough analysis of the dream which is linked to the parapraxis. I once dreamt, as part of a longish dream, that I had lost my purse. In the morning while I was dressing I found that it was really missing. While undressing the night before I had the dream, I had forgotten to take it out of my trouser pocket and put it in it usual place. I was therefore not ignorant of my forgetfulness and it was probably meant to give expression to an unconscious thought which was prepared for making its appearance in the content of the dream.[2]

1. [This paragraph was added in 1912; the reference to Rank's second paper was inserted in 1917.]

2. [*Footnote added* 1924:] It is not so rare an event for a parapraxis like losing or mislaying something to be undone by means of a dream – by one's learning in the dream where the missing object is to be found; but this has nothing about it in the nature of the occult, so long as dreamer and loser are the same person. [Cf. below, p. 325.] A young lady writes: 'About four months ago at the bank I [noticed that I had] lost a very beautiful ring. I hunted in every nook and cranny of my room without finding it. A week ago I dreamt it was lying beside the cupboard by the radiator. Naturally the dream gave me no rest, and next morning I did in fact really find it in that very spot.' She is surprised at this

I do not mean to assert that cases of combined parapraxes like these can teach us anything new that could not already be observed in the simple cases. And yet this situation, of there being a change in the form taken by the parapraxis while the outcome remains the same, gives a vivid impression of a will striving for a definite aim, and contradicts in a far more energetic way the notion that a parapraxis is a matter of chance and needs no interpretation. We may also be struck by the fact that a conscious intention should in these examples fail so completely to prevent the success of the parapraxis. My friend failed in spite of everything to attend the meeting of the society, and the lady found it impossible to part from the medal. The unknown factor that opposed these intentions found another outlet after the first path had been barred to it. For what was required to overcome the unconscious motive was something other than a conscious counter-intention; it called for a piece of psychical work, which could make what was unknown known to consciousness.

---

incident, and maintains that it often happens that her thoughts and wishes are fulfilled in this way, but omits to ask herself what change had occurred in her life between the loss and the recovery of the ring.

CHAPTER XII

DETERMINISM, BELIEF IN
CHANCE AND SUPERSTITION –
SOME POINTS OF VIEW[1]

THE general conclusion that emerges from the previous individual discussions may be stated in the following terms.
Certain shortcomings in our psychical functioning – whose common
characteristics will in a moment be defined more closely – *and
certain seemingly unintentional performances prove, if psychoanalytic
methods of investigation are applied to them, to have valid motives and
to be determined by motives unknown to consciousness.*

In order to be included in the class of phenomena explicable
in this way, a psychical parapraxis must fulfil the following
conditions:

(*a*) It must not exceed certain dimensions fixed by our judgement, which we characterize by the expression 'within the
limits of the normal'.

(*b*) It must be in the nature of a momentary and temporary
disturbance. The same function must have been performed by
us more correctly before, or we must at all times believe ourselves capable of carrying it out more correctly. If we are corrected by someone else, we must at once recognize the rightness
of the correction and the wrongness of our own psychical
process.

(*c*) If we perceive the parapraxis at all, we must not be aware
in ourselves of any motive for it. We must rather be tempted to
explain it by 'inattentiveness', or to put it down to 'chance'.

There thus remain in this group the cases of forgetting ['*Vergessen*'], the errors in spite of better knowledge, the slips of the
tongue ['*Versprechen*'], misreadings ['*Verlesen*'], slips of the pen

1. [Except where otherwise indicated, the early part of this chapter
(up to p. 304) dates back to 1901.]

['*Verschreiben*'], bungled actions ['*Vergreifen*'] and the so-called 'chance actions'. Language points to the internal similarity between most of these phenomena: they are compounded alike [in German] with the prefix '*ver-*'.[1]

The explanation of the psychical processes which are defined in this way leads on to a series of observations which should in part excite a wider interest.

(A) If we give way to the view that a part of our psychical functioning cannot be explained by purposive ideas, we are failing to appreciate the extent of determination[2] in mental life. Both here and in other spheres this is more far-reaching than we suspect. In an article in [the Vienna daily paper] *Die Zeit* by R. M. Meyer, the literary historian, which I came across in 1900, the view was put forward and illustrated by examples that it is impossible intentionally and arbitrarily to make up a piece of nonsense. I have known for some time that one cannot make a number occur to one at one's own free choice any more than a name. Investigation of a number made up in an apparently arbitrary manner – one, let us say, of several digits uttered by someone as a joke or in a moment of high spirits – reveals that it is strictly determined in a way that would really never have been thought possible. I will begin by briefly discussing an instance of an arbitrarily chosen first name, and then analyse in some detail an analogous example of a number 'thrown out without thinking'.

(1) With a view to preparing the case history[3] of one of my women patients for publication I considered what first name I should give her in my account. There appeared to be a very wide choice; some names, it is true, were ruled out from the

1. [The prefix '*ver-*' in German corresponds closely to the English prefix '*mis-*' in such words as 'mis-hear', 'mis-lay' and 'mis-read'.]

2. [I.e. the degree to which the principle of determinism operates.]

3. [This was the 'Fragment of an Analysis of a Case of Hysteria' (1905*e*). Though the greater part of this was written in January, 1901 (that is to say, before the present work appeared), Freud did not publish it till the autumn of 1905.]

start – the real name in the first place, then the names of members of my own family, to which I should object, and perhaps some other women's names with an especially peculiar sound. But otherwise there was no need for me to be at a loss for a name. It might have been expected – and I myself expected – that a whole host of women's names would be at my disposal. Instead, one name and only one occurred to me – the name 'Dora'.

I asked myself how it was determined. Who else was there called Dora? I should have liked to dismiss with incredulity the next thought to occur to me – that it was the name of my sister's nursemaid; but I have so much self-discipline or so much practice in analysing that I held firmly to the idea and let my thoughts run on from it. At once there came to my mind a trivial incident from the previous evening which provided the determinant I was looking for. I had seen a letter on my sister's dining-room table addressed to 'Fräulein Rosa W.'. I asked in surprise who there was of that name, and was told that the girl I knew as Dora was really called Rosa, but had had to give up her real name when she took up employment in the house, since my sister could take the name 'Rosa' as applying to herself as well. 'Poor people,' I remarked in pity, 'they cannot even keep their own names!' After that, I now recall, I fell silent for a moment and began to think of a variety of serious matters which drifted into obscurity, but which I was now easily able to make conscious. When next day I was looking for a name for someone *who could not keep her own,* 'Dora' was the only one to occur to me. The complete absence of alternatives was here based on a solid association connected with the subject-matter that I was dealing with: for it was a person employed in someone else's house, a governess, who exercised a decisive influence on my patient's story, and on the course of the treatment as well.

Years later[1] this little incident had an unexpected sequel. Once, when I was discussing in a lecture the long since pub-

1. [This paragraph was added in 1907.]

lished case history of the girl now called Dora, it occurred to
me that one of the two ladies in my audience had the same
name Dora that I should have to utter so often in a whole
variety of connections. I turned to my young colleague, whom
I also knew personally, with the excuse that I had not in fact
remembered that that was her name too, and added that I was
very willing to replace it in my lecture by another name. I was
now faced with the task of rapidly choosing another one, and I
reflected that I must at all costs avoid selecting the first name
of the other lady in the audience and so setting a bad example
to my other colleagues, who were already well grounded in
psychoanalysis. I was therefore very much pleased when the
name 'Erna' occurred to me as a substitute for Dora, and I
used it in the lecture. After the lecture I asked myself where the
name Erna could possibly have come from, and I could not
help laughing when I noticed that the possibility I had been
afraid of when I was choosing the substitute name had nevertheless come about, at least to some extent. The other lady's
family name was Lucerna, of which Erna is a part.

(2) In a letter to a friend I informed him I had just then
finished correcting the proofs of *The Interpretation of Dreams*
and did not intend to make any more changes in the work,
'even if it contains 2467 mistakes'.[1] I at once tried to explain this
number to myself and added the little analysis as a postscript
to my letter. The best plan will be to quote it as I wrote it
down at the time, just after I had caught myself in the act:

'Let me hastily add a contribution to the psychopathology
of everyday life. You will find that in the letter I put down the
number 2467 as a bold arbitrary estimate of the number of mistakes which will be found in the dream book. What I meant
was some very big number; but that particular one emerged.
However, nothing in the mind is arbitrary or undetermined.
You will therefore rightly expect that the unconscious had

1. [The friend was Wilhelm Fliess of Berlin, to whom Freud sent this
analysis in a postscript to his letter of August 27, 1899 (Freud, 1950a,
Letter 116).]

hastened to determine the number which was left open by consciousness. Now, immediately before, I had read in the newspaper that a General E. M. had retired from the post of Master of Ordnance. I should explain that I am interested in this man. While I was serving as a medical officer-cadet he came to the sick quarters one day (he was then a colonel) and said to the medical officer: 'You must make me well in a week, because I have some work to do for which the Emperor is waiting.' After that episode I decided to follow his career, and lo and behold! now he has reached the end of it, having become Master of Ordnance, and is already (1899) on the retired list. I wanted to work out how long he had taken over this. Assuming that it was in 1882 that I saw him in hospital, it must have been seventeen years. I told my wife this and she remarked: "Oughtn't you to be on the retired list too, then?" "Heaven forbid!" I exclaimed. After this conversation I sat down to write to you. But the earlier train of thought went on in my mind, and with good reason. I had miscalculated; I have a fixed point in my memory to prove it. I celebrated my majority, i.e. my twenty-fourth birthday, under military arrest (having been absent without leave). So that was in 1880, or nineteen years ago. That gives you the "24" in 2467. Now take my present age – 43 – add 24, and you have 67. In other words, in answer to the question whether *I* meant to retire too, my wish gave me another twenty-four years' work. I was obviously annoyed at having failed to get very far myself during the period in which I have followed Colonel M.'s career; and yet I was celebrating a kind of triumph over his career being at an end, while I still have everything in front of me. So one can say with justice that not even the number 2467 which I threw out unthinkingly was without its determinants from the unconscious.'

(3)[1] Since this first example in which an apparently arbitrarily chosen number was explained I have often repeated the same experiment, and with the same result; but the content of

1. [Example 3, apart from this first sentence which dates back to 1901, was added in 1907.]

the majority of cases is so intimate that they cannot be reported.

For that very reason, however, I will take the opportunity of adding here a very interesting analysis of a 'numerical association', which Dr Adler (1905) of Vienna obtained from a 'perfectly healthy' informant. 'Yesterday evening', this informant reports, 'I got down to *The Psychopathology of Everyday Life*, and would have read the whole of the book straight away if I had not been prevented by a remarkable incident. For what happened was that, when I read that every number which we summon seemingly arbitrarily into consciousness has a definite meaning, I decided to make an experiment. There came to my mind the number 1734. The following ideas then rapidly occurred to me: $1734 \div 17 = 102$; $102 \div 17 = 6$. I then divided the number into 17 and 34. I am 34 years old. I believe, as I think I once told you, that 34 is the last year of youth, and for that reason I felt very miserable on my last birthday. The end of my 17th year saw the beginning of a very pleasant and interesting period in my development. I divide my life into portions of 17 years. What do the divisions mean? In thinking of the number 102 it occurred to me that No. 102 in the Reclam Universal Library is Kotzebue's play *Menschenhass und Reue* [*Misanthropy and Remorse*].[1]

'My present psychical state is one of misanthropy and remorse. No. 6 in the U.L. (I know a whole quantity of its numbers by heart) is Müllner's *Die Schuld* [*Guilt*].[2] The thought plagues me constantly that the guilt is mine for my failure to become what I could have been with my abilities. It further occurred to me that No. 34 in the U.L. contains a tale by the same Müllner entitled *Der Kaliber* [*The Calibre*]. I divided the word into "Ka" and "Liber"; it further occurred to me that it contains the words "Ali" and "Kali" ["potassium"]. This re-

---

1. [The Reclam Universal Library was an old-established and very comprehensive series of paper-bound reprints. Kotzebue (1761–1819) is still known in England for another of his plays, *Lovers' Vows*, which was *not* performed at *Mansfield Park*.]

2. [Adolf Müllner (1774–1829).]

minded me of my once making up rhymes with my (six-year-old) son Ali. I asked him to find a rhyme to Ali. He could not think of any, and as he wanted me to give him one I said: "*Ali reinigt den Mund mit hypermangansaurem Kali.*" ["Ali cleans his mouth with potassium permanganate."] We laughed a lot and Ali was very *lieb* [sweet]. During the last few days I have been obliged to notice with regret that he is "*ka (kein) lieber Ali*" ["not the sweet Ali" ("*ka lieber*" pronounced as "*Kaliber*")].

'I then asked myself: what is No. 17 in the U.L.? but I could not bring it to mind. But I quite certainly knew it earlier, so I assumed I wanted to forget that number. All reflection was in vain. I wanted to go on reading, but I only read mechanically, without understanding a word, as the 17 was tormenting me. I put out the light and continued my search. Finally I came to the conclusion that No. 17 must be a play of Shakespeare's. But which one? I thought of *Hero and Leander* – clearly a stupid attempt on the part of my will to lead me astray. Finally I got up and looked in the catalogue of the U.L. – No. 17 is *Macbeth*. To my bewilderment I was forced to realize that I knew almost nothing at all of the play, although I had given it as much attention as other plays of Shakespeare's. I only thought of: murderer, Lady Macbeth, witches, "fair is foul" and that at one time I had found Schiller's version of Macbeth very fine. There is no doubt then that I wished to forget the play. The further thought occurred to me that 17 and 34 divided by 17 gives the result 1 and 2. Numbers 1 and 2 in the U.L. are Goethe's *Faust*. Formerly I found very much of Faust in myself.'

We must regret that the physician's discretion did not allow us any insight into the significance of this series of associations. Adler observes that the man did not succeed in synthesizing his remarks. They would seem to us scarcely worth reporting if something had not emerged during their continuation which gave us the key to understanding the number 1734 and the whole series of associations.

'This morning indeed I had an experience that strongly supports the correctness of the Freudian view. My wife, whom I had woken up when I got out of bed the night before, asked me why I had wanted the U.L. catalogue. I told her the story. She found it was all hair-splitting, only – a very interesting point – she accepted *Macbeth*, which I had resisted so forcibly. She said that nothing whatever came to her mind when she thought of a number. I answered: "Let us test it." She gave the number 117. I immediately replied: "17 is a reference to what I have told you. Moreover I said to you yesterday that when a wife is in her 82nd year and her husband in his 35th year there is gross incompatibility." For the last few days I have been teasing my wife by saying she is a little old woman of 82. $82 + 35 = 117$.'

Thus the man, who was not able to find determinants for his own number, found the solution at once when his wife gave him a number purporting to be arbitrarily chosen. In reality the wife understood very well what complex her husband's number was derived from, and chose her own number from the same complex – which was certainly common to both of them, for in his case it concerned their relative ages. It is therefore easy for us to translate the number that had occurred to the husband. It expresses, as Adler suggests, a suppressed wish of his which, fully developed, would run: 'Only a wife of 17 is suitable for a man of 34 like me.'

In case anyone should think too lightly of such 'trifles', I may add that I recently learned from Dr Adler that a year after the publication of this analysis the man was divorced from his wife.[1]

Adler gives similar explanations of the origin of obsessive numbers.

1. In explanation of *Macbeth*, No. 17 in the U.L., Adler informs me that in his seventeenth year this man joined a society of anarchists with regicide as its aim. This was no doubt why the content of *Macbeth* was forgotten. At that time, too, he had invented a code in which letters were replaced by numbers.

(4)[1] Moreover the choice of what have been called 'favourite numbers' is not unrelated to the life of the person concerned and is not without a certain psychological interest. A man who admitted having a special preference for the numbers 17 and 19 was able to specify after a little reflection that at the age of 17 he had gone to the university and so attained the academic freedom he had long desired, and that at 19 he had taken his first long journey and soon after had made his first scientific discovery. But the fixation of this preference occurred a decade later, when the same numbers took on a significance in his erotic life. – Indeed, even those numbers which a person uses especially often in a particular connection, in an apparently arbitrary way, can be traced by analysis to an unexpected meaning. Thus it struck a patient of mine one day that when annoyed he was especially fond of saying: 'I've told you that already from 17 to 36 times', and he asked himself whether there was any motive for it. It at once occurred to him that he was born on the 27th day of the month whereas his younger brother was born on the 26th, and that he had good reason to complain that fate so often robbed him of the good things in life in order to bestow them on this younger brother. He therefore represented this partiality on the part of fate by deducting ten from the date of his own birthday and adding it to his brother's. 'I am the elder and yet I am cut short like this.'

(5)[2] I shall dwell longer on analyses of numerical associations, since I know of no other separate observations that would prove so forcefully the existence of highly composite thought-processes which are yet quite unknown to consciousness. At the same time I know of no better example of analyses in which the part contributed by the physician (suggestion) – so often held responsible – is so definitely ruled out. I shall therefore give a report here (with his consent) of the analysis of a number which occurred to a patient of mine. I need only add that he is the youngest child in a large family and at an early age lost his greatly admired father. While he was in a particularly cheerful

1. [Added 1910.]   2. [Added 1912.]

mood the number 426718 came to his mind, and he asked himself: 'What ideas occur to me in that connection? First of all, a joke I have heard: "When a doctor treats a cold it lasts for 42 days; when it is not treated, it lasts 6 weeks."' This corresponds to the first figures in the number ($42=6\times7$). In the stoppage that followed this first solution I drew his attention to the fact that the six-figure number he had chosen contained all the first digits except for 3 and 5. He then immediately found the continuation of the interpretation. 'There are 7 of us brothers and sisters, and I am the youngest. In the order of our age, 3 corresponds to my sister A., and 5 to my brother L.; they were my two enemies. As a child I used to pray to God every night for him to remove these two tormenting spirits from life. It seems to me now that in this choice of numbers I was myself fulfilling this wish; 3 and 5, the wicked brother and the hated sister, are passed over.' – If the number represents the order of your brothers and sisters, what does the 18 at the end mean? There were only 7 of you after all. – 'I have often thought that if my father had lived longer I should not have remained the youngest child. If there had been 1 more we should have been 8 and I should have had a younger child after me to whom I should have played the elder brother.'

With this the number was explained, but we had still to establish the connection between the first part of the interpretation and the second one. This followed very easily from the necessary precondition of the last figures: 'if my father had lived longer'. '$42=6\times7$' signified scorn towards the doctors who had not been able to help his father, and, in this form, therefore, it expressed his wish for his father to go on living. The whole number [426718] in fact corresponded to the fulfilment of his two infantile wishes about his family circle – that his bad brother and sister should die and that a baby should be born after him, or, expressed in the shortest form: 'If only those two had died instead of my beloved father!'[1]

1. In the interests of simplicity I have omitted some of the patient's intermediate associations which were equally to the point.

(6)[1] Here is a brief example from a correspondent. The manager of a telegraph office in L. writes that his eighteen-and-a-half-year-old son, who wants to study medicine, is already taken up with the psychopathology of everyday life, and is trying to convince his parents of the correctness of my assertions. I reproduce one of the experiments he undertook, without expressing an opinion on the discussion attached to it.

'My son was talking to my wife about what we call "chance" and was demonstrating to her that she could not name any song or any number that really occurred to her simply "by chance". The following conversation ensued. Son: "Give me any number you like." – Mother: "79." – Son: "What occurs to you in that connection?" – Mother: "I think of the lovely hat I was looking at yesterday." – Son: "What did it cost?" – Mother: "158 marks." – Son: "That explains it: $158 \div 2 = 79$. The hat was too dear for you and no doubt you thought: 'If it were half the price, I would buy it.'"

'To these assertions of my son's I first raised the objection that women are not in general particularly good at figures and that anyway his mother had certainly not worked out that 79 was half 158. His theory was therefore based on the sufficently improbable fact that the subconscious is better at arithmetic than normal consciousness. "Not at all", was the answer I received; "it may well be that my mother did not work out the sum $158 \div 2 = 79$, she may perfectly well have happened to see this equation – indeed she may have thought about the hat while dreaming and then realized what it would cost if it were only half the price."'

(7)[2] I take another numerical analysis from Jones (1911b, 478). A gentleman of his acquaintance let the number 986 occur to him and then defied Jones to connect it with anything he thought of. 'Using the free-association method he first recalled

1. [Added 1920.]
2. [Added 1912. – Jones's original text, which differs in very small points from Freud's version, is given here.]

a memory, which had not previously been present in his mind, to the following effect: Six years ago, on the hottest day he could remember, he had seen a joke in an evening newspaper, which stated that the thermometer had stood at 986° F., evidently an exaggeration of 98·6° F. We were at the time seated in front of a very hot fire from which he had just drawn back, and he remarked, probably quite correctly, that the heat had aroused this dormant memory. However, I was curious to know why this memory had persisted with such vividness as to be so readily brought out, for with most people it surely would have been forgotten beyond recall, unless it had become associated with some other mental experience of more significance. He told me that in reading the joke he had laughed uproariously, and that on many subsequent occasions he had recalled it with great relish. As the joke was obviously a very tenuous one, this strengthened my expectation that more lay behind. His next thought was the general reflection that the conception of heat had always greatly impressed him; that heat was the most important thing in the universe, the source of all life, and so on. This remarkable attitude of a quite prosaic young man certainly needed some explanation, so I asked him to continue his free associations. The next thought was of a factory-stack which he could see from his bedroom window. He often stood of an evening watching the flame and smoke issuing out of it, and reflecting on the deplorable waste of energy. Heat, fire, the source of life, the waste of vital energy issuing from an upright, hollow tube – it was not hard to divine from such associations that the ideas of heat and fire were unconsciously linked in his mind with the idea of love, as is so frequent in symbolic thinking, and that there was a strong masturbation complex present, a conclusion which he presently confirmed.'

Those who wish to get a good impression[1] of the way in which the material of numbers is worked over in unconscious

1. [This paragraph was also added in 1912; the following one dates back to 1901.]

thinking may be referred to the papers by Jung (1911) and Jones (1912).

In analyses of this kind which I conduct on myself I find two things particularly striking: firstly, the positively somnambulistic certainty[1] with which I set off for my unknown goal and plunge into an arithmetical train of thought which arrives all at once at the desired number, and the speed with which the entire subsequent work is completed; and secondly, the fact that the numbers are so freely at the disposal of my unconscious thinking, whereas I am a bad reckoner and have the greatest difficulties in consciously noting dates, house numbers and such things. Moreover in these unconscious thought-operations with numbers I find I have a tendency to superstition, whose origin for long remained unknown to me.[2] [Cf. p. 323, n. 3.]

---

1. [See footnote, p. 221 above.]

2. [In 1901 and 1904, this sentence ended: '. . . whose origin is still unknown to me myself.' The paragraph continued: 'I generally come upon speculations about the duration of my own life and the lives of those dear to me; and the fact that my friend in B[erlin] has made the period of human life the subject of his calculations, which are based on biological units, must have acted as a determinant of this unconscious juggling. I am not now in agreement with one of the premisses from which this work of his proceeds; from highly egoistic motives I should be very glad to carry my point against him, and yet I appear to be imitating his calculations in my own way.' The whole of this passage was omitted, and the sentence preceding it was given its present form, from 1907 onwards. The references in the omitted passage are to Freud's friend and correspondent in Berlin, Wilhelm Fliess, and to the analysis of the number 2467 (p. 303 above) which (in 1901 and 1904) immediately preceded it. The hypothesis of Fliess's with which Freud had egoistic motives for disagreeing was no doubt that with which predicted his death at the age of 51 in 1907 – the year in which the passage was cancelled. See *The Interpretation of Dreams* (1900*a*), *P.F.L.*, 4, 565 ff., 569 *n.* and 657; cf. also Jones (1953, 341).]

[*Footnote added* 1920:] Herr Rudolf Schneider (1920) of Munich has raised an interesting objection to the conclusiveness of such analyses of numbers. He experimented with numbers that were presented to him – for example, with the number that first caught his eye when he opened a history book – or he presented someone else with a number he had chosen; and he then noticed whether associations emerged to the imposed number which had the appearance of having determined it. This was in fact what did happen. In one instance which he relates that concerned himself, the associations provided determinants just as abundant and full of meaning as in our analyses of numbers that have arisen spontaneously, whereas the number of Schneider's experiments, having been presented from outside, called for no determinant. In a second experiment carried out on someone else, he clearly made the problem too easy, for the number he set him was 2, and everybody has *some* material which would enable him to find a determinant for that number. – From his experiments Schneider then draws two conclusions: first, that 'the mind possesses the same potentialities for finding associations to numbers as to concepts'; and secondly, that the emergence of determining associations to numbers that occur to the mind spontaneously does not in any way prove that these numbers originated from the thoughts discovered in the 'analysis' of them. The former conclusion is undoubtedly correct. It is just as easy to find an appropriate association to a number which is presented as it is to a word which is called out – indeed it is perhaps easier, since the ability of the few digits to form connections is particularly great. The situation in which one finds onself is then simply that of what are called 'association experiments', which have been studied from the greatest variety of angles by the school of Bleuler and Jung. In this situation the association (reaction) is determined by the word presented (stimulus-word). This reaction could however still be of very diverse kinds, and Jung's experiments have shown that even these further distinctions are not left to 'chance', but that unconscious 'complexes' participate in the determination if they have been touched on by the stimulus-word. – Schneider's second conclusion goes too far. The fact that appropriate associations arise to numbers (or words) which are *presented* tells us nothing more about the origin of numbers (or words) which emerge *spontaneously* than could already be taken into consideration before that fact was known. These spontaneous ideas (words or numbers) may be undetermined, or may have been determined by the thoughts that come out in the analysis, or by other thoughts not disclosed in the analysis – in which last case the analysis will have led us astray. The important thing is to get rid of the impression that this problem is different for numbers from what it is for verbal associations. A critical examination of the problem and with it a justification of the psychoanalytic technique of association lie outside the scope of this book. In analytic practice we proceed on the presupposition that the second of the possibilities mentioned above

It will not surprise us[1] to find that not only numbers but also verbal associations of another kind regularly prove an analytic investigation to be fully determined.

(8) A good example of the derivation of an obsessive word – a word that cannot be got rid of – is to be found in Jung (1906). 'A lady told me that for some days the word "Taganrog"[2] had been constantly on her lips without her having any idea where it came from. I asked the lady for information about the affectively stressed events and repressed wishes of the very recent past. After some hesitation she told me that she would very much like a morning gown [*Morgenrock*], but her husband did not take the interest in it that she had hoped. "*Morgenrock*", "*Tag-an-rock*" [literally "day-on-gown"] – their partial similarity in sound and meaning is obvious. The Russian form was determined by the fact that at about the same time the lady had come to know someone from Taganrog.'

(9) I am indebted to Dr E. Hitschmann for the elucidation of another case, in which in a particular locality a line of poetry repeatedly forced its way up as an association, without its origin and connections having been apparent.

'E., a doctor of law, relates: Six years ago I travelled from Biarritz to San Sebastian. The railway line crosses the River Bidassoa, which at this point forms the frontier between France and Spain. From the bridge there is a fine view – on one side, of a broad valley and the Pyrenees, and on the other, of the distant sea. It was a beautiful, bright summer's day; everything was filled with sun and light, I was on my holiday travels

---

meets the facts and that in the majority of instances use can be made of it. The investigations of an experimental psychologist (Poppelreuter [1914]) have demonstrated that it is by far the most probable one. See further in this connection the valuable findings in Section 9 of Bleuler's book on autistic thinking (1919).

1. [This sentence, and Examples 8 and 9, were added in 1912.]

2. [The name of a port in South Russia.]

and was happy to be coming to Spain. At that point the following lines occurred to me:

> Aber frei ist schon die Seele,
> Schwebet in dem Meer von Licht.[1]

'I recall that at the time I pondered on where the lines came from and could not recollect the place. To judge by the rhythm the words must have come from a poem, which, however, had entirely escaped my memory. I believe that later, when the lines came to my mind repeatedly, I asked a number of people about them without being able to learn anything.

'Last year, when I was returning from Spain I passed over the same stretch of railway. It was a pitch-dark night and it was raining. I looked out of the window to see whether we were already coming into the frontier station, and noticed that we were on the Bidassoa bridge. Immediately the lines given above returned to my memory, and again I could not recall their origin.

'Several months later when I was at home, I came across a copy of Uhland's poems. I opened the volume and my glance fell on the lines: "Aber frei ist schon die Seele, schwebet in dem Meer von Licht", which form the conclusion of a poem called "Der Waller".[2] I read the poem and had a very dim recollection of having once known it many years ago. The scene of action is in Spain and this seemed to me to form the only connection between the quoted lines and the place on the railway line described by me. I was only half satisfied with my discovery and went on mechanically turning the pages of the book. The lines "Aber frei ist schon . . ." etc. are printed at the bottom of a page. On turning over the page I found a poem on the other side with the title "Bidassoa Bridge".

'I may add that the contents of this poem seemed almost more unfamiliar than those of its predecessor, and that its first lines run:

1. ['But the soul is already free, it floats in the sea of light.']
2. ['The Pilgrim.']

'Auf der Bidassoabrücke steht ein Heiliger altersgrau,
Segnet rechts die span'schen Berge, segnet links den fränk'schen
   Gau.'[1]

(B)[2] Perhaps the insight we have gained into the determining of names and numbers that are chosen with apparent
arbitrariness may help to solve another problem. Many people,
as is well known, contest the assumption of complete psychical
determinism by appealing to a special feeling of conviction that
there is a free will. This feeling of conviction exists; and it does
not give way before a belief in determinism. Like every normal
feeling it must have something to warrant it. But so far as I
can observe, it does not manifest itself in the great and important
decisions of the will; on these occasions the feeling that we have
is rather one of psychical compulsion, and we are glad to
invoke it on our behalf. ('Here I stand: I can do no other.')[3] On
the other hand, it is precisely with regard to the unimportant,
indifferent decisions that we would like to claim that we could
just as well have acted otherwise: that we have acted of our free
– and unmotivated – will. According to our analyses it is not
necessary to dispute the right to the feeling of conviction of
having a free will. If the distinction between conscious and unconscious motivation is taken into account, our feeling of conviction informs us that conscious motivation does not extend to
all our motor decisions. *De minimis non curat lex.* But what is
thus left free by the one side receives its motivation from the
other side, from the unconscious; and in this way determination
in the psychical sphere is still carried out without any gap.[4]

1. ['On the Bidassoa bridge there stands a saint grey with age: on the
right he blesses the Spanish mountains, on the left he blesses the
Frankish land.']

2. [Except where otherwise specified, the whole of Sections B and C
dates back to 1901.]

3. [Martin Luther's declaration at the Diet of Worms.]

4. [*Footnote added* 1907:] These conceptions of the strict determination
of apparently arbitrary psychical acts have already borne rich fruit in
psychology, and perhaps also in the juridical field. By applying them,
Bleuler and Jung have made intelligible the reactions in what is known

(C) Although the motivation of the parapraxes described in the preceding chapters is something of which from the very nature of the case conscious thought must lack knowledge, it would nevertheless be desirable to discover a psychological proof of the existence of that motivation; indeed, for reasons which a closer knowledge of the unconscious reveals, it is probable that such proofs are somewhere discoverable. There are in fact two spheres in which it is possible to demonstrate phenomena that appear to correspond to an unconscious, and therefore displaced, knowledge of that motivation.

(a) A striking and generally observed feature of the behaviour of paranoics is that they attach the greatest significance to the minor details of other people's behaviour which we ordinarily neglect, interpret them and make them the basis of far-reaching conclusions. For example, the last paranoic seen by me concluded that there was a general understanding in his environment, because when his train was moving out of the station the people had made a particular movement with one hand. Another noted the way people walked in the street, how they flourished their walking sticks, and so on.[1]

The category of what is accidental and requires no motiva-

---

as the 'association experiment', in which the subject of the test, when he hears a word called out (the stimulus-word), answers it with one that comes to his mind in connection with it (the reaction), the intervening time being measured (the reaction-time). In his *Studies in Word Association* (1906), Jung has shown what a subtle reagent for psychical states we possess in the association experiment as thus interpreted. Wertheimer and Klein [1904], both pupils of Hans Gross, the Professor of Criminal Law in Prague, have developed out of these experiments a technique for the establishment of the facts in criminal proceedings which is at present being examined by psychologists and jurists. – [Freud had himself recently written a paper on the subject (1906c). – Hans Gross (1847–1915) is generally regarded as one of the founders of modern scientific criminal investigation.]

1. From other points of view this interpretation of immaterial and accidental indications given by other people has been classed as a 'delusion of reference'.

tion, in which the normal person includes a part of his own psychical performances and parapraxes, is thus rejected by the paranoic as far as the psychical manifestations of other people are concerned. Everything he observes in other people is full of significance, everything can be interpreted. How does he reach this position? Probably here as in so many similar cases he projects on to the mental life of other people what is unconsciously present in his own. In paranoia many sorts of things force their way through to consciousness whose presence in the unconscious of normal and neurotic people we can demonstrate only through psychoanalysis.[1] In a certain sense, therefore, the paranoic is justified in this, for he recognizes something that escapes the normal person: he sees more clearly than someone of normal intellectual capacity, but the displacement on to other people of the state of affairs which he recognizes renders his knowledge worthless. I hope I shall not now be expected to justify the various paranoic interpretations. But the partial justification which we concede to paranoia in respect of this view taken by it of chance actions will help us towards a psychological understanding of the sense of conviction that the paranoic attaches to all these interpretations. *There is in fact some truth in them*;[2] those, too, of our errors of judgement which are

1. For example, the phantasies of hysterics concerning sexual and cruel maltreatment correspond, at times even down to details, with the complaints of persecuted paranoics. It is curious, but not unintelligible, that we meet the identical content in the form of reality in the contrivances of perverts for the satisfaction of their desires. [Cf. the discussion of this in Section I of the 'Dora' case history, which had been written before the publication of the present work but did not appear till four years later (1905*e*). See *P.F.L.*, **8**, 80–86.]

2. [The notion of there being a core of truth in paranoic delusions has a long course of development in Freud's writings. Among its later appearances may be mentioned one in Chapter III of the *Gradiva* essay (1907*a*), and another, which seems to follow closely some of the present discussions, in the paper on 'Some Neurotic Mechanisms' (1922*b*). In Freud's latest writings the idea was extended. He now applied the notion of a historical core of truth firstly to myths, in the paper on the origin of fire (1932*a*), and then to religion, in *Moses and Monotheism* (1939*a*),

not to be counted as pathological acquire their sense of conviction in just the same way. This feeling is justified for a certain part of the erroneous train of thought, or for its source of origin; and it is then extended by us to the rest of the context.

(b) Another indication that we possess unconscious and displaced knowledge of the motivation in chance actions and parapraxes is to be found in the phenomenon of superstition. I will make my meaning clear by a discussion of the small experience that started me on these reflections.

On my return fom my holidays my thoughts immediately turned to the patients who were to claim my attention in the year's work that was just beginning. My first visit was to a very old lady for whom I had for many years performed the same professional services twice every day (p. 218 [and 232]). Owing to the uniformity of the circumstances, unconscious thoughts have very often managed to find expression while I was on my way to the patient and while I was treating her. She is over ninety years old; it is therefore natural to ask oneself at the beginning of each year's treatment how much longer she is likely to live. On the day I am speaking about I was in a hurry and called a cab to take me to her house. Every cabman on the rank in front of my house knew the old lady's address, as they had all often taken me there. But on this day it happened that the cabman did not draw up in front of her house but in front of a house with the same number in a nearby street which ran parallel and was in fact of a similar appearance. I noticed the error and reproached the cabman with it, and he apologized. Now is it of any significance that I was driven to a house where the old lady was not to be found? Certainly not to me, but if I were *superstitious* I should see an omen in the incident, the finger of fate announcing that this year would be the old lady's last. Very many omens recorded by history have been based on a symbolism no better than this. *I* of course explain the occurrence as an accident without any further meaning.

Essay III, Part I, Section D and Part II, Section G. In these later discussions Freud elaborates a distinction between 'material' and 'historical' truth.]

The case would have been quite different if I had made the journey on foot, and while 'deep in thought', or through 'absent-mindedness' had come to the house in the parallel street instead of the right one. This I should not explain as an accident but as an action that had an unconscious aim and required interpretation. My interpretation of 'going astray' like this would probably have had to be that I did not expect to see the old lady for much longer.

I am therefore different from a superstitious person in the following way:

I do not believe that an event in whose occurrence my mental life plays no part can teach me any hidden thing about the future shape of reality; but I believe that an unintentional manifestation of my own mental activity *does* on the other hand disclose something hidden, though again it is something that belongs only to my mental life [not to external reality]. I believe in external (real) chance, it is true, but not in internal (psychical) accidental events. With the superstitious person it is the other way round. He knows nothing of the motivation of his chance actions and parapraxes, and believes in psychical accidental events; and, on the other hand, he has a tendency to ascribe to external chance happenings a meaning which will become manifest in real events, and to regard such chance happenings as a means of expressing something that is hidden from him in the external world. The differences between myself and the superstitious person are two: first, he projects outwards a motivation which I look for within; secondly, he interprets chance as due to an event, while I trace it back to a thought. But what is hidden from him corresponds to what is unconscious for me, and the compulsion not to let chance count as chance but to interpret it is common to both of us.[1]

1. [*Footnote added* 1924:] At this point I may quote a neat example which Ossipow (1922) has used for discussing the difference between the superstitious, psychoanalytic and mystical points of view. He had been married in a small Russian provincial town and immediately afterwards started for Moscow with his young wife. At a station two hours before his destination he had a wish to go to the station exit and take

I assume that this conscious ignorance and unconscious knowledge of the motivation of accidental psychical events is one of the psychical roots of superstition. *Because* the superstitious person knows nothing of the motivation of his own chance actions, and *because* the fact of this motivation presses for a place in his field of recognition, he is forced to allocate it, by displacement, to the external world. If such a connection exists, it can hardly be limited to this single application. In point of fact I believe that a large part of the mythological view of the world, which extends a long way into the most modern religions, *is nothing but psychology projected into the external world.* The obscure recognition[1] (the endopsychic perception, as it were)[2] of psychical factors and relations in the unconscious is mirrored – it is difficult to express it in other terms, and here the analogy with paranoia must come to our aid – in the construction of a *supernatural reality*, which is destined to be changed back once more by science into the *psychology of the unconscious.* One could venture to explain in this way the myths of paradise and the fall of man, of God, of good and evil, of immortality, and so on,

---

a look at the town. The train was due to halt there long enough, as he thought, but when he returned a few minutes later it had already left with his young wife. When he told his old nurse at home of this accident, she shook her head and declared: 'No good will come of this marriage.' At the time Ossipow laughed at this prophecy. But when, five months later, he was separated from his wife, he could not avoid in retrospect viewing his action in leaving the train as an 'unconscious protest' against his marriage. Years later, the town where this parapraxis happened took on a great importance for him, as a person lived there with whom fate later linked him closely. This person, and even the fact of this person's existence, had been completely unknown to him at the time. But the *mystical* explanation of his behaviour would be that he had left the Moscow train and his wife at that town because the future that was in store for him in relation to this other person was seeking to declare itself.

1. A recognition which, of course, has nothing of the character of a [true] recognition.

2. [The words in parenthesis were added in 1907. Freud refers to the passage in the theoretical section, II (B), of the 'Rat Man' case history (1909*d*), *P.F.L.*, 9, 111 f.]

and to transform *metaphysics* into *metapsychology*.[1] The gap between the paranoic's displacement and that of the superstitious person is less wide than it appears at first sight. When human beings began to think, they were, as is well known, forced to explain the external world anthropomorphically by means of a multitude of personalities in their own image; chance events, which they interpreted superstitiously, were thus actions and manifestations of persons. They behaved, therefore, just like paranoics, who draw conclusions from insignificant signs given them by other people, and just like all normal people, who quite rightly base their estimate of their neighbours' characters on their chance and unintentional actions. It is only in our modern, scientific but as yet by no means perfected *Weltanschauung* that superstition seems so very much out of place; in the *Weltanschauung* of pre-scientific times and peoples it was justified and consistent.[2]

The Roman who gave up an important undertaking if he saw an ill-omened flight of birds was therefore in a relative sense justified; his behaviour was consistent with his premises. But if he withdrew from the undertaking because he had stumbled on the threshold of his door ('*un Romain retournerait*'[3]) he was also in an absolute sense superior to us unbelievers; he was a better psychologist than we are striving to be. For his stumbling must have revealed to him the existence of a doubt, a counter-current at work within him, whose force might at the moment of execution subtract from the force of his intention. For we are only sure of complete success if all our mental forces are united in striving towards the desired goal. How did Schiller's Tell, who hesitated so long to shoot the apple on his

1. [This was the first published appearance of the word. Freud did not use it again for fourteen years – in 'The Unconscious' (1915e).]

2. [Freud's views on the part played by projection in superstition, paranoia and the origins of religion were developed in the case histories of the 'Rat Man' (1909d) and of Schreber (1911c), P.F.L., 9, 109–16 and 204 f; and in *Totem and Taboo* (1912–13), Essays II (3c) and III (4).]

3. [This apparent quotation has not been traced.]

son's head, answer the Governor's question why he had provided himself with a second arrow?

> Mit diesem zweiten Pfeil durchschoss ich – Euch,
> Wenn ich mein liebes Kind getroffen hätte,
> Und *Euer* – wahrlich, hätt' ich *nicht* gefehlt.[1]

(D)[2] Anyone who has had the opportunity of studying the hidden mental impulses of human beings by means of psycho-analysis can also say something new about the *quality* of the unconscious motives that find expression in superstition. It can be recognized most clearly in neurotics suffering from obsessional thinking or obsessional states – people who are often of high intelligence – that superstition derives from suppressed hostile and cruel impulses.[3] Superstition is in large part the expectation of trouble; and a person who has harboured frequent evil wishes against others, but has been brought up to be good and has therefore repressed such wishes into the unconscious, will be especially ready to expect punishment for his unconscious wickedness in the form of trouble threatening him from without.

Though we admit that these remarks of ours in no way exhaust the psychology of superstition, we shall at least have to

1. [Schiller, *Wilhelm Tell*, Act III, Scene 3: 'With this second arrow I would have transfixed – you, if I had struck my dear child; and *you*, truly, I should *not* have missed.']

2. [Section D first appeared in 1907 and was expanded in subsequent editions. The first six paragraphs date back to 1907.]

3. [See for example, the 'Rat Man' (1909*d*), *P.F.L.*, **9**, 113-14. In Freud's interleaved copy of the 1904 edition (see Editor's Introduction, p. 35) the following remarks are to be found at a slightly earlier point in the text. 'Rage, anger and consequently a murderous impulse is the source of superstition in obsessional neurotics: a sadistic component, which is attached to love and is therefore directed against the loved person and repressed precisely because of this link and because of its intensity.' – 'My own superstition has its roots in suppressed ambition (immortality) and in my case takes the place of that anxiety about death which springs from the normal uncertainty of life . . .']

touch on the question of whether we are to deny entirely that superstition has any real roots: whether there are definitely no such things as true presentiments, prophetic dreams, telepathic experiences, manifestations of supernatural forces and the like. I am far from meaning to pass so sweeping a condemnation of these phenomena, of which so many detailed observations have been made even by men of outstanding intellect, and which it would be best to make the subject of further investigations. We may even hope that some portion of these observations will then be explained by our growing recognition of unconscious mental processes, without necessitating radical alterations in the views we hold to-day.[1] If the existence of still other phenomena – those, for example, claimed by spiritualists – were to be established, we should merely set about modifying our 'laws' in the way demanded by the new discovery, without being shaken in our belief in the coherence of things in the world.

In the compass of these discussions the only answer I can give to the questions raised here is a subjective one – that is, one in accordance with my personal experience. To my regret I must confess that I am one of those unworthy people in whose presence spirits suspend their activity and the supernatural vanishes away, so that I have never been in a position to experience anything myself which might arouse a belief in the miraculous. Like every human being, I have had presentiments and experienced trouble, but the two failed to coincide with one another, so that nothing followed the presentiments, and the trouble came upon me unannounced. During the days when I was living alone in a foreign city – I was a young man at the time[2] – I quite often heard my name suddenly called by an unmistakable and beloved voice; I then noted down the exact moment of the hallucination and made anxious enquiries of those at home about what had happened at that time. Nothing

1. [Footnote added 1924:] See Hitschmann (1910 and 1916).
2. [The reference is to Freud's stay in Paris in 1885–6. Cf. above, pp. 13–14.]

had happened. To balance this, there was a later occasion when I went on working with my patients without any disturbance or foreboding while one of my children was in danger of bleeding to death. Nor have I ever been able to regard any of the presentiments reported to me by patients as veridical. – I must however confess that in the last few years I have had a few remarkable experiences which might easily have been explained on the hypothesis of telepathic thought-transference.[1]

Belief in prophetic dreams can claim many adherents, because it can take support from the fact that a number of things do in reality turn out in the future in the way in which the wish has previously arranged them in the dream.[2] But there is little that is surprising in that, and as a rule, too, there are extensive differences between the dream and its fulfilment, which the dreamer's credulity prefers to neglect. A good example of a dream which may justly be called prophetic was once brought to me for detailed analysis by an intelligent and truthful woman patient. Her story was that she had once dreamt she met a former friend of hers and family doctor in front of a certain shop in a certain street; and that when next morning she went into the Inner Town [p. 187] she in fact met him at the very spot named in the dream. I may observe that no subsequent event proved the importance of this miraculous coincidence,[3] which could not therefore be accounted for by what lay in the future.

Careful questioning established that there was no evidence of her having had any recollection of the dream on the morning

1. [The last sentence was added in 1924. – Freud wrote a good deal on the subject of telepathy at about this time: the posthumous paper on 'Psycho-Analysis and Telepathy' (1941d [1921]), the note on 'The Occult Significance of Dreams' (1925i), and Lecture 30 on 'Dreams and Occultism' in the New Introductory Lectures (1933a [1932]), in addition to the paper quoted by him in his next footnote.]

2. [Footnote added 1924:] See my paper on 'Dreams and Telepathy' (1922a).

3. [The German 'Zusammentreffen' means both 'coincidence' and 'meeting'.]

after she dreamt it – that is, until after her walk and the meeting. She could produce no objection to an account of what happened which robbed the episode of anything miraculous and left nothing but an interesting psychological problem. She was walking along the street in question one morning and met her old family doctor in front of a particular shop, and thereupon, on seeing him, she felt convinced that she had dreamt the night before of having this meeting at that precise spot. Analysis was then able to show with great probability how she arrived at this sense of conviction, which, according to general rules, cannot fairly be denied a certain right to be considered authentic. A meeting at a particular place, which has been expected beforehand, amounts in fact to a *rendezvous*. The old family doctor awakened her memory of former days, when meetings with a *third* person, also a friend of the doctor, had played a very important part in her life. Since then she had continued her relations with that gentleman and had waited for him in vain on the day before the dream was supposed to have taken place. If I were able to report the circumstances of the case in greater detail it would be easy for me to show that her illusion, when she saw her friend of former days, of having had a prophetic dream was equivalent to some such remark as this; 'Ah! doctor – you remind me now of past times when I never had to wait in vain for N. if we'd arranged a meeting.'[1]

The 'remarkable coincidence' of meeting a person we were at that very moment thinking about is a familiar one. I have observed a simple and easily explained example of it in myself, which is probably a good model for similar occurrences. A few days after I had been awarded the title of professor[2] – which carries considerable authority with it in countries under monarchical rule – my thoughts, while I was walking through

1. [This incident is reported in much greater detail in Freud's posthumously published paper 'A Premonitory Dream Fulfilled' (1941c), *Standard Ed.*, 5, 623, the manuscript of which is dated November 10, 1899.]

2. [In March, 1902.]

the Inner Town, suddenly turned to a childish phantasy of revenge directed against a particular married couple. Some months earlier they had called me in to see their little daughter, who had developed an interesting obsessional symptom following upon a dream. I took a great interest in the case, whose genesis I thought I understood. My offer of treatment was however declined by her parents and I was given to understand that they thought of changing over to a foreign authority who effected cures by hypnotism. My present phantasy was that after the total failure of that attempt the parents begged me to start my treatment, saying that now they had complete confidence in me, and so on. I however answered: 'Yes, *now* you have confidence in me – now that I too have become a professor. The title has done nothing to alter my capacities; if you could not make use of me as a university lecturer you can do without me as a professor as well.' – At this point my phantasy was interrupted by a loud 'Good day to you, Professor!' and I looked up and saw walking past me the very married couple on whom I had just taken my revenge by rejecting their offer. Immediate reflection destroyed the impression of something miraculous. I had been walking towards the couple along a wide, straight and almost deserted street; when I was about twenty paces from them I had glanced up for a moment and caught a glimpse of their impressive figures and recognized them, but had set the perception aside – on the pattern of a negative hallucination – for the emotional reasons which then took effect in the phantasy that arose with apparent spontaneity.[1]

Here is another 'resolution of an apparent presentiment', this time from Otto Rank (1912):[2]

'Some time ago I myself experienced an unusual variation of the "remarkable coincidence" of meeting someone one was at the very moment thinking about. Shortly before Christmas I was on my way to the Austro-Hungarian Bank to get some

1. [Cf. similar occurrences in the case of the 'Rat Man' (1909*d*), Section II (B), *P.F.L.*, 9, 110–11.]
2. [Added 1912.]

change in the form of ten new silver kronen for giving as presents. While I was absorbed in ambitious phantasies which had to do with the contrast between my small assets and the piles of money stored in the bank building, I turned into a narrow street in which the bank stood. I saw a car standing at the door and many people going in and out. I said to myself: No doubt the cashiers will have time even for my few kronen. In any case I shall be quick about it. I shall put down the banknote I want changed and say "Let me have *gold*, please". I immediately noticed my error – I should, of course, have asked for *silver* – and awoke from my phantasies. I was now only a few steps from the entrance and saw a young man coming towards me whom I thought I recognized, but as I am short-sighted I was not yet able to identify him for certain. As he drew nearer I recognized him as a school-friend of my *brother's* called *Gold*. Gold's *brother* was a well-known writer from whom I had expected considerable help at the beginning of my literary career. This help, however, had not been forthcoming, and in consequence I failed to win the material success I had hoped for, which had been the subject of my phantasy on the way to the bank. While I was absorbed in my phantasies, therefore, I must have unconsciously perceived the approach of Herr Gold; and this was represented in my consciousness (which was dreaming of material success) in such a form that I decided to ask for gold at the counter, instead of the less valuable silver. On the other hand, however, the paradoxical fact that my unconscious is able to perceive an object which my eyes can recognize only later seems partly to be explained by what Bleuler [1910] terms "complexive preparedness [*Complexbereit-schaft*]". This was, as we have seen, directed to material matters and had from the beginning, contrary to my better knowledge, directed my steps to the building where only gold and paper money is changed.'

We must also include[1] in the category of the miraculous and

1. [What follows from here up to the words 'a wish to improve the situation' on p. 331 dates from 1907.]

the 'uncanny' the peculiar feeling we have, in certain moments
and situations, of having had exactly the same experience once
before or of having once before been in the same place, though
our efforts never succeed in clearly remembering the previous
occasion that announces itself in this way. I am aware that I am
merely following loose linguistic usage when I call what arises
in a person at such moments a 'feeling'. What is no doubt in
question is a judgement, and, more precisely, a perceptual
judgement; but these cases have nevertheless a character quite
of their own, and we must not leave out of account the fact that
what is looked for is never remembered. I do not know whether
this phenomenon of '*déjà vu*' has ever been seriously offered
in proof of an individual's previous psychical existence; but
psychologists have certainly turned their attention to it and
have endeavoured to solve the problem in a whole variety of
speculative ways. None of the attempted explanations which
they have brought forward seems to me to be correct, because
none of them takes into consideration anything other than the
concomitant manifestations and the conditions which favour
the phenomenon. Those psychical processes which according
to my observations are alone responsible for the explanation of
'*déjà vu*' – namely, unconscious phantasies – are still generally
neglected by psychologists even to-day.

It is in my view wrong to call the feeling of having experienced
something before an illusion. It is rather that at such moments
something is really touched on which we have already experienced once before, only we cannot consciously remember it
because it has never been conscious. To put it briefly, the feeling of '*déjà vu*' corresponds to the recollection of an unconscious
phantasy. There exist unconscious phantasies (or day-dreams)
just as there exist conscious creations of the same kind which
everybody knows from his own experience.

I know that the subject would merit the most exhaustive
treatment; but I shall here do no more than give the analysis
of a single case of '*déjà vu*' where the feeling was characterized
by especial intensity and persistence. A lady who is now thirty-

seven claimed to have a most distinct memory of having at the age of twelve and a half paid her first visit to some school-friends in the country. When she entered the garden, she had an immediate feeling of having been there before. This feeling was repeated when she went into the reception rooms, so that she felt she knew in advance what room would be the next one, what view there would be from it, and so on. But the possibility that this feeling of familiarity could have owed its origin to an earlier visit to the house and garden, perhaps one in her earliest childhood, was absolutely ruled out and was disproved as a result of her questioning her parents. The lady who reported this was not in search of any psychological explanation, but saw the occurrence of this feeling as a prophetic indication of the significance for her emotional life which these same school-friends later acquired. However, a consideration of the circumstances in which the phenomenon occurred in her shows us the way to another view of the matter. At the time when she paid the visit she knew that these girls had an only brother, who was seriously ill. During the visit she actually set eyes on him, though he looked very ill and she said to herself that he would die soon. Now, her own only brother had been dangerously ill with diphtheria a few months earlier; during his illness she had spent several weeks away from her parents' house, staying with a relative. She believed that her brother had been with her on this visit to the country; she even thought it had been his first considerable journey after his illness; but her memory was remarkably uncertain on these points while of all the other details, and in particular of the dress she was wearing that day, she had an ultra-clear picture. [Cf. footnote, p. 50 f.] Anyone who is well-informed will find no difficulty in concluding from these hints that the expectation that her brother would die had at that time played an important part in the girl's thoughts and either had never become conscious or, after the favourable termination of the illness, had succumbed to energetic repression. If things had turned out otherwise, she would have had to wear a different dress – mourning. She found an analogous situation in the home of her friends, whose only brother was in danger of dying soon, as in fact he did shortly after. She ought to have remembered consciously that she herself had lived through this situation a few months before: instead of remembering it – which was prevented by repression – she transferred her feeling of remembering something to her surroundings, the garden and the house, and fell a victim to the '*fausse reconnaissance*' of having seen all this exactly the same once before. From the fact that repression occurred we may conclude that her former expectation of her brother's death had not been far removed from a wishful phantasy. She would then have been the only child. In her later neurosis she suffered most severely from a fear of losing her parents, behind which, as usual, analysis was able to reveal the unconscious wish with the same content.

I have been able in a similar way to derive my own fleeting experiences of '*déjà vu*' from the emotional constellation of the moment. 'This would once more be an occasion for wakening the (unconscious and unknown) phantasy which was formed in me at this or that time as a wish to improve the situation.'– This explanation of '*déjà vu*'[1] has so far been taken into consideration by only one observer. Dr Ferenczi, to whom the third [1910] edition of this book is indebted for so many valuable contributions, writes to me on this subject as follows: 'From my own case, as well as that of others, I have convinced myself that the unaccountable feeling of familiarity is to be traced to unconscious phantasies of which one is unconsciously reminded in a situation of the present time. With one of my patients what happened was apparently something different, but in reality it was quite analogous. This feeling returned to him very often, but it regularly proved to have originated from a *forgotten (repressed) portion of a dream of the preceding night*. It seems there-

---

1. [The remainder of this paragraph was added as a footnote in 1910, and the following paragraph was added as a footnote in 1917. They were both transferred to the text in 1924.]

fore that "*déjà vu*" can derive not only from day-dreams but from night-dreams as well.'

I have later learnt that Grasset (1904) has given an explanation of the phenomenon which comes very close to my own.[1]

In 1913[2] I wrote a short paper describing another phenomenon that is very similar to '*déjà vu*' [1914a]. This is '*déjà raconté*', the illusion of having already reported somethirg of special interest when it comes up in the course of psychoanalytic treatment. On these occasions the patient maintains with every sign of subjective certainty that he has already recounted a particular memory a long time ago. The physician is however sure of the contrary and is as a rule able to convince the patient of his error. The explanation of this interesting parapraxis is probably that the patient has felt an urge to communicate this information and intended to do so, but has failed to carry it into effect, and that he now takes the memory of the former as a substitute for the latter, the carrying out of his intention.

A similar state of affairs, and probably also the same mechanism, is to be seen in what Ferenczi (1915) has called 'supposed' parapraxes. We believe there is something - some object - that we have forgotten or mislaid or lost; but we are able to convince ourselves we have done nothing of the kind and that everything is as it should be. For example, a woman patient returns to the doctor's room, giving as a reason that she wants to collect the umbrella she has left behind there; but the doctor sees that she is in fact holding it in her hand.[3] There was therefore an impulse towards this parapraxis, and the impulse was sufficient to serve as a substitute for its actual execution. Except for this difference, the supposed parapraxis is equivalent to the real one. It is, however, what one might call cheaper.

1. [For a discussion of a phenomenon allied to '*déjà vu*' - that of 'depersonalization' - see Freud's paper on 'A Disturbance of Memory on the Acropolis' (1936a), *P.F.L.*, **11**, 443 f.]

2. [The last two paragraphs in this section were added in 1924.]

3. [This example is taken from Ferenczi's paper.]

(E)[1] When I recently had occasion to report some examples of the forgetting of names, with their analyses, to a colleague with a philosophical education, he hastened to reply: 'That's all very well; but in my case the forgetting of names happens differently.' The matter can obviously not be dealt with as easily as this; I do not suppose that my colleague had ever before thought of analysing the forgetting of a name, nor could he say how it happened differently in his case. But his comment nevertheless touches on a problem which many people will be inclined to put in the foreground. Does the elucidation given here of parapraxes and chance actions apply quite generally or only in certain cases? and if the latter, what are the conditions under which it can be called in to explain phenomena that might also have been brought about in another way? In answering this question my experiences leave me in the lurch. I can but utter a warning against supposing that a connection of the kind here demonstrated is only rarely found; for every time I have made the test on myself or on my patients, a connection has been clearly shown to exist just as in the examples reported, or there have at least been good grounds for supposing that it did. It is not surprising if success in finding the hidden meaning of a symptomatic act is not achieved every time, for the magnitude of the internal resistances opposing the solution comes into account as a deciding factor. Equally, it is not possible to interpret every single dream of one's own or of one's patients; to prove that the theory holds good in general it is enough if one can penetrate a part of the way into the hidden connection. It often happens that a dream which proves refractory during an attempt to solve it the next day will allow its secret to be wrested from it a week or a month later, after a real change has come about in the meantime and has reduced the contending psychical values.[2] The same applies to the solving of parapraxes and symptomatic acts. The example of

1. [The first two paragraphs in this section date back to 1901.]

2. [Cf. some remarks of Freud in *The Interpretation of Dreams* (1900a), P.F.L., 4, 671.]

misreading on page 154 ('Across Europe in a Tub') gave me the opportunity of showing how a symptom that is at first insoluble becomes accessible to analysis when the *real interest* in the repressed thoughts has passed away.[1] As long as the possibility existed of my brother obtaining the envied title before me, this misreading resisted every one of my repeated efforts to analyse it; after it had turned out to be unlikely that he would be preferred to me in this way, the path that led to its solution was suddenly cleared. It would therefore be incorrect to maintain that all the cases which resist analysis are due to a mechanism other than the psychical mechanism disclosed here. Such an assumption would need more than negative evidence. Furthermore, the readiness to believe in a different explanation of parapraxes and symptomatic acts, which is probably to be found in all healthy people, is quite devoid of evidential value; it is obviously a manifestation of the same mental forces which produced the secret and which therefore also devote themselves to preserving it and resist its elucidation.

On the other hand we must not overlook the fact that repressed thoughts and impulses certainly do not achieve expression in symptomatic acts and parapraxes by their own unaided efforts. The technical possibility for such side-slipping on the part of the innervations must be presented independently; this will then be readily exploited by the intention of the repressed to make itself felt consciously. In the case of verbal parapraxes, detailed investigations by philosophers and philologists have endeavoured to determine what are the structural

1. [*Footnote added* 1924:] At this point very interesting problems of an *economic* nature come in, questions taking into consideration the fact that the psychical processes aim at gaining pleasure and removing unpleasure. There is already an economic problem in how it becomes possible by way of substitutive associations to recapture a name that has been forgotten through motives of unpleasure. An excellent paper by Tausk (1913) gives good examples of how the forgotten name becomes accessible once more if one succeeds in connecting it with a pleasurably-toned association, which can counterbalance the unpleasure to be expected from the reproduction of the name.

and functional relations that put themselves at the service of such an intention. If we distinguish, among the determinants of parapraxes and symptomatic acts, between the unconscious motive on the one hand and the physiological and psycho-physical relations that come to meet it on the other, it remains an open question whether there are, within the range of normality, yet other factors that can – like the unconscious motive, and in place of it – create parapraxes and symptomatic acts along the lines of these relations. It is not my task to answer this question.

Nor is it my purpose[1] to exaggerate the differences, sufficiently large as they are, between the psychoanalytic and the popular view of parapraxes. I would rather call attention to cases in which these differences lose much of their sharpness. As regards the simplest and most inconspicuous examples of slips made by the tongue or the pen – in which, perhaps, words are merely contracted, or words and letters left out – the more complicated interpretations come to nothing. From the point of view of psychoanalysis we must maintain that *some* disturbance of intention has revealed its existence in these cases, but we cannot say from what the disturbance derived and what its aim was. In fact it has achieved nothing apart from demonstrating its existence. In such cases we can also see how a parapraxis is encouraged by phonetic resemblances and close psychological associations: this is a fact that we have never disputed. It is, however, a reasonable scientific demand that such rudimentary cases of slips of the tongue or slips of the pen should be judged on the basis of the more clearly marked cases, whose investigation yields such unambiguous conclusions as to the way in which parapraxes are caused.

(F)[2] Since our discussion of slips of the tongue [p. 94 ff.] we have been content with demonstrating that parapraxes have a

1. [This paragraph was added in 1917.]

2. [With the exception of the footnotes on pp. 336 and 339, the remainder of the chapter dates back to 1901.]

hidden motivation, and by the help of psychoanalysis we have traced our way to a knowledge of this motivation. We have so far left almost without consideration the general nature and the peculiarities of the psychical factors that find expression in parapraxes; at any rate we have not yet attempted to define them more closely and to test whether they conform to laws. Nor shall we attempt now to deal with the matter in a radical way, since the subject can better be explored from another angle, as our first steps will show us in a moment.[1] Here several questions can be raised which I will at least bring forward and describe in outline. (1) What is the content and origin of the thoughts and impulses which are indicated in erroneous and chance actions? (2) What are the determinants which compel a thought or an impulse to make use of such actions as a means of expression and which put it in a position to do so? (3) Is it possible to establish constant and unambiguous relations between the kind of parapraxis and the qualities of what is expressed by means of it?

I will begin by bringing together material for answering the last question. In discussing the examples of slips of the tongue [p. 94 ff.] we found it necessary to go beyond the content of what was intended to be said, and were obliged to look for the cause of the speech-disturbance in something outside the intention. What this was was obvious in a number of cases, and was known to the speaker's consciousness. In the examples that seemed simplest and most transparent it was another version of the same thought – one which sounded as if it had an equal right [to express the thought], and which disturbed the expression of the thought without its being possible to explain why the one version had succumbed and the other had won the day. (These are Meringer and Mayer's

1. [*Footnote added* 1924:] This book is of an entirely popular character; it merely aims, by an accumulation of examples, at paving the way for the necessary assumption of *unconscious yet operative* mental processes, and it avoids all theoretical considerations on the nature of this unconscious.

'contaminations' [p. 95].) In a second group of cases the motive for the defeat of one version was a consideration which, however, did not prove strong enough to withhold it completely ('*zum Vorschwein gekommen*' [p. 98]). The version which was withheld was perfectly conscious too. Only of the third group can it be asserted unreservedly that the disturbing thought differed from the one intended, and only in their case can a distinction which is apparently essential be established. The disturbing thought is either connected with the disturbed thought by thought associations (disturbance as a result of internal contradiction), or it is unrelated to it in its nature and the disturbed word happens to be connected with the disturbing thought – which is *often* unconscious – by an unexpected *external* association. In the examples I have given from my psychoanalyses the entire speech is under the influence of thoughts which have become active but have at the same time remained entirely unconscious; either these are betrayed by the disturbance itself ('*Klapperschlange*' – '*Kleopatra*' [p. 108]) or they exercise an indirect influence by making it possible for the different parts of the consciously intended speech to disturb each other ('*Ase natmen*', where '*Hasenaur* Street' and reminiscences of a Frenchwoman are in the background [p. 105]). The withheld or unconscious thoughts from which the disturbance in speech derives are of the most varied origin. This survey therefore does not enable us to generalize in any direction.

A comparative examination of my examples of misreading and slips of the pen leads to the same conclusions. As with slips of the tongue, certain cases appear to owe their origin to a work of condensation which has no further motivation (e.g. the '*Apfe*' [p. 103]). It would however be satisfactory to learn whether special conditions may not have to be fulfilled if such a condensation, which is normal in dream-work but a fault in our waking thought, is to take place. No information on this problem can be obtained from the examples themselves. I should however refuse to conclude from this that there are in fact no conditions other than, for instance, a relaxation of conscious attention, since I know from other sources that it is precisely automatic activities[1] which are characterized by correctness and reliability. I should prefer to stress the fact that here, as so often in biology, normal circumstances or those approaching the normal are less favourable subjects for investigation than pathological ones. I expect that what remains obscure in the elucidation of these very slight disturbances will be illuminated by the explanation of serious disturbances.

In misreading and slips of the pen there are also plenty of examples in which we can discern a more remote and complicated motivation. 'Across Europe in a Tub' [p. 154] is a disturbance in reading which is explained as being due to the influence of a remote thought, foreign in its essence, arising from a repressed impulse of jealousy and ambition, and utilizing the 'switch-word' '*Beförderung*' to form a connection with the indifferent and innocent topic that was being read. In the case of 'Burckhard' [p. 165 f.] the name itself forms a 'switch-word' of this kind.[2]

There is no doubt that disturbances in the functions of speech occur more readily, and make smaller demands on the disturbing forces, than do those in other psychical activities. [Cf. p. 281 above.]

One is on different ground when it comes to examining forgetting in its proper sense – that is, the forgetting of past experiences. (To distinguish them from forgetting in this stricter sense, we might speak of the forgetting of proper names and of foreign words, described in Chapter I and II, as 'slipping the memory', and the forgetting of intentions as 'omissions'.) The basic determinants of the *normal* process of forgetting are

1. [I.e. activities from which conscious attention is withdrawn. Cf. p. 181 f. above.]

2. [This term is used at two or three points in the contemporary 'Dora' case history (1905e), e.g. *P.F.L.*, 8, 100 *n*. Freud also uses the term 'verbal bridge', as, for instance, above on p. 90. Cf. similarly 'associative bridge' on p. 156 above.]

unknown.[1] We are also reminded that not everything is forgotten that we believe to be. Our explanation has here to do only with cases where the forgetting causes us surprise, in so far as it breaks the rule that unimportant things are forgotten but important ones are preserved by memory. Analysis of the examples of forgetting that seem to require a special explanation reveals that the motive for forgetting is invariably an unwillingness to remember something which can evoke distress-

1. [*Footnote added* 1907:] I may perhaps put forward the following suggestions as regards the mechanism of forgetting in its proper sense. Mnemic material is subject in general to two influences, condensation and distortion. Distortion is the work of the dominant trends in mental life, and is directed above all against the memory traces which have remained affectively operative and which show considerable resistance to condensation. The traces that have grown indifferent succumb unresistingly to the process of condensation; yet it can be observed that in addition to this, the distorting trends feed on the indifferent material if they have remained unsatisfied at the place at which they sought to manifest themselves. As these processes of condensation and distortion continue for long periods, during which every fresh experience acts in the direction of transforming the mnemic content, it is generally thought that it is time which makes memory uncertain and indistinct. It is highly probable that there is no question at all of there being any direct function of time in forgetting. [For an earlier draft of some of these ideas, cf. footnote 2, p. 184 above.]— In the case of *repressed* memory-traces it can be demonstrated that they undergo no alteration even in the course of the longest period of time. The unconscious is quite timeless. The most important as well as the strangest characteristic of psychical fixation is that all impressions are preserved, not only in the same form in which they were first received, but also in all the forms which they have adopted in their further developments. This is a state of affairs which cannot be illustrated by comparison with another sphere. Theoretically every earlier state of the mnemic content could thus be restored to memory again, even if its elements have long ago exchanged all their original connections for more recent ones. [This seems to be the earliest explicit mention of the 'timelessness' of the unconscious. — An attempt at an illustration, by a comparison taken from the archaeology of the city of Rome, was made by Freud and abandoned as useless in Chapter I of his later work, *Civilization and its Discontents* (1930*a*), where there is another long discussion of the nature of memory and forgetting.]

ing feelings. We come to suspect that this motive aims at manifesting itself quite generally in mental life, but is prevented from putting itself into effect at all regularly by other forces which work against it. The extent and the significance of this unwillingness to remember distressing impressions would seem to deserve the most careful psychological examination; moreover we cannot separate from this wider context the question of what special conditions make this forgetting, that is universally aimed at, possible in individual cases.

In the forgetting of intentions another factor comes into the foreground. The conflict, which could only be *surmised* in the repression of what was distressing to remember, here becomes tangible, and in the analysis of the examples a counter-will can regularly be recognized which opposes the intention without putting an end to it. As in the parapraxes already described, two types of psychical process can be recognized here. [Cf. pp. 336–7.] Either the counter-will is turned directly against the intention (in cases where the latter's purpose is of some importance), or it is unrelated in its nature to the intention itself and establishes its connection with it by means of an *external* association (in the case of intentions that are almost indifferent).

The same conflict governs the phenomena of bungled actions. The impulsion which manifests itself in disturbing the action is often a counter-impulsion, but still more often it is an entirely unrelated one, which merely takes the opportunity of achieving expression by disturbing the action while it is being carried out. The cases where the disturbance results from an internal contradiction are the more significant ones; they also involve the more important actions.

In chance actions or in symptomatic actions the internal conflict becomes less and less important. These motor manifestations, to which consciousness attaches little value, or which it overlooks entirely, thus serve to express a wide variety of unconscious or withheld impulses; for the most part they are symbolic representations of phantasies or wishes.

In regard to the first question – as to what is the origin of the thoughts and impulses which find expression in parapraxes [p. 336] – we can say that in a number of cases it is easy to show that the disturbing thoughts are derived from suppressed impulses in mental life. In healthy people, egoistic, jealous and hostile feelings and impulsions, on which the pressure of moral education weighs heavily, make frequent use of the pathway provided by parapraxes in order to find some expression for their strength, which undeniably exists but is not recognized by higher mental agencies. Acquiescence in these parapraxes and chance actions is to a large extent equivalent to a compliant tolerance of the immoral. Among these suppressed impulses no small part is played by the various sexual currents. That these particular ones should in fact appear so rarely among the thoughts disclosed by analysis in my examples is an accident of my material. Since the examples I have analysed are to a great extent taken from my own mental life, the selection was partial from the first and aimed at excluding sexual matters. At other times it appears to be from perfectly innocent objections and considerations that the disturbing thoughts arise.

We have now reached the moment for answering the second question – that is, what psychological determinants are responsible for a thought being compelled to seek expression not in its complete form but in a kind of parasitic form, as a modification and disturbance of another thought [p. 336]. The most striking examples of parapraxes make it seem probable that these determinants must be looked for in a relation to admissibility to consciousness: in the question, that is, of the greater or less degree to which they bear the marked character of being 'repressed'. But if we follow this character through the series of examples, it dissolves into ever vaguer indications. The inclination to dismiss something as a waste of time, or the consideration that the thought in question is not properly relevant to the matter in hand, appear, as motives for pushing back a thought (which is then left to find expression by disturbing another thought), to play the same part as does the moral condemnation of an insubordinate emotional impulse or as does derivation from totally unconscious trains of thought. Insight into the general nature of how parapraxes and chance actions are determined cannot be gained along these lines. One single fact of significance emerges from these enquiries. The more innocent the motivation of a parapraxis, and the less objectionable – and therefore the less inadmissible to consciousness – the thought finding expression in it, the easier it is to explain the phenomenon, once one's attention has been turned to it. The slightest cases of slips of the tongue are noticed immediately, and spontaneously corrected. Where the motivation comes from really repressed impulses, the case has to be elucidated by careful analysis, which may itself at times come up against difficulties or prove unsuccessful.

We are therefore no doubt justified in taking the result of this last enquiry as evidence that the satisfactory explanation of the psychological determinants of parapraxes and chance actions is to be looked for along other lines and by a different approach. The indulgent reader may accordingly see in these discussions signs of the broken edges where this subject has been somewhat artificially detached from a wider context.

(G) A few words should be said to indicate at least in what direction this wider context lies. The mechanism of parapraxes and chance actions, as we have come to know it by our employment of analysis, can be seen to correspond in its most essential points with the mechanism of dream-formation which I have discussed in the chapter on the 'dream-work' in my *Interpretation of Dreams*. In both cases we find condensations and compromise-formations (contaminations). We have the same situation: by unfamiliar paths, and by the way of external associations, unconscious thoughts find expression as modifications of other thoughts. The incongruities, absurdities and errors of the dream-content, which result in the dream being scarcely recognized as the product of psychical activity, originate in the same way, though it is true with a freer use of the means at hand, as our common mistakes in everyday life. In both cases *the appearance of an incorrect function is explained by the peculiar mutual interference between two or several correct functions.*

An important conclusion can be drawn from this conformity. The peculiar mode of working, whose most striking achievement we see in the content of dreams, cannot be attributed to the sleeping state of mental life if we possess such abundant evidence in the form of parapraxes that it operates during our waking life as well. The same connection also forbids our assuming that these psychical processes, which strike us as abnormal and strange, are determined by a deep-seated decay in mental activity or by pathological states of functioning.[1]

We shall not be able to form a correct picture of the strange psychical work which brings about the occurrence of both parapraxes and dream images until we have learnt that psychoneurotic symptoms, and especially the psychical formations of hysteria and obsessional neurosis, repeat in their mechanism all the essential features of this mode of working. This is therefore the starting-point for the continuation of our researches. For us, however, there is yet another special interest in considering parapraxes, chance actions and symptomatic actions in the light of this last analogy. If we compare them to the products of the psychoneuroses, to neurotic symptoms, two frequently repeated statements – namely, that the borderline between the normal and the abnormal in nervous matters is a fluid one, and that we are all a little neurotic – acquire meaning and support. Without any medical experience we can construct various types of nervous illness of this kind which are merely hinted at – *formes frustes*[2] of the neuroses: cases in which the symptoms are few, or occur rarely or not severely – in other words, cases whose comparative mildness is located in the number, intensity and duration of their pathological manifestations. But we might perhaps never arrive by conjecture at precisely the type that appears most frequently to form the

1. See *The Interpretation of Dreams* (1900*a*), *P.F.L.*, 4, 767–9.
2. ['Blurred forms.' The French word '*fruste*' applies primarily to coins or medals that are 'rubbed' or 'worn'.]

transition between health and illness. For the type we are considering, whose pathological manifestations are parapraxes and symptomatic acts, is characterized by the fact that the symptoms are located in the least important psychical functions, while everything that can lay claim to higher psychical value remains free from disturbance. Where the symptoms are distributed in the reverse way – that is, where they make their appearance in the most important individual and social functions and are able to disturb nutrition, sexual intercourse, professional work and social life – this is the mark of severe cases of neurosis and is more characteristic of them than, for example, are the variety and vigour of their pathological manifestations.

But there is one thing which the severest and the mildest cases all have in common, and which is equally found in parapraxes and chance actions: *the phenomena can be traced back to incompletely suppressed psychical material, which, although pushed away by consciousness, has nevertheless not been robbed of all capacity for expressing itself.*

BIBLIOGRAPHY
AND AUTHOR INDEX

Titles of books and periodicals are in italics, titles of papers are in inverted commas. Abbreviations are in accordance with the *World List of Scientific Periodicals* (London, 1963–5). Further abbreviations used in this volume will be found in the List at the end of this bibliography. Numerals in bold type refer to volumes, ordinary numerals refer to pages. The figures in round brackets at the end of each entry indicate the page or pages of this volume on which the work in question is mentioned.

In the case of the Freud entries, only English translations are given. The initial dates are those of the German original publications. (The date of writing is added in square brackets where it differs from the latter.) The letters attached to the dates of publication are in accordance with the corresponding entries in the complete bibliography of Freud's writings included in Volume **24** of the *Standard Edition*. Details of the original publication, including the original German title, are given in the editorial introduction to each work in the *Penguin Freud Library*.

For non-technical authors, and for technical authors where no specific work is mentioned, see the General Index.

ABRAHAM, K. (1922*a*) 'Über Fehlleistungen mit überkompensierender Tendenz', *Int. Z. Psychoanal.*, **8**, 345. (126–7)
    [*Trans.*: 'Mistakes with an Over-compensating Tendency', *Clinical Papers and Essays on Psycho-Analysis*, London and New York, 1955, Part I: Clinical Papers, XVI.]
  (1922*b*) 'Vaterrettung und Vatermord in den neurotischen Phantasiegebilden', *Int. Z. Psychoanal.*, **8**, 71. (202)
    [*Trans.*: 'The Rescue and Murder of the Father in Neurotic Phantasy-Formations', *Clinical Papers and Essays on Psycho-Analysis*, London and New York, 1955, Part I: Clinical Papers, XV.]
  (1965) With FREUD, S. *See* FREUD, S. (1965*a*)

ADLER, A. (1905) 'Drei Psycho-Analysen von Zahleneinfällen und obsedierenden Zahlen', *Psychiat.-neurol. Wschr.*, **7**, 263. (305–7)

ANDREAS-SALOMÉ, L., and FREUD, S. (1966) *See* FREUD, S. (1966a)

BERNHEIM, H. (1891) *Hypnotisme, suggestion et psychothérapie: études nouvelles*, Paris. (204)

BLEULER, E. (1906) *Affektivität, Suggestibilität, Paranoia*, Halle. (158)
[*Trans.*: *Affectivity, Suggestibility, Paranoia*, New York, 1912.]

(1910) 'Die Psychoanalyse Freuds', *Jb. psychoanalyt. psychopath. Forsch.*, **2**, 623. (328)

(1919) *Das autistisch-undisziplinierte Denken in der Medizin und seine Überwindung*, Berlin. (49, 314)

BREUER, J., and FREUD, S. (1895) *See* FREUD, S. (1895d)

BRILL, A. A. (1909) 'A Contribution to the Psychology of Everyday Life', *Psychotherapy*, **2**, 5. (148)

(1912) *Psychanalysis: its Theories and Practical Application*, Philadelphia and London. (2nd ed., 1914; 3rd ed., 1922.) (134–5, 193, 211, 283)

DARWIN, C. (1958) *The Autobiography of Charles Darwin 1809–1882. With Original Omissions Restored* (ed. N. Barlow), London. (199)

DATTNER, B. (1911) 'Eine historische Fehlleistung', *Zentbl. Psychoanal.*, **1**, 550. (177–8)

EIBENSCHÜTZ, M. (1911) 'Ein Fall von Verlesen im Betrieb der philologischen Wissenschaft', *Zentbl. Psychoanal.*, **1**, 242. (158–60)

EITINGON, M. (1915) 'Ein Fall von Verlesen', *Int. Z. ärztl. Psychoanal.*, **3**, 349. (162–3)

EMDEN, J. E. G. VAN (1912) 'Selbstbestrafung wegen Abortus', *Zentbl. Psychoanal.*, **2**, 467. (238–40)

FERENCZI, S. (1915) 'Über vermeintliche Fehlhandlungen', *Int. Z. ärztl. Psychoanal.*, **3**, 338. (332)
[*Trans.:* 'On Supposed Mistakes', *Further Contributions to the Theory and Technique of Psycho-Analysis*, London, 1926, Chap. LXXVIII.]

FREUD, M. (1957) *Glory Reflected*, London. (22)

FREUD, S. (1891b) *On Aphasia*, London and New York, 1953. (14, 26, 94)

(1892a) Translation of H. Bernheim's *Hypnotisme, suggestion et psychothérapie: études nouvelles*, Paris, 1891, under the title *Neue Studien über Hypnotismus, Suggestion und Psychotherapie*, Vienna. (204)

(1892–94) Translation with Preface and Footnotes of J.-M. Charcot's *Leçons du mardi (1887–8)*, Paris, 1888, under the title
Poliklinische Vorträge, I, Vienna. (213)
[*Trans.*: Preface and Footnotes to Charcot's *Poliklinische Vorträge*, I, *Standard Ed.*, I, 131.]

(1893a) With BREUER, J., 'On the Psychical Mechanism of
Hysterical Phenomena: Preliminary Communication', in *Studies
on Hysteria, Standard Ed.*, **2**, 3; *P.F.L.*, **3**, 53. (26)

(1895d) With BREUER, J., *Studies on Hysteria*, London, 1956;
Standard Ed., **2**; *P.F.L.*, **3**. (26, 102)

(1897a) *Die infantile Cerebrallähmung*, II. Theil, II. Abt. of Nothnagel's *Specielle Pathologie und Therapie*, **9**, Vienna. (213)

(1898b) 'The Psychical Mechanism of Forgetfulness', *Standard Ed.*,
3, 289. (34, 37–42, 50–51)

(1899a) 'Screen Memories', *Standard Ed.*, **3**, 301. (34, 83–4,
90)

(1900a) *The Interpretation of Dreams*, London and New York, 1955;
Standard Ed., **4–5**; *P.F.L.*, **4**. (21, 26, 32, 33, 34, 36, 47, 49, 51, 100,
148, 154, 155, 156, 166, 179, 200, 212–13, 232, 255, 276–8, 281,
303–4, 312, 333, 342–3)

(1900b) 'Cerebrale Kinderlähmung [III]' (22 reviews and abstracts),
Jbr. Leist. Neurol., **3** (1899), 611. (165)

(1901a) *On Dreams*, London and New York, 1951; *Standard Ed.*, **5**,
633. (34, 169, 187, 212–13)

(1901b) *The Psychopathology of Everyday Life, Standard Ed.*, **6**;
P.F.L., **5**. (21, 26)

(1905c) *Jokes and their Relation to the Unconscious, Standard Ed.*, **8**;
P.F.L., **6**. (33, 160, 182, 224, 277)

(1905d) *Three Essays on the Theory of Sexuality*, London, 1962;
Standard Ed., **7**, 125; *P.F.L.*, **7**, 31. (26, 32, 87)

(1905e) [1901]) 'Fragment of an Analysis of a Case of Hysteria',
Standard Ed., **7**, 3; *P.F.L.*, **8**, 29. (34, 301, 318, 338)

(1906c) 'Psycho-Analysis and the Establishment of the Facts in
Legal Proceedings', *Standard Ed.*, **9**, 99. (317)

(1907a) *Delusions and Dreams in Jensen's 'Gradiva', Standard Ed.*,
9, 3; *P.F.L.*, **14**. (281, 318)

(1909b) 'Analysis of a Phobia in a Five-Year-Old Boy', *Standard
Ed.*, **10**, 3; *P.F.L.*, **8**, 165. (27)

(1909d) 'Notes upon a Case of Obsessional Neurosis', *Standard
Ed.*, **10**, 155; *P.F.L.*, **9**, 31. (198, 321, 322, 323, 327)

FREUD, S. (cont.)

(1910a [1909]) *Five Lectures on Psycho-Analysis*, Standard Ed., **11**, 3; in *Two Short Accounts of Psycho-Analysis*, Penguin Books, Harmondsworth, 1962. (16, 27)

(1910c) *Leonardo da Vinci and a Memory of his Childhood*, Standard Ed., **11**, 59; *P.F.L.*, **14**. (88, 93)

(1911c [1910]) 'Psycho-Analytic Notes on an Autobiographical Account of a Case of Paranoia (Dementia Paranoides)', Standard Ed., **12**, 3; *P.F.L.*, **9**, 129. (27, 322)

(1911i) ['A Contribution to the Forgetting of Proper Names'], included in 1901b, Standard Ed., **6**, 30; *P.F.L.*, **5**, 70. (70–71)

(1912–13) *Totem and Taboo*, London, 1950; New York, 1952; Standard Ed., **13**, 1; *P.F.L.*, **13**, 43. (27, 322)

(1913j) 'The Claims of Psycho-Analysis to Scientific Interest', Standard Ed., **13**, 165; *P.F.L.*, **15**, 27. (35)

(1914a) 'Fausse Reconnaissance ("déjà raconté") in Psycho-Analytic Treatment', Standard Ed., **13**, 201. (332)

(1914d) 'On the History of the Psycho-Analytic Movement', Standard Ed., **14**, 3; *P.F.L.*, **15**, 57. (27)

(1915e) 'The Unconscious', Standard Ed., **14**, 161; *P.F.L.*, **11**. (321–2)

(1916–17 [1915–17]) *Introductory Lectures on Psycho-Analysis*, New York, 1966; London, 1971; Standard Ed., **15–16**; *P.F.L.*, **1**. (27, 32, 35, 97, 101, 143, 144, 160, 277, 290)

(1917b) 'A Childhood Recollection from *Dichtung und Wahrheit*', Standard Ed., **17**, 147; *P.F.L.*, **14**, 321. (93)

(1918b [1914]) 'From the History of an Infantile Neurosis', Standard Ed., **17**, 3; *P.F.L.*, **9**, 225. (27)

(1920g) *Beyond the Pleasure Principle*, London, 1961; Standard Ed., **18**, 7; *P.F.L.*, **11**, 269. (27)

(1921c) *Group Psychology and the Analysis of the Ego*, London and New York, 1959; Standard Ed., **18**, 69; *P.F.L.*, **12**, 91. (27)

(1922a) 'Dreams and Telepathy', Standard Ed., **18**, 197. (325)

(1922b) 'Some Neurotic Mechanisms in Jealousy, Paranoia and Homosexuality', Standard Ed., **18**, 223; *P.F.L.*, **10**, 195. (318)

(1923a) 'Two Encyclopaedia Articles', Standard Ed., **18**, 235; *P.F.L.*, **15**, 129. (35)

(1923b) *The Ego and the Id*, London and New York, 1962; Standard Ed., **19**, 3; *P.F.L.*, **11**, 339. (27)

(1923d) 'A Seventeenth-Century Demonological Neurosis', Standard Ed., **19**, 69; *P.F.L.*, **14**, 377. (279)

(1925*d* [1924]) *An Autobiographical Study*, Standard Ed., 20, 3; P.F.L., 15, 183. (12)

(1925*i*) 'Some Additional Notes upon Dream-Interpretation as a Whole', *Standard Ed.*, 19, 125. (325)

(1926*d* [1925]) *Inhibitions, Symptoms and Anxiety*, London, 1960; *Standard Ed.*, 20, 77; *P.F.L.*, 10, 227. (27)

(1927*a*) 'Postscript to *The Question of Lay Analysis*', Standard Ed., 20, 251; *P.F.L.*, 15, 355. (12)

(1927*c*) *The Future of an Illusion*, London, 1962; Standard Ed., 21, 3; *P.F.L.*, 12, 179. (27–8)

(1930*a*) *Civilization and its Discontents*, New York, 1961; London, 1963; *Standard Ed.*, 21, 59; *P.F.L.*, 12, 243. (28, 339)

(1932*a*) 'The Acquisition and Control of Fire', Standard Ed., 22, 185; *P.F.L.*, 13, 225. (318–19)

(1933*a* [1932]) *New Introductory Lectures on Psycho-Analysis*, New York, 1966; London, 1971; Standard Ed., 22, 3; P.F.L., 2. (325)

(1935*a*) Postscript (1935) to *An Autobiographical Study*, new edition, London and New York; *Standard Ed.*, 20, 71; *P.F.L.*, 15, 256. (12)

(1936*a*) Letter to Romain Rolland: 'A Disturbance of Memory on the Acropolis', *Standard Ed.*, 22, 239; *P.F.L.*, 11, 443. (332)

(1939*a* [1934–8]) *Moses and Monotheism*, Standard Ed., 23, 3; P.F.L., 13, 237. (28, 318–19)

(1940*a* [1938]) *An Outline of Psycho-Analysis*, New York, 1968; London, 1969; *Standard Ed.*, 23, 141; *P.F.L.*, 15, 369. (28)

(1941*c* [1899]) 'A Premonitory Dream Fulfilled', *Standard Ed.*, 5, 623. (326)

(1941*d* [1921]) 'Psycho-Analysis and Telepathy', *Standard Ed.*, 18, 177. (325)

(1950*a* [1887–1902]) *The Origins of Psycho-Analysis*, London and New York, 1954. (Partly, including 'A Project for a Scientific Psychology', in *Standard Ed.*, 1, 175.) (16, 24, 26, 34–5, 90, 91, 148, 303)

(1960*a*) *Letters 1873–1939* (ed. E. L. Freud) (trans. T. and J. Stern), New York, 1960; London, 1961. (23, 24)

(1963*a* [1909–39]) *Psycho-Analysis and Faith. The Letters of Sigmund Freud and Oskar Pfister* (ed. H. Meng and E. L. Freud) (trans. E. Mosbacher), London and New York, 1963. (24)

(1905*a* [1907–26]) *A Psycho-Analytic Dialogue. The Letters of Sigmund Freud and Karl Abraham* (ed. H. C. Abraham and E. L.

FREUD, S. (*cont.*)

Freud) (trans. B. Marsh and H. C. Abraham), London and New York, 1965. (24)

(1966*a* [1912–36]) *Sigmund Freud and Lou Andreas-Salomé: Letters* (ed. E. Pfeiffer) (trans. W. and E. Robson-Scott), London and New York, 1972. (24)

(1968*a* [1927–39]) *The Letters of Sigmund Freud and Arnold Zweig* (ed. E. L. Freud) (trans. W. and E. Robson-Scott), London and New York, 1970. (24)

(1970*a* [1919–35]) *Sigmund Freud as a Consultant. Recollections of a Pioneer in Psychoanalysis* (Letters from Freud to Edoardo Weiss, including a Memoir and Commentaries by Weiss, with Foreword and Introduction by Martin Grotjahn), New York, 1970. (24)

(1974*a* [1906–23]) *The Freud/Jung Letters* (ed. W. McGuire) (trans. R. Manheim and R. F. C. Hull), London and Princeton N.J., 1974. (24)

GRASSET, J. (1904) 'La sensation du déjà vu; sensation du déjà entendu; du déjà éprouvé; illusion de fausse reconnaissance', *J. psychol. norm. et path.*, **I**, 17. (332)

GROSS, H. (1898) *Kriminalpsychologie*, Graz. (199)

HAIMAN, H. (1917) 'Eine Fehlhandlung im Felde', *Int. Z. ärztl. Psychoanal.*, **4**, 269. (114)

HAUPT, J. (1872) 'Über das mittelhochdeutsche Buch der Märterer', *Sitzb. kais. Akad. Wiss. Wien*, **70**. (159–60)

HEIJERMANS, H. (1914) *Schetsen van Samuel Falkland*, **18**, Amsterdam. (245–6)

HENRI, V. and C. (1897) 'Enquête sur les premiers souvenirs de l'enfance', *L'année psychologique*, **3**, 184. (86, 90)

HITSCHMANN, E. (1910) 'Zur Kritik des Hellsehens', *Wien. klin. Rundsch.*, **24**, 94. (324)

(1913*a*) 'Zwei Fälle von Namenvergessen', *Int. Z. ärztl. Psychoanal.*, **I**, 266. (71–2)

(1913*b*) 'Ein wiederholter Fall von Verschreiben bei der Rezeptierung', *Int. Z. ärztl. Psychoanal.*, **I**, 265. (171–4)

(1916) 'Ein Dichter und sein Vater, Beitrag zur Psychologie religiöser Bekehrung und telepathischer Phänomene', *Imago*, **4**, 337. (324)

HUG-HELLMUTH, H. VON (1912) 'Beiträge zum Kapitel "Verschreiben" und "Verlesen"', *Zentbl. Psychoanal.*, **2**, 277. (176–7)

JEKELS, L. (1913) 'Ein Fall von Versprechen', *Int. Z. ärztl. Psycho-anal.*, **1**, 258. (149–52)

JONES, E. (1910*a*) 'Beitrag zur Symbolik im Alltagsleben', *Zentbl. Psychoanal.*, **1**, 96. (251–4)

(1910*b*) 'Freud's Theory of Dreams', *Am. J. Psychol.*, **21**, 283; in *Papers on Psycho-Analysis*, London and New York, 1913. (5th ed., London and Baltimore, 1948.) (253–4)

(1911*a*) 'Analyse eines Falles von Namenvergessen', *Zentbl. Psychoanal.*, **2**, 84. (79)

(1911*b*) 'The Psychopathology of Everyday Life', *Am. J. Psychol.*, **22**, 477; in *Papers on Psycho-Analysis*, London and New York, 1913. (5th ed., London and Baltimore, 1948.) (128–9, 144–6, 165, 171, 175, 178, 193, 196, 199, 206, 209, 217, 273, 291, 310–11)

(1912) 'Unbewusste Zahlenbehandlung', *Zentbl. Psychoanal.*, **2**, 241. (311–12)

[*English text:* 'Dream Manipulation of Numbers', in *Papers on Psycho-Analysis*, 2nd ed., London and New York, 1918.]

(1953) *Sigmund Freud: Life and Work*, Vol. 1, London and New York. (Page references are to the English edition.) (24, 59, 195, 312)

(1955) *Sigmund Freud: Life and Work*, Vol. 2, London and New York. (Page references are to the English edition.) (24, 71, 90, 130)

(1957) *Sigmund Freud: Life and Work*, Vol. 3, London and New York. (Page reference is to the English edition.) (24, 223)

JUNG, C. G. (1906) (ed.) *Diagnostische Assoziationsstudien* (Vol. 1), Leipzig. (314, 316–17)

[*Trans.: Studies in Word-Association*, London, 1918; New York, 1919.]

(1907) *Über die Psychologie der Dementia praecox*, Halle. (56–7, 64, 274)
[*Trans.: The Psychology of Dementia Praecox*, New York, 1909.]

(1911) 'Ein Beitrag zur Kenntnis des Zahlentraumes', *Zentbl. Psychoanal.*, **1**, 567. (311–12)

(1974) With FREUD, S. *See* FREUD, S. (1974*a*)

KLEIN, J., and WERTHEIMER, M. (1904) *See* WERTHEIMER, M. (1904)

KLEINPAUL, R. [1892] *Menschenopfer und Ritualmorde*, Leipzig. (47)

LICHTENBERG, G. C. VON (The Elder) (1853) *Witzige und satirische Einfälle*, Leipzig. (160)

MAEDER, A. (1906) 'Contributions à la psychopathologie de la vie
    quotidienne', *Archives de psychologie*, **6**, 148. (216–17, 261)

    (1908) 'Nouvelles contributions à la psychopathologie de la vie
    quotidienne', *Archives de psychologie*, **7**, 283. (285–6)

    (1909) 'Une voie nouvelle en psychologie – Freud et son école',
    Coenobium, **3**, 100. (274)

MAYER, C., and MERINGER, R. (1895) *See* MERINGER, R. (1895)

MERINGER, R. (1895) With MAYER, C., *Versprechen und Verlesen,
eine psychologisch-linguistische Studie*, Vienna. (94–102, 104, 106,
125, 126–8, 181, 215, 336–7)

    (1900) 'Wie man sich versprechen kann', *Neue Freie Presse*, August
    23. (100–102)

    (1908) *Aus dem Leben der Sprache*, Berlin. (215)

MÜLLER, D. (1915) 'Automatische Handlungen im Dienste bewus-
ster, jedoch nicht durchführbarer Strebungen', *Int. Z. ärztl.
Psychoanal.*, **3**, 41. (193–4)

OSSIPOW, N. (1922) 'Psychoanalyse und Aberglaube', *Int. Z.
Psychoanal.*, **8**, 348. (320–21)

PFISTER, O., and FREUD, S. (1963) *See* FREUD, S. (1963*a*)

PICK, A. (1905) 'Zur Psychologie des Vergessens bei Geistes- und
Nervenkranken', *Arch. KrimAnthrop.*, **18**, 251. (198)

POPPELREUTER, W. (1914) 'Bemerkungen zu dem Aufsatz von G.
Frings "Über den Einfluss der Komplexbildung auf die effek-
tuelle und generative Hemmung"', *Arch. ges. Psychol.*, **32**, 491.
(314)

POTWIN, E. (1901) 'Study of Early Memories', *Psycholog. Rev.*, **8**,
596. (86)

RANK, O. (1907) *Der Künstler, Ansätze zu einer Sexualpsychologie*,
Leipzig and Vienna. (202–3)

    (1910) 'Ein Beispiel von poetischer Verwertung des Versprechens',
    Zentbl. Psychoanal., **1**, 109. (143–4)

    (1911) 'Das Verlieren als Symptomhandlung', *Zentbl. Psychoanal.*,
    1, 450. (266)

    (1912) 'Fehlleistungen aus dem Alltagsleben', *Zentbl. Psychoanal.*,
    2, 265. (292–5, 298, 327–8)

    (1913) 'Zwei witzige Beispiele von Versprechen', *Int. Z. ärztl.
    Psychoanal.*, **1**, 267. (120–21, 137)

    (1915*a*) 'Ein determinierter Fall von Finden', *Int. Z. ärztl. Psycho-
    anal.*, **3**, 157. (266–8)

(1915*b*) 'Fehlhandlung und Traum', *Int. Z. ärztl. Psychoanal.*, **3**, 158. (298)

REIK, T. (1915) 'Fehlleistungen im Alltagsleben', *Int. Z. ärztl. Psychoanal.*, **3**, 43. (112–13, 136–7, 262)

(1920) 'Über kollektives Vergessen', *Int. Z. Psychoanal.*, **6**, 202. (81–2)

ROSCHER, W. H. (ed.) (1884–97) *Ausführliches Lexikon der griechischen und römischen Mythologie.* Leipzig. (277)

RUTHS, W. (1898) *Experimentaluntersuchungen über Musikphantome*, Darmstadt. (153–4)

SACHS, H. (1917) 'Drei Fälle von "Kriegs"-Verlesen', *Int. Z. ärztl. Psychoanal.*, **4**, 159. (163-4)

SCHNEIDER, R. (1920) 'Zu Freuds Untersuchungsmethode des Zahleneinfalls', *Int. Z. Psychoanal.*, **6**, 75. (312–14)

SILBERER, H. (1922) 'Tendenziöse Druckfehler', *Int. Z. Psychoanal.*, **8**, 350 (179)

SPITZER, D. (1912) *Wiener Spaziergänge II, Gesammelte Werke*, **2**, Munich. (63)

STÄRCKE, J. (1916) 'Aus dem Alltagsleben', *Int. Z. ärztl. Psychoanal.*, **4**, 21 and 98. (76–9, 136, 191, 241, 245–6, 288–9, 295–7)

STEKEL, W. (1904) 'Unbewusste Geständnisse', *Berliner Tageblatt*, January 4. (111–12)

(1910) 'Ein Beispiel von Versprechen', *Zentbl. Psychoanal.*, **1**, 40. (148–9)

STORFER, A. J. (1914) 'Zur Psychopathologie des Alltagsleben', *Int. Z. ärztl. Psychoanal.*, **2**, 170. (74–5, 166–7, 179)

(1915) 'Ein politischer Druckfehler', *Int. Z. ärztl. Psychoanal.*, **3**, 45. (179–80)

STOUT, G. F. (1938) *A Manual of Psychology* (5th ed.), London. (42)

TAUSK, V. (1913) 'Entwertung des Verdrängungsmotivs durch Rekompense', *Int. Z. ärztl. Psychoanal.*, **1**, 230. (334)

(1917) 'Zur Psychopathologie des Alltagslebens', *Int. Z. ärztl. Psychoanal.*, **4**, 156. (138–9, 286–7)

WAGNER, R. (1911) 'Ein kleiner Beitrag zur "Psychopathologie des Alltagslebens"', *Zentbl. Psychoanal.*, **1**, 594. (175–6)

WEISS, E., and FREUD, S. (1970) *See* FREUD, S. (1970*a*)

WEISS, K. (1912) 'Über einen Fall von Vergessen', *Zentbl. Psychoanal.*, **2**, 532. (291–2)

(1913) 'Strindberg über Fehlleistungen', *Int. Z. ärztl. Psychoanal.*, **1**, 268. (270–71)

WERTHEIMER, M. (1904) With KLEIN, J., 'Psychologische Tat-
    bestandsdiagnostik', *Arch. KrimAnthrop.*, 15, 72. (317)
WILSON, P. (1922) 'The Imperceptible Obvious', *Rev. Psiquiat.*,
    Lima, 5. (50)
WUNDT, W. (1900) *Völkerpsychologie*, 1, Part 1, Leipzig. (102–3,
    125, 181)
ZWEIG, A. (1968) With FREUD, S. *See* FREUD, S. (1968a)

LIST OF ABBREVIATIONS

Gesammelte Schriften	= Freud, *Gesammelte Schriften* (12 vols), Vienna, 1924–34.
Gesammelte Werke	= Freud, *Gesammelte Werke* (18 vols), Vols 1–17 London, 1940–52, Vol. 18 Frankfurt am Main, 1968. From 1960 the whole edition published by S. Fischer Verlag, Frankfurt am Main.
Standard Edition *Standard Ed.*	= *The Standard Edition of the Complete Psychological Works of Sigmund Freud* (24 vols), Hogarth Press and The Institute of Psycho-Analysis, London, 1953–74.
P.F.L.	= *Pelican Freud Library* (15 vols), Penguin Books, Harmondsworth, from 1973.

INDEX OF PARAPRAXES

This list does not entirely follow Freud's grouping of parapraxes according to the titles of the various chapters. Items have been classified under the most appropriate headings, regardless of whereabouts they appear in the book. The source of each parapraxis is given in brackets where it is other than Freud himself.

GENERAL INDEX

This index includes the names of non-technical authors. It also includes the names of technical authors where no reference is made in the text to specific works. For reference to specific technical works, the Bibliography should be consulted. – The compilation of the index was undertaken by Mrs R. S. Partridge.

READ MORE IN PENGUIN

In every corner of the world, on every subject under the sun, Penguin represents quality and variety – the very best in publishing today.

For complete information about books available from Penguin – including Puffins, Penguin Classics and Arkana – and how to order them, write to us at the appropriate address below. Please note that for copyright reasons the selection of books varies from country to country.

In the United Kingdom: Please write to *Dept. EP, Penguin Books Ltd, Bath Road, Harmondsworth, West Drayton, Middlesex UB7 ODA*

In the United States: Please write to *Consumer Sales, Penguin Putnam Inc., P.O. Box 12289 Dept. B, Newark, New Jersey 07101-5289.* VISA and MasterCard holders call 1-800-788-6262 to order Penguin titles

In Canada: Please write to *Penguin Books Canada Ltd, 10 Alcorn Avenue, Suite 300, Toronto, Ontario M4V 3B2*

In Australia: Please write to *Penguin Books Australia Ltd, P.O. Box 257, Ringwood, Victoria 3134*

In New Zealand: Please write to *Penguin Books (NZ) Ltd, Private Bag 102902, North Shore Mail Centre, Auckland 10*

In India: Please write to *Penguin Books India Pvt Ltd, 11 Community Centre, Panchsheel Park, New Delhi 110017*

In the Netherlands: Please write to *Penguin Books Netherlands bv, Postbus 3507, NL-1001 AH Amsterdam*

In Germany: Please write to *Penguin Books Deutschland GmbH, Metzlerstrasse 26, 60594 Frankfurt am Main*

In Spain: Please write to *Penguin Books S. A., Bravo Murillo 19, 1° B, 28015 Madrid*

In Italy: Please write to *Penguin Italia s.r.l., Via Benedetto Croce 2, 20094 Corsico, Milano*

In France: Please write to *Penguin France, Le Carré Wilson, 62 rue Benjamin Baillaud, 31500 Toulouse*

In Japan: Please write to *Penguin Books Japan Ltd, Kaneko Building, 2-3-25 Koraku, Bunkyo-Ku, Tokyo 112*

In South Africa: Please write to *Penguin Books South Africa (Pty) Ltd, Private Bag X14, Parkview, 2122 Johannesburg*

THE PENGUIN FREUD LIBRARY

Based on James Strachey's Standard Edition, this collection of fifteen volumes is the first full paperback edition of Freud's works in English. The first eleven volumes were edited by Angela Richards, and subsequent volumes by Albert Dickson.